THE DIVINE AUTHENTICITY OF SCRIPTURE

RETRIEVING AN EVANGELICAL HERITAGE

A. T. B. MCGOWAN

IVP Academic

An imprint of InterVarsity Press
Downers Grove, Illinois

InterVarsity Press
P.O. Box 1400, Downers Grove, IL 60515-1426
World Wide Web: www.ivpress.com
E-mail: email@ivpress.com

InterVarsity Press® is the book-publishing division of InterVarsity Christian Fellowship/USA®, a student movement active on campus at hundreds of universities, colleges and schools of nursing in the United States of America, and a member movement of the International Fellowship of Evangelical Students. For information about local and regional activities, write Public Relations Dept., InterVarsity Christian Fellowship/USA, 6400 Schroeder Rd., P.O. Box 7895, Madison, WI 53707-7895, or visit the IVCF website at <www.intervarsity.org>.

Design: Cindy Kiple

Images: Bernardo Strozzi/Getty Images

ISBN 978-0-8308-2879-1

Printed in the United States of America ∞

Library of Congress Cataloging-in-Publication Data

McGowan, A. T. B. (Andrew Thomson Blake)
    The divine authenticity of Scripture: retrieving an evangelical
heritage / A.T.B. McGowan.
        p. cm.
    Includes bibliographical references and index.
    ISBN 978-0-8308-2879-1 (pbk.: alk. paper)
    1. Bible—Evidences, authority, etc. I. Title.
BS480.M387 2008
220.1'3—dc22

                                                                                2008008872

P	22	21	20	19	18	17	16	15	14	13	12	11	10	9	8	7	6	5	4	3	2	1
Y	27	26	25	24	23	22	21	20	19	18	17	16	15	14	13	12	11	10	09	08		

For my three sons:

Scott B. McGowan
David R. McGowan
Christopher W. McGowan

CONTENTS

1. **Introduction**   **9**
The *locus* of Scripture reconsidered   12
The vocabulary of Scripture reconsidered   12
The doctrine of Scripture reconsidered   12
The use of Scripture in the church reconsidered   13

2. **Reconstructing the doctrine**   **17**
Introduction   17
Revelation   17
The work of the Holy Spirit   21
Reconstructing the vocabulary   38

3. **The Enlightenment and liberal theology**   **50**
Introduction   50
The Enlightenment   50
Liberal theology   53
The response to liberal theology   61
Conclusion   83

4. **Fundamentalism and inerrancy**   **84**
Introduction   84
Warfield and Hodge   85

Fundamentalism   87
The modern inerrancy debate   97
Arguments against inerrancy   105
The rationalist implication   113
Rejecting the incarnational model   119
Conclusion   121

5. **Infallibility: an evangelical alternative**   **123**
Introduction   123
An evangelical alternative   124
James Orr   126
Orr and the Dutchmen   137
Herman Bavinck   139
Bavinck's doctrine of Scripture   143
G. C. Berkouwer   161
Summary   162
Conclusion   164

6. **Scripture and confession**   **165**
Introduction   165
Scripture and confession   166
Scripture and tradition   175
Defining the relationship   179
Conclusion   187

7. **Preaching Scripture**   **188**
Introduction   188
Scripture and the believer   189
The preaching of Scripture   191
Reformed preaching   192
Application   205

8. **Conclusion**   **207**
Summary of chapters 2–7   207
Anticipating the critique   210
Charting the way forward   212
Conclusion   214

Bibliography   215
Index of names   225

1. INTRODUCTION

The purpose of this book is to contribute to discussions about the nature and function of Scripture in evangelical Christianity.[1] I shall argue that, in formulating our doctrine of Scripture, we need to review both our vocabulary and our theology, in order to clarify precisely what we mean when we speak about Scripture as the Word of God. I shall also argue that the way Scripture functions in the church ought to be revisited, first, by analysing the relationship between Scripture, confessional statements and tradition, and second, by a reassessment of how Scripture is to be preached.

Christian theologians must give attention to many difficult issues, but it seems to me that none is more vital than the doctrine of Scripture. I say this because what we believe about Scripture determines what we believe about everything else. If we take the view that the Scriptures are God-given, then our views on every other subject will be determined with reference to Scripture. It stands to reason that if God has spoken and if what he said has been written down under the supervisory action of the Holy Spirit, then God speaking in

---

1. Sometimes I shall use the expressions 'Scripture' and 'the Scriptures' in what follows, instead of the word 'Bible' (which simply means 'book'). But when I use these expressions I am referring to the sixty-six books gathered in the Christian Bible.

and through the Scriptures becomes the final authority for decision-making and the ultimate arbiter of truth. If, on the other hand, we believe that the Scriptures are simply an interesting record of what Jews and Christians have believed over the centuries but that these beliefs are not binding upon believers today, then we may reach quite different decisions in respect of doctrine, ethics and the life of faith.

Since the 1850s, the church has been deeply affected by types of theology that advocate this latter view of Scripture. The dramatic changes in philosophy and theology in the years since the Enlightenment have brought the doctrine of Scripture into sharp relief. There is a sense in which one of the early church Fathers, together with one of the sixteenth-century magisterial Reformers and, for example, a seventeenth-century Scottish minister, might happily have agreed on the doctrine of Scripture. That harmony and unity has all been changed by the Enlightenment, the birth of liberal theology,[2] the philosophical influence of existentialism and, even more so, by the recent advent of such views as postmodernism and relativism.

These movements in theology have also affected the evangelical movement. Until fairly recently, one of the clearest identifying marks of an evangelical was a 'high' view of Scripture as the Word of God. Unfortunately, it is no longer possible to take it for granted that those who call themselves 'evangelical' will hold to the same position on Scripture held by those who were described in this way even in the 1960s. Indeed, the very word 'evangelical' has lost something of its clarity and is used to refer to a range of positions. Francis Schaeffer's final book was called *The Great Evangelical Disaster*, where he argued that evangelicals had abandoned a truly evangelical view of the Bible and were giving way to other views.[3] In that book, Schaeffer said that an

---

2. Given that certain theological terms have been used in different ways, it is important to define usage. I use the term 'liberal theology' to refer to the school of thought associated with Schleiermacher, Ritschl, Harnack, Hermann and others, which had substantially run its course by the end of the Second World War. I use the term 'neo-orthodoxy' to refer to the school of thought associated with Karl Barth, including those who have been profoundly influenced by Barth while not agreeing with him on every point. I use the term 'conservative evangelicalism' to refer to those whose position is largely defined by adherence to the set of documents known as 'The Fundamentals', which I shall deal with in chapter 4.

3. Francis A. Schaeffer, *The Complete Works of Francis Schaeffer*, vol. 4: *A Christian View of The Church* (Westchester, Ill.: Crossway, 1982), pp. 301–405.

orthodox view of the Bible is the 'Watershed of the Evangelical World'. In other words, it is a defining position, such that our view of Scripture determines whether or not we are truly evangelical. It seems to me that he was correct in this assessment.

As an evangelical, there have been many influences on my own understanding of Scripture. Naturally, the first influences were my family and church. Next was my involvement with two key organizations within the British evangelical movement, namely Scripture Union and the Inter-Varsity Fellowship.[4] From those earliest days, I was taught that the Bible was the Word of God and that the voice of God speaking by his Spirit through his Word is the final authority on all matters. I have never seriously questioned that commitment and do not do so today. Nevertheless, I have gradually become concerned that some ways of defining and using Scripture within evangelicalism are open to serious criticism and could do us more harm than good if we continue to maintain them in their present form. Through a failure to understand the differences between evangelicalism and fundamentalism, through a failure to engage with biblical scholarship, and sometimes through sheer obscurantist and anti-intellectual approaches, evangelicals have often damaged rather than helped the case for a high view of Scripture. We do not properly state and defend the evangelical doctrine of Scripture by retreating into an untenable ghetto mentality and ignoring genuine matters of concern. Rather, we must engage with those who take a different position and we must do so graciously. In what follows, I shall seek to address these issues and advocate a doctrine of Scripture that is truly evangelical but that avoids some of the problems and challenges rightly laid at our door by those who do not share our position.

When I first began to write this book, I had in mind a rather different project than the one that has unfolded. At the time, I was teaching a course on the doctrine of Scripture and was struggling to find a suitable textbook to cover the whole scope of the module. It seemed to me that I might usefully write such a textbook. As I studied the subject, however, I came to the conclusion that there was a more pressing issue, namely the need for me as an evangelical to clarify my own understanding of the doctrine of Scripture and to make a contribution to the debate among evangelicals regarding its significance for today. With these concerns in mind, I propose to offer some suggestions regarding the nature and use of Scripture that I hope will be theologically productive and ecclesiastically

---

4. Now the Universities and Colleges Christian Fellowship.

useful. My proposal essentially has four parts, which will be divided up as follows.

The *locus* of Scripture reconsidered

First, I shall reconsider the place of Scripture in the theological *corpus*. For a long time now, in my own Reformed tradition, it has been taken for granted that Scripture comes at the beginning of the theological system, as it does in the Westminster Confession of Faith, where the doctrine of Scripture is chapter 1. A study of this matter has led me to conclude that this is a mistake that needs to be corrected. I shall argue that the doctrine of Scripture should be relocated, in order to emphasize that it is an aspect of God's self-revelation. Hence the doctrine of Scripture will be moved to its true theological *locus* within the doctrine of God, more precisely as an aspect of the work of the Holy Spirit. Although most theologians have spoken about the work of the Holy Spirit in relation to Scripture, there has been insufficient emphasis upon this theme.

The vocabulary of Scripture reconsidered

Second, I shall revisit the vocabulary of the doctrine. Words like 'inspiration' and 'illumination' have come to mean rather different things since they were first used in theological discourse and there is a question as to whether 'inspiration' was ever a good rendering of what Paul is saying in 2 Timothy 3:16. I shall argue that we should cease to use the word 'inspiration', both on exegetical grounds and because of the confusion that arises through modern English usage of the word, opting instead for 'divine spiration'. Similarly, I shall argue that we should supplement the words 'illumination' and 'perspicuity' with 'recognition' and 'comprehension', so as to underline the work of the Holy Spirit in enabling human beings both to identify the Scriptures as God's Word and to gain understanding of them.

The doctrine of Scripture reconsidered

Third, I shall address the important differences between two ways in which evangelicals have traditionally sought to define their doctrine of Scripture, the 'inerrantist' position on the one hand and the 'infallibilist' position on the other. This being a major part of my proposal, it will occupy several chapters. I shall argue that we should cease to use the word 'inerrancy' in relation to our doctrine of Scripture, using instead the word 'infallibility'. I shall demonstrate that the debate in the USA between inerrantists and errantists represents a false dichotomy, which can be avoided by following several leading Reformed theologians in their advocacy of the word 'infallibility'. In this context, I shall argue that if it was necessary for evangelicals in response to liberal theology to emphasize the divine speaking, it is time to redress the balance by saying more about the human authors of Scripture. I shall further demonstrate that, far from weakening an evangelical doctrine of Scripture, this move actually strengthens it.

The use of Scripture in the church reconsidered

Fourth, believing as I do that all theology is 'church' theology, I shall address two ecclesial issues. First, I shall consider the relationship between Scripture and our creeds and confessions. This will include some discussion of the need for an evangelical theology of tradition. Then, finally, I shall deal with the church's preaching of Scripture. One of the worst consequences of the classical liberal theology has been that the academy and the church have been separated. If we as evangelicals believe that the Bible is the Word of God, then we should not discuss its nature and significance without dealing with the matter of how we open up the Scriptures in the context of the life of the church.

From this brief outline, it should be clear that at least two things are not attempted in this book. First, there will be no attempt to delve deeply into issues of canonicity, although I do believe that our understanding of 'divine spiration' enables us to say some useful things about the final form of the text. The subject of canonicity, however, is too complex to be dealt with in passing and, in any case, a number of important books address the subject.[5] For the purposes of this book, I accept the canonical decisions of the church

---

5. See e.g. Bruce M. Metzger, *The Canon of the New Testament: Its Origins, Development and Significance* (Oxford: Clarendon, 1987); F. F. Bruce, *The Canon of Scripture* (Downers Grove: IVP, 1988); L. M. McDonald and J. A. Sanders (eds.), *The Canon Debate* (Peabody, Mass.: Hendrickson, 2002); and L. M. McDonald, *The Biblical Canon: Its Origin, Transmission and Authority* (Peabody, Mass.: Hendrickson, 2007).

and work with the canon as we have received it. Second, I do not attempt any sustained study of hermeneutical issues, except briefly in the context of chapter 7, on preaching Scripture. In my personal engagement with Scripture and in my preaching of Scripture, however, I am indebted to a number of books written on this subject.[6]

One further comment is perhaps necessary before I enter the substance of the argument. Among evangelicals in the USA, the word 'inerrancy' has become something of a sacred talisman and there is a deep sensitivity in respect of any questioning of this word. Indeed, one might reasonably expect something of a firestorm directed against any challenge to its continued usage. I would plead with my fellow evangelicals to listen carefully to the argument and to consider it on its merits rather than adopting a knee-jerk, defensive position. We might usefully recall that, at the turn of the twentieth century, the great Reformed theologians of the day were B. B. Warfield, James Orr and Abraham Kuyper. These men took different positions on the doctrine of Scripture (Warfield was an inerrantist, while Orr and Kuyper were infallibilists), but, as we shall see later, there was a recognition that their differences on the doctrine of Scripture although significant, were not sufficient to damage their fellowship in Christ. There has been a tendency in more recent days towards a less tolerant position, particularly in the American context, such that anyone who dares to challenge the use of the word 'inerrancy' is regarded as heading down the 'slippery slope' towards liberal theology. This is unfortunate and is symptomatic of the fact that evangelicals have often failed to observe the highest standards in theological debate and dialogue. My hope is that this proposal will provoke a constructive and helpful discussion within the fellowship of the evangelical community.

Finally, there are some acknowledgments I ought to make. First, I would like to express my thanks to the various bodies that cooperated to provide me with a four-month sabbatical, which enabled me to undertake some of the initial groundwork for this book. Thanks to the UHI Millennium Institute for

---

6. See e.g. A. Thiselton, *New Horizons in Hermeneutics* (Carlisle: Paternoster, 1992); Gerald Bray, *Biblical Interpretation, Past and Present* (Leicester: IVP, 1996); Kevin J. Vanhoozer, *Is There a Meaning in This Text?* (Leicester: Apollos, 1998); Grant Osborne, *The Hermeneutical Spiral: A Comprehensive Introduction to Biblical Interpretation* (Nottingham: Apollos, 2006); Francis Watson, *Text, Church and World: Biblical Interpretation in Theological Perspective* (Edinburgh: T. & T. Clark, 1994); and Stephen E. Fowl, *Engaging Scripture: A Model for Theological Interpretation* (Oxford: Blackwell, 1998).

providing funding for three months of that sabbatical and to my own college, the Highland Theological College, for providing me with additional leave for a further month. I am grateful to the University of Aberdeen, where I hold an honorary Professorship in Reformed Doctrine, for providing me with an office for the first three months of the sabbatical and to John Webster who not only invited me to attend his weekly postgraduate seminar in systematic theology (which was a master class in how to run a seminar) but also discussed with me some of the themes on which I was working. It was an additional privilege to be able to discuss this work with Howard Marshall, one of my former teachers, whose own work on the doctrine of Scripture has been so helpful to me. Thanks also to Reformed Theological Seminary in Jackson, Mississippi, where I spent the fourth month of the sabbatical. As always, the seminary provided me with a house and an office and the gracious southern hospitality I have come to appreciate so much during my visits there over the years as an Adjunct Professor.

It is a great privilege to work in a context where academic life is set in the context of a worshipping community and where the environment is both spiritually supportive and intellectually stimulating. I am grateful for my academic colleagues who share this environment with me: Hector Morrison, Jamie Grant, Mike Bird, Innes Visagie, Nick Needham and Rob Shillaker, with whom I have discussed various aspects of this work over the past several years. I am also grateful for specific comments on this book. No work of this nature would be possible without the help of libraries and librarians, so thanks to Martin Cameron, our librarian at Highland Theological College, for his unfailing support and help in the writing of the book. He always seemed to be able to get anything I needed almost as soon as I asked for it. Thanks also to the library staff at Reformed Theological Seminary, especially Ken Elliott and John McCarty (Mac), whose help and kindness are much appreciated.

A special word of thanks to my personal assistant, Fiona Cameron, who has not only helped directly in a variety of ways but has also, when necessary, acted as a very firm doorkeeper, thus allowing me to have peace and quiet to work.

Thanks also to Howard Marshall, Paul Wells, Stephen Williams, John Webster and Alan Carter for reading sections of this book for me and for their most helpful comments. The book is in much better shape than it would otherwise have been!

I would also like to pay tribute to my family. I met my wife June in the Scripture Union group at Uddingston Grammar School in 1971 and we have been married now for over thirty years. She has been my best friend for most of my life and has lovingly and generously put up with a husband whose lifestyle has often involved working at college from early in the morning until late into the night and who is often away for weeks at a time. Her love and support mean more than I can say. Finally, I would like to mention my three sons, Scott, David and Christopher, to whom this book is dedicated, in the hope that they will continue to build their lives on the truth that God has revealed to us by his Spirit in his Word.

2. RECONSTRUCTING THE DOCTRINE

Introduction

The argument of this chapter is that the traditional evangelical doctrine of Scripture requires some reconstruction. First, I shall argue that any understanding of Scripture must be set in the context of God's self-revelation. Second, I shall argue that the doctrine of Scripture must be viewed as an aspect of the work of the Holy Spirit and that this pneumatological focus requires us to relocate the doctrine of Scripture within the theological *corpus*. Third, I shall argue that, in order most adequately to express this pneumatological approach and to take account of certain linguistic changes, we must recast the vocabulary of the doctrine of Scripture.

Revelation

Everything to be said in this book is based on the conviction that the God who has eternally existed in Trinity as Father, Son and Holy Spirit has chosen to make himself known to the human beings he created in his own image. The knowledge of God that comes through this self-revelation is not merely an intellectual conviction that such a God exists but is rather a knowledge that leads to life and salvation, as we discover God's love and grace made known to us in the incarnation, life, death, resurrection and heavenly session of his eternal Son, Jesus Christ. Without God's self-revelation, we could know nothing of him.

Throughout most of Christian history, it was axiomatic that Christian theology is only possible because God has chosen to reveal himself. As John Calvin put it, 'the pious mind does not dream up for itself any god it pleases, but contemplates the one and only true God. And it does not attach to him whatever it pleases, but is content to hold him to be as he manifests himself . . .'[1] This belief in God's self-revelation, taken for granted in earlier centuries, has become in modern times one of the most controverted issues in theology. There can be little doubt that it is also one of the most vital issues. As G. C. Berkouwer says, 'There is no more significant question in the whole of theology and in the whole of human life than that of the nature and reality of revelation.'[2] In order to understand the departure from orthodoxy that took place through the rise and ultimate dominance of classical liberal theology, we must pause and emphasize the key place revelation plays in Christian theology, noting the two constituent types of revelation, 'general revelation' and 'special revelation'. Calvin did not use these terms but wrote that there is a twofold knowledge of God: 'First, as much in the fashioning of the universe as in the general teaching of Scripture the Lord shows himself to be simply the Creator. Then in the face of Christ [cf. 2 Cor. 4:6] he shows himself the Redeemer.'[3]

'General revelation' is the term used to describe those ways in which God reveals himself to all humanity without exception, for example, in creation, in conscience and in history. In speaking of general revelation, however, it is important to make two things clear. First, and rather obviously, general revelation is revelation. That is to say, it is not to be confused with any kind of natural knowledge, obtainable by human reason apart from God's self-revelation. Hence I argue that the term 'natural revelation' is unhelpful, since it can so easily be confused with 'natural theology'. Second, as John Calvin argued (see below), general revelation is sufficient to render us without excuse before God but not sufficient to bring us to salvation. This was well summarized in the Westminster Confession of Faith, which says, 'Although the light of nature, and the works of creation and providence do so far manifest the goodness, wisdom, and power of God, as to leave men unexcusable; yet are they not sufficient to give that

---

1. John Calvin, *Institutes of the Christian Religion*, ed. F. L. Battles (Philadelphia: Westminster, 1977), 1.2.2.

2. G. C. Berkouwer, *General Revelation* (Grand Rapids: Eerdmans, 1955), p. 17.

3. Calvin, *Institutes* 1.2.1.

knowledge of God, and of His will, which is necessary unto salvation.'[4] We can press this further, as Paul does in Romans 1, pointing out that every human being has direct and innate knowledge of God but that sinful human beings deliberately suppress that knowledge. In other words, at the very core of our being, having been made in the image of God, we know that there is a God. Calvin put it like this, 'There is within the human mind, and indeed by natural instinct, an awareness of divinity. This we take to be beyond controversy. To prevent anyone from taking refuge in the pretence of ignorance, God himself has implanted in all men a certain understanding of his divine majesty.'[5] This knowledge does not bring us salvation but it does mean that no-one will be able to say on the Day of Judgment, 'I did not know that there was a God.'

'Special revelation' is the term used to describe those ways in which God makes himself known more directly and more personally. We can identify several forms of special revelation: Jesus Christ (the incarnate Word), Scripture (the written Word) and preaching (the spoken Word). It should also be noted that this special revelation is necessary even for a proper understanding of general revelation. Calvin said that God's Word is necessary because human beings, due to sin, are blind to the light of God given to them in their 'sense of divinity' and in creation.[6] He uses a much-discussed simile to explain this need for Scripture:

> Just as old or bleary-eyed men and those with weak vision, if you thrust before them a most beautiful volume, even if they recognise it to be some sort of writing, yet can scarcely construe two words, but with the aid of spectacles will begin to read distinctly; so Scripture, gathering up the otherwise confused knowledge of God in our minds, having dispersed our dullness, clearly shows us the true God.[7]

F. L. Battles, the editor of the 1977 Westminster edition of Calvin's *Institutes of the Christian Religion*, directs us to various discussions of this simile in Calvin studies.[8]

Although each aspect of God's special revelation is important, the revelation that takes place in and through Christ is the heart and centre of God's

---

4. J. W. Ross (ed.), *The Westminster Confession of Faith* (Glasgow: Free Presbyterian, 1986), ch. 1, sect. 1.
5. Calvin, *Institutes* 1.3.1.
6. Ibid. 1.6.1.
7. Ibid.
8. Ibid. p. 70, n. 1.

self-revelation. As the writer to the Hebrews says, 'Long ago, at many times and in many ways, God spoke to our fathers by the prophets, but in these last days he has spoken to us by his Son, whom he appointed the heir of all things, through whom also he created the world' (1:1–2). Both the written Word and the preached Word testify to Christ, the incarnate Word. The fact that the written Word testifies to him was affirmed by Christ himself, when he told some Jews, 'You search the Scriptures because you think that in them you have eternal life; and it is they that bear witness about me, yet you refuse to come to me that you may have life' (John 5:39–40). It is also evident in the post-resurrection narrative of the disciples on the way to Emmaus: 'And beginning with Moses and all the Prophets, he interpreted to them in all the Scriptures the things concerning himself' (Luke 24:27). The preached Word also testifies to Christ, since preaching is the declaration of the gospel of the Lord Jesus Christ. Since God supremely reveals himself in and through his Son, who is himself God, all other special revelation must stand in the proper relationship to this self-revelation.

As I indicated at the beginning, however, we must not make the mistake of imagining that revelation is simply the communication of information, as if God used prophets and apostles to communicate certain facts that human beings need to know. Rather, we must view revelation as part of the overall plan and purpose of God whereby he acts to save his people. As John Webster writes, 'revelation is the self-presentation of the triune God, the free work of sovereign mercy in which God wills, establishes and perfects saving fellowship with himself in which humankind comes to know, love and fear him above all things'.[9] Notice particularly Webster's emphasis on revelation as 'the establishment of *saving fellowship*. Revelation is purposive. Its end is not simply divine self-display but the overcoming of human opposition, alienation and pride, and their replacement by knowledge, love and fear of God. In short: revelation is reconciliation.'[10]

Revelation, then, 'is not so much an action in which God informs us of other acts of his through which we are reconciled to him; rather, revelation is a way of indicating the communicative force of God's saving, fellowship-creating presence. God is present as saviour, and so communicatively present.'[11]

---

9. John Webster, *Holy Scripture: A Dogmatic Sketch* (Cambridge: Cambridge University Press, 2003), p. 13.

10. Ibid., pp. 15–16.

11. Ibid., p. 16.

This is important because it means that revelation is 'not simply the bridging of a noetic divide (though it includes that) but is reconciliation, salvation and therefore fellowship. The idiom of revelation is as much moral and relational as it is cognitional.'[12] In affirming this broadening of the term 'revelation' by Webster, I am not thereby accepting that revelation is pure 'event' and that it occurs only in the context of an existential encounter between the individual and God. It is possible to understand revelation in this wider sense, while still affirming that God has revealed himself in history and that the record of this revelation in history has been written down for us.

When we attempt to define our doctrine of Scripture, then, we must do so in the context of this self-revelation of God. But in what does this self-revelation consist? Historically, God's self-revelation originates in the very beginning, when he speaks to our first parents, whom he made in his own image. After the fall, God's self-revelation is directed towards an elect people from whom would ultimately come the Messiah. Then, with the incarnation, God's self-revelation comes to believers in Christ and in the witness to him. Theologically, God's self-revelation is centred upon Jesus Christ, who is himself God incarnate and in whom therefore all the fulness of the godhead lives in bodily form.

In the context of describing this self-revelation of God, we may say that the Scriptures are the record of the revelation that God has given to his church, often written down long after the revelatory events they describe but used of God to bring that revelation afresh to every generation. The Scriptures are vital to the life of the church because they are God's Word to us. They have come into existence supernaturally, through a dual authorship of God and human writers and are entirely trustworthy. The Scriptures do not deceive us and infallibly achieve the purposes for which God has given them.

The work of the Holy Spirit

If the Holy Spirit was once regarded as the 'forgotten' person of the Trinity, that is certainly no longer the case. This is illustrated by the dramatic rise of Pentecostalism out of the American 'holiness movement', with its early beginnings in the 'Azusa Street' experience of 1906, when the Apostolic Faith Gospel Mission was born. Just over fifty years later, Henry Van Dusen could

---

12. Ibid.

describe Pentecostalism as the 'Third Force' in Christendom alongside
Protestantism and Roman Catholicism.[13] By the end of the twentieth century,
the explosion of interest in the charismatic renewal, not least in mainstream
denominations, extended the discussion of the person and work of the Holy
Spirit even further. Hundreds of popular books have been published since the
1970s, and the flow continues.

In the academy, however, there has been relatively little work done on the
doctrine of the person and work of the Holy Spirit, although some monographs have been published.[14] In addition, the recent welcome resurgence of
interest in trinitarian theology has produced some stimulating studies.[15]
Overall, however, there has been a dearth of interest in the subject and we
should perhaps not be surprised by this. It is undoubtedly the case that
Western rationalism and secularism have affected Christian theology more
than we would normally care to admit. Why is it that Western theology has
tended to say so little about the Holy Spirit and about the supernatural? It is
surely because many theologians have been somewhat embarrassed by such
language and have been determined to demonstrate that their theological
views are rational and modern, based upon sound philosophical foundations,
believing that these standards are somewhat threatened by an appeal to the
supernatural! They recognize that the New Testament uses supernatural concepts and language, but either they see no need to dwell on these matters or,
like Bultmann, they argue that belief in a supernatural world of spirits and evil
powers and so on is quite unacceptable in the modern world and that the

---

13. Henry Van Dusen, 'The Third Force in Christendom', *Life* 44 (9 June 1958),
     pp. 113–121.

14. See e.g. Alasdair I. C. Heron, *The Holy Spirit: The Holy Spirit in the Bible, the History of
     Christian Thought, and Recent Theology* (Philadelphia: Westminster, 1983); Sinclair B.
     Ferguson, *The Holy Spirit* (Leicester: IVP, 1996); Donald G. Bloesch, *The Holy Spirit:
     Works and Gifts* (Downers Grove: IVP, 2000); Gary D. Badcock, *Light of Truth and
     Fire of Love: A Theology of the Holy Spirit* (Grand Rapids: Eerdmans, 1997); and
     Graham Cole, *Engaging with the Holy Spirit* (Nottingham: Apollos, 2007).

15. See e.g. Thomas G. Weinandy, *The Father's Spirit of Sonship* (Edinburgh: T. & T. Clark,
     1995); Thomas F. Torrance, *The Christian Doctrine of God, One Being Three Persons*
     (Edinburgh: T. & T. Clark, 1996); Colin E. Gunton, *Father, Son and Holy Spirit:
     Toward a Fully Trinitarian Theology* (London: T. & T. Clark, 2003); Michael Welker,
     God the Spirit, trans. John F. Hoffmeyer (Minneapolis: Fortress, 1994); and Jürgen
     Moltmann, *God in Creation: A New Theology of Creation and the Spirit of God*, trans.
     Margaret Kohl (San Francisco: Harper & Row, 1985).

Scriptures must be 'demythologized'.[16] Such beliefs are attributed to the primitive nature of first-century society and the superstitious character of the people who lived at that time. With the advance of science and technology, they say, we know better. In short, most modern theologians have accepted the Enlightenment consensus, which I shall discuss in the next chapter, arguing that real knowledge must be obtained from rational reflection upon the information received through sense perception. This world is all there is. In such an environment, it is no wonder that there is little talk in the academy of the Holy Spirit and his work.

It can also be argued with some cogency that this rationalist and secularist world view has affected those who *do* affirm the Scriptures, including what they say about the supernatural, the Holy Spirit, miracles, evil spirits, Satan and so on. There are probably two reasons for this somewhat negative approach to the supernatural and to spiritual powers. First, some evangelicals in the northern hemisphere have been so determined to present themselves within the academy as intellectuals whose theology is rational, that the respect of their academic peers has become more important to them than their self-designation as evangelicals. Second, many evangelicals in the northern hemisphere, perhaps especially in my own Reformed tradition, have articulated their position in contradistinction to Pentecostalism and the charismatic movements and so have been wary of saying too much about the Holy Spirit lest they be regarded as having abandoned their cessationist position.

In Africa, Asia and much of the southern hemisphere, however, theologians take a quite different approach. Spirits, supernatural powers, exorcism and so on are part of the everyday life of the church. Indeed, the issues that confront Christianity in those places where it is a fast-growing religion are remarkably like the issues faced by the early Christians, as described in the New Testament. Is it a coincidence that the churches in the northern hemisphere are moribund, whereas the churches in the southern hemisphere are growing and are now beginning to exercise leadership in the world church? As Andrew Walls has said for many years, the centre of Christianity and Christian leadership is now very firmly in the southern hemisphere.[17] This

---

16. See Bultmann's essay on this subject together with a series of essays in which scholars debate with Bultmann, in Hans-Werner Bartsch, *Kerygma and Myth: A Theological Debate* (London: SPCK, 1972).

17. See Andrew F. Walls, *The Missionary Movement in Christian History: Studies in the Transmission of Faith* (Maryknoll: Orbis, 1996); and Andrew F. Walls, *The Cross-Cultural Process in Christian History: Studies in the Transmission and Appropriation of Faith*

has been strikingly demonstrated in the recent controversies within the Anglican communion on the subject of the ordination of homosexual clergy. It is the African and other southern hemisphere bishops who are driving a biblical agenda in opposition to the pro-homosexual agenda of the northern liberal clergy, especially in North America. The fact that many episcopal churches in the USA have now rejected the oversight of their diocesan bishops and sought oversight from Nigerian and Ugandan bishops is an extraordinary example of how leadership within the Anglican communion is moving south. Attempts by liberal intellectuals in the northern hemisphere to dismiss the theologians from these developing southern hemisphere nations as primitive and uneducated sound increasingly hollow. The churches in the northern hemisphere must listen to the plea from our brothers and sisters in Africa, Asia and South America that we return to basics, recover the essence of authentic Christianity and affirm the supernatural without shame or apology.

The argument of this chapter is that such a recovery of authentic Christianity, and particularly a renewed emphasis on the person and work of the Holy Spirit, will affect our doctrine of Scripture. Clearly, if a supernatural being (God) has chosen to reveal himself to humanity by his Spirit through his Word (living, written and preached), then we cannot continue to take seriously any doctrine of Scripture that has been constructed in order to conform to the dictates of modernity. In this chapter, I shall attempt to reconstruct the doctrine of Scripture in the light of our doctrine of the Holy Spirit.

Stanley Grenz advocated this pneumatological approach to the doctrine of Scripture in his *Revisioning Evangelical Theology*.[18] He said that 'our bibliology must revision the link between the Holy Spirit and Scripture' on the grounds that 'the purpose of Scripture is instrumental to the work of the Spirit'.[19] He argued that, although Reformed theology in its confessional documents advocated a pneumatological approach to Scripture, this had often been neglected or forgotten, sometimes due to the adoption of a particular theological method. 'Consequently, the reestablishment of the

---

Footnote 17 (*continues*)

      (Maryknoll: Orbis, 2002). Also a recent volume in the same vein: Philip Jenkins, *The Next Christendom: The Coming of Global Christianity* (New York: Oxford University Press, 2002).

18. Stanley J. Grenz, *Revisioning Evangelical Theology: A Fresh Agenda for the 21st Century* (Downers Grove: IVP, 1993).

19. Ibid., p. 113.

integral link between Spirit and Scripture must begin methodologically through the reorientation of the doctrine of Scripture under the doctrine of the Holy Spirit.'[20]

I begin that process now by considering the place we give to Scripture in our systematic theology, arguing that it must be situated in the context of the knowledge of God that comes by revelation through the Holy Spirit. Thus I seek to relocate the doctrine within the theological *corpus*, from where it has more recently been placed in Reformed theology, to be subsumed under the doctrine of God.

Historical survey

In the earliest creeds and confessional statements of the Christian church, Scripture was either not mentioned at all, or came towards the end of the statement. We see this if we consider the 'Ecumenical Symbols', being the Apostles' Creed, the Niceno-Constantinopolitan Creed and the Athanasian Creed, together with a statement of equal importance, the Chalcedonian Definition.

There is no mention of Scripture in the Apostles' Creed, although the Scriptures provide the basic teaching the Creed affirms. The Niceno-Constantinopolitan Creed makes only one reference to Scripture, being a quotation from 1 Corinthians 15:4, affirming that Christ 'rose again, according to the Scriptures'. Once again, Scripture provides the content of faith, although worshippers were not required to affirm belief in any particular doctrine of Scripture. Similarly, the Athanasian Creed focuses exclusively on the Trinity and on Christology, with no mention of Scripture. The Chalcedonian Definition, given its context, is concerned primarily with Christology. The fact that Jesus Christ was both God and man having been established at the Council of Nicaea in AD 325, the Council of Chalcedon in AD 451 was convened largely to explain how this was possible, concluding that Christ was one person with two natures. Once again, there is no doctrine of Scripture to be affirmed in its tenets, but it does contain a statement at the end concerning the basis for its teaching: 'as the prophets from the beginning [have declared] concerning him, and the Lord Jesus Christ himself has taught us, and the Creed of the holy Fathers has handed down to us'.[21]

---

20. Ibid., p. 114.

21. Philip Schaff, *The Creeds of Christendom*, vol. 1: *The History of the Creeds* (New York: Harper & Brothers, 1877), pp. 62–63.

The church accepted no significant creedal or confessional statement from this early period until the sixteenth century.[22] The period in between produced various doctrinal statements and many a theologian produced his *summa*, but there was no universally accepted symbol, creed or confession. The doctrinal statements produced during this period, however, especially from the thirteenth century onwards, placed the doctrine of Scripture under 'prolegomena', rather than in the core doctrinal statement itself. As Richard Muller has said, 'The doctrine of Scripture was, after all, not an independent *locus* or *quaestio* in the theological system until the second half of the sixteenth century, and even then it remained closely linked to its systematic place of origin, the prolegomena.'[23]

The earliest Protestant confessional statement, the Lutheran Augsburg Confession of 1530, begins its outline of Christian theology with the doctrine of God, and there is no statement on Scripture. This was very much in line with the Ecumenical Creeds and with the medieval pattern. Similarly, the Scots Confession of 1560 begins with the doctrine of God. It does contain a short statement on Scripture, although not until chapter 19. The Belgic Confession of 1561 also begins with a chapter on God but then immediately launches into several detailed chapters on the doctrine of Scripture. The Thirty-Nine Articles of the Church of England of 1571 begins with five chapters on God and only then turns to deal with Scripture.

If, however, we look at some of the other confessional statements of the period we see a different pattern beginning to emerge, as more statements were produced.[24] A brief examination of some of the Reformation and post-Reformation confessional statements helps to demonstrate the move.[25]

The Genevan Confession of 1536 was a twenty-one-article confession John Calvin appended to the Catechism of Geneva, which 'was to be binding upon all the citizens of Geneva – probably 'the first instance of a formal pledge to a symbolical book in the history of the Reformed Church'.[26] The first article

---

22. With the possible exception of the creed of the Sixth Ecumenical Council against the Monothelites. See Philip Schaff, *The Creeds of Christendom*, vol. 2 of *The Creeds of Christendom* (Grand Rapids: Baker, 1983), p. 72.

23. Richard A. Muller, *Post-Reformation Reformed Dogmatics*, vol. 2: *Holy Scripture: The Cognitive Foundation of Theology* (Grand Rapids: Baker, 1993), p. 3.

24. Ibid., pp. 69–70.

25. For a more detailed analysis of these confessional statements see ibid., pp. 69–86.

26. Schaff, *Creeds*, vol. 2, p. 468.

of the confession is not on God but on Scripture. It is a very brief, non-technical statement, completely lacking in the detail to be seen in later statements, but its position at the beginning of the confession was instrumental in influencing other, later statements. For example, the Second Helvetic Confession of 1566, written by Heinrich Bullinger, begins with a long chapter on the Scriptures as the Word of God, followed by a chapter on interpreting Scripture. Only then does it turn to speak of God. This trend is intensified when we come to the Irish Articles of 1615. This confession begins with six articles on Scripture, then includes a chapter affirming the Ecumenical Creeds, and only in article 7 does it turn to speak of God. Finally, the Westminster Confession of Faith of 1647 begins with a long chapter on the doctrine of Scripture, a chapter similar in form and content to that of the Irish Articles.

There were many differences between the Reformers and the Protestant orthodox in their interpretation of Scripture and in the place they gave to the *locus* of Scripture. Muller examines these in significant detail.[27] He notes that there is continuity and discontinuity between the medieval view and that of the Reformers and again between that of the Reformers and that of the Protestant orthodox. In particular,

> we are in a position to recognize both the continuity of the scholastic view of Scripture as *principium* of theology from the thirteenth through the seventeenth centuries and the discontinuity in the approach to Scripture between the late Middle Ages and the Reformation. This discontinuity, moreover, can be seen at the root of both the Reformers' kerygmatic appeal to *sola Scriptura* and the Protestant orthodox theologians' massive development of a distinctively Protestant *locus de Scriptura* separate from the prolegomena (where the medieval doctors had placed it) and far more elaborate than the discussions of Scripture available to the orthodox in medieval systems.[28]

In the Reformation confessions and catechisms, then, there was a gradual move towards putting the doctrine of Scripture at the beginning, with everything thereafter being deduced from that first premise. Logically, this makes perfect sense. The Reformers and those who followed in their tradition wanted to emphasize that all of their teaching was drawn from Scripture; hence they began with a strong statement on the authority, sufficiency and perspicuity of Scripture before dealing with any other doctrine. In this way, they were underlining the

---

27. Muller, *Post-Reformation Reformed Dogmatics*, vol. 2, pp. 96–117.
28. Ibid., p. 68.

fact that when they came to speak about God, salvation, the church or any other matter, everything they said would be drawn from the Scripture principle. Although making sense 'logically', however, this positioning of the doctrine of Scripture creates many problems when viewed 'theologically'. In fact, this positioning of Scripture at the beginning of the theological system takes the primary focus away from God.

Within my own Reformed tradition, placing Scripture as the first *locus* in our theology, after the pattern of the Westminster Confession of Faith, has long been generally accepted as the basic methodology for systematic theology. Interestingly, however, in the twentieth century there was a curious anomaly. Most Reformed seminaries in the USA and many evangelical theological colleges elsewhere used as a standard text for systematic theology Louis Berkhof's *Systematic Theology*. The problem was that Berkhof had written an earlier volume entitled *Introductory Volume to Systematic Theology* in which he dealt with matters of prolegomena, including the nature, history, method and *principia* of dogmatics, not least the doctrines of revelation and inspiration. This volume, however, intended by Berkhof to be read before turning to his *Systematic Theology*, gradually went out of print and so generations of theological students read only the *Systematic Theology*, which had no chapter on the doctrine of Scripture. This meant that in practice they began with the doctrine of God, while theologically they held to a different view! Only recently has the *Introductory Volume to Systematic Theology* been republished and bound with the *Systematic Theology* into one volume.[29]

Scripture and the Holy Spirit

If we accept that the scholastic approach to Scripture, as epitomized by the Westminster Confession of Faith, made sense logically but not theologically, where should we place the doctrine of Scripture in our theological formulations?

When the apostle Peter addressed himself specifically to the question of the origins of Scripture, his answer focused on the Holy Spirit. He wrote, 'knowing this first of all, that no prophecy of Scripture comes from someone's own interpretation. For no prophecy was ever produced by the will of man, but men spoke from God as they were carried along by the Holy Spirit' (2 Pet. 1:20–21). Peter is saying here that the writers of the Bible did not simply sit down one day and decide to write something for posterity. Rather, they were

---

29. Louis Berkhof, *Systematic Theology: New Combined Edition* (Grand Rapids: Eerdmans, 1996).

under the constraint of the Holy Spirit. They could do no other! In other words, Peter is here testifying to the divine origin of the Bible in the work of God the Holy Spirit. As we shall see later, the work of the Holy Spirit is also the key both to recognizing Scripture *as* Scripture and also to understanding its meaning and significance. The writing of Scripture, then, ought to be seen as an aspect of the work of the Holy Spirit, and this ought to be reflected in the place Scripture is given in our theological formulations. This means that Scripture ought not to be placed at the beginning of the theological system, to provide an epistemological basis for what follows, but rather ought to be placed under the doctrine of God – more specifically, under the work of the Holy Spirit. The rationale for this argument concerns the nature of Scripture itself, as part of God's self-revelation. Thus theology proper begins with God, not with the Scriptures. It is God himself who brought the Scriptures into existence. How then can these writings have a logical or theological priority over the God who caused them to be written?

The logical argument that the Scriptures must come first in the theological system, because until we have established the authority of the Scriptures we cannot say anything about God or about anything else, does not stand up to close examination. This argument confuses two things: (1) the place of Scripture in God's self-revelation (a theological issue) and (2) the place of Scripture in the teaching office of the church (a practical issue). No-one denies that the truths we express in our systematic theologies are to be found in the Scriptures, but to put God's Word prior to God himself in our theological system has often led to serious errors. The most serious of these errors is to imply that the Scriptures can stand alone as a source of epistemological certainty, quite apart from the work of God the Holy Spirit. This error results in the Scriptures taking on a life of their own, whereby men and women sometimes imagine (even if they would never express it this way) that they hold in their hands the final written revelation of God that can be read, understood and applied, without any further involvement of God.

Please do not misunderstand this point. I am not arguing that the Scriptures are a dead letter that somehow 'become' the Word of God in a moment of revelation through the work of the Holy Spirit in the life of the believer, as some neo-orthodox have argued. These scholars, in my view, have confused the origin of the Scriptures (inspiration) with the spiritual recognition of the Scriptures (illumination). Rather, I hold that the Scriptures are objectively the Word of God, whether or not any individual has come to the place of recognizing them as such. Nevertheless, neither the origin nor the function of the Scriptures can be properly articulated outside the context of the work of God the Holy Spirit.

Within the structure of a systematic theology, the doctrine of Scripture might be expressed as follows. First, we speak of God (Father, Son and Holy Spirit) as a self-existent being, noting the Creator–creature distinction. Second, we speak of God's self-revelation, as in Hebrews 1, noting that he first of all spoke through prophets and apostles but supremely in the person and work of his Son, Jesus Christ. Then third, we go on to speak of the person and work of the Holy Spirit, the agent of this self-revelation, both in terms of Jesus Christ himself (conceived and empowered by the Holy Spirit) and of the Scriptures (breathed-out by the Holy Spirit). By this means, the doctrine of Scripture is placed in a solidly trinitarian context and thus in a thoroughly theological, Christological and pneumatological context. When we do this, the doctrine of Scripture can be articulated in a fresh way, liberated from the human quest for epistemological certainty and rooted in the God-centred context of revelation.

It might be thought that the location of the doctrine of Scripture is not important so long as it is included somewhere, but there is an issue here concerning the nature and content of revelation. John Webster has demonstrated that when the doctrine of Scripture 'migrates to the beginning of the dogmatic corpus' it then takes on the function of 'furnishing the epistemological warrants for Christian claims'.[30] Webster sees this as a failure to understand the true nature of revelation and as a misunderstanding of the relationship between Scripture and revelation. In particular, he insists that

> the content of revelation is God's own proper reality. Revelation is not to be thought of as the communication of arcane information or hidden truths, as if in revelation God were lifting the veil on something other than his own self and indicating it to us. Talk of revelation is not talk of some reality separable from God's own being, something which God as it were deposits in the world and which then becomes manipulable. Revelation is divine *self*-presentation; its content is identical with God.[31]

It is vital, then, that Scripture be set in the wider context of revelation and that revelation be firmly rooted within the doctrine of God. As Webster says, 'The doctrinal under-determination and mislocation of the idea of revelation can only be overcome by its reintegration into the comprehensive structure of Christian doctrine, and most especially the Christian doctrine of God.'[32] The

---

30. Webster, *Holy Scripture*, p. 12.

31. Ibid., p. 14.

32. Ibid., p. 13.

case being made in this chapter is that, within the doctrine of God, the proper place to discuss Scripture is as an aspect of the work of the Holy Spirit.

Scripture and epistemology

The argument that Scripture ought not to be placed as the first head in a theological system should not be taken to mean that epistemological concerns are to be ignored. Indeed, it is vital that we explain the way in which our epistemology relates to our doctrine of Scripture. In 1962, during a visit to America where he lectured at Princeton Theological Seminary and at the Chicago Divinity School, a reporter asked Karl Barth to sum up the teaching of his *Church Dogmatics*. Barth quoted the children's hymn 'Jesus loves me, this I know/ for the Bible tells me so'. In one sense, this was a media 'sound bite', long before such things became the normal currency of debate. In another sense, it was a profound epistemological statement of the relationship between Scripture and our knowledge of God. Barth was arguing that our knowledge of the love of God in Christ comes to us through the voice of God speaking in the Scriptures.

Christians have always believed that the Bible is the Word of God, meaning that it has its origins in the revelatory activity of the personal God of whom it speaks, and that it is a means by which he communicates with the creatures he has made. This God, eternally existing in Trinity as Father, Son and Spirit, creator of all things and yet distinct from creation, has chosen to make himself known and communicates with human beings by his Spirit through his Word. Now to declare that the Bible is God-given and therefore different from all other books would not have seemed a remarkable claim for Christians to make during the first millennium and a half of Christian history. Today, however, in the prevailing intellectual climate, it requires some justification and explanation. On what basis do Christians believe that the Bible ought to be received as having its origin in a personal, speaking God? The answer is that we believe the Bible to be the Word of God because God the Holy Spirit, working in our hearts and minds, persuades and assures us that this is the case. As Herman Bavinck puts it:

> Holy Scripture is self-attested (αυτοπιστος) and therefore the final ground of faith. No deeper ground can be advanced. To the question 'Why do you believe Scripture?' the only answer is: 'Because it is the word of God.' But if the next question is 'Why do you believe that Holy Scripture is the word of God?' a Christian cannot answer.[33]

---

33. Herman Bavinck, *Reformed Dogmatics*, vol. 1: *Prolegomena* (Grand Rapids: Baker Academic, 2003), p. 589.

This is not to say that Christian belief is irrational or consists in a blind fideism: quite the reverse is the case. This has been best argued by Cornelius Van Til[34] through his presuppositional theology and his transcendental argument.[35] As Van Til argued, we cannot prove the existence of God or the truth of the Bible. Indeed, we can come to accept the Bible only through the work of the Holy Spirit in our lives. This being the case, we must begin with the Bible, assuming it to be true, and work everything out from that starting point. His opponents said that this was a circular argument, but Van Til insisted that for a human being this was the only kind of argument. In recognizing that we are creatures of God, we must also recognize that God has the right to speak to us. If we try to judge whether or not the Bible has come to us from God, the question then becomes 'By what standard or criterion can we make such a judgment?' If we reply 'reason' or 'logic' or 'evidence', then we are setting these things as a higher authority than the voice of God speaking in Scripture. We must argue, rather, that reason, logic and evidence have their place in our thinking only because we live in a world God has created, which is therefore inherently rational. If we do not assume that God has created and sustains all things, then why should we expect to find any kind of rationality, structure or consistent form in our world? It is only when, by the internal testimony of the Holy Spirit, we accept the Bible as God's Word, that we can understand the nature and purpose of all created reality.

There has been a long Christian tradition of 'evidentialism', which stands in marked contrast to Van Til's 'presuppositionalism'. This traditional method of apologetics was developed in the early history of the Christian church and given classic form in the writings of Thomas Aquinas. It remains today the position of most Roman Catholic and most Protestant theologians. This method of defending Christian belief involves two stages. In the first stage, the task is to prove that there is a god, using the various proofs that have been developed over the centuries, such as the ontological, teleological and moral

---

34. Cornelius Van Til, *The Defense of the Faith* (Philadelphia: Presbyterian & Reformed, 1976); and Cornelius Van Til, *A Christian Theory of Knowledge* (Phillipsburg, N. J.: Presbyterian & Reformed, 1969).

35. For two different but sympathetic analyses of Van Til's thought see Greg L. Bahnsen, *Van Til's Apologetic: Readings and Analysis* (Phillipsburg, N. J.: Presbyterian & Reformed, 1998); and John M. Frame, *Cornelius Van Til – An Analysis of His Thought* (Phillipsburg, N. J.: Presbyterian & Reformed, 1995).

arguments. In the second stage, the task is to describe this god and call people to faith in this god. In practice, Christian theologians have normally laid out the arguments for the existence of God and then gone to the Bible to describe what this God is like.

There are four significant problems with this traditional method of apologetics. First, no-one has ever developed a compelling and conclusive proof capable of demonstrating, without reasonable doubt, that God exists. The proofs have more often served as helpful confirmations to the faith of those who already believe. To this degree, we must not reject the importance of evidence. Van Til himself never rejected the value of evidence in this sense.[36] Nor does John Frame, perhaps the leading presuppositionalist of our day, who is not only a critical and constructive expositor of Van Til's theological perspective[37] but a careful dialogue partner with evidentialists and others.[38] Van Til and Frame are simply demonstrating themselves to be good Reformed theologians in affirming that our 'full persuasion and assurance' of the Bible's truth and authority comes from the internal witness of the Holy Spirit, while at the same time recognizing, with the Westminster Confession of Faith, that there are many factors that would support this belief and help to strengthen this conviction.[39]

The second problem with evidentialism is that it involves a logical leap at the connecting point between the two stages of the traditional apologetic. In other words, having demonstrated (at least to his own satisfaction) that there is a god, the evidentialist theologian has traditionally gone on to use the Bible

---

36. Thom Notaro, *Van Til and the Use of Evidence* (Phillipsburg, N. J.: Presbyterian & Reformed, 1980).

37. Frame, *Cornelius Van Til*.

38. John M. Frame, *Apologetics to the Glory of God* (Phillipsburg, N. J.: Presbyterian & Reformed, 1994).

39. 'We may be moved and induced by the testimony of the Church to an high and reverent esteem of the Holy Scripture. And the heavenliness of the matter, the efficacy of the doctrine, the majesty of the style, the consent of all the parts, the scope of the whole (which is, to give all glory to God), the full discovery it makes of the only way of man's salvation, the many other incomparable excellencies, and the entire perfection thereof, are arguments whereby it does abundantly evidence itself to be the Word of God: yet notwithstanding, our full persuasion and assurance of the infallible truth and divine authority thereof, is from the inward work of the Holy Spirit bearing witness by and with the Word in our hearts' (ch. 1, sect. 5).

to describe this god. There is, however, no clear logical step from proving the existence of 'a' god to then speaking about 'the' God described in the Bible. How do we know that the 'god' thus proven is the God who has revealed himself in and through the person of Jesus Christ?

The third problem with evidentialism is its support for a 'natural theology', which precedes a 'revealed theology'. This problem is compounded by the fact that even among theologians who believe in natural theology there are major differences of view. For example, the Roman Catholic view of natural theology is based on the conviction that human beings are able, by unaided reason alone, to come to real knowledge of God. G. C. Berkouwer describes those who hold to this position and says of their version of natural theology that it seeks a way to God 'via the *undisturbed natural reason* and it assigns to special revelation an *augmenting* function'.[40] The evangelical evidentialist method known as the Ligonier Apologetic, developed by R. C. Sproul, John Gerstner and Arthur Lindsley, also holds that a natural theology is possible. It does not, however, accept the view of Roman Catholic theology regarding human nature. All of the Ligonier scholars regard human beings as totally depraved, in the sense that every aspect of their human nature is tainted by sin. They are, however, convinced that there is common ground between the believer and the unbeliever and that this common ground is 'where believer and unbeliever can stand on equal terms and engage in meaningful discourse'.[41] They identify three 'common assumptions' that 'are held by theists and nontheists alike'.[42] These are as follows:

1. The validity of the law of non-contradiction.
2. The validity of the law of causality.
3. The basic reliability of sense perception.[43]

The key point in such discussions becomes the 'point of contact' with the unregenerate human being. In other words, if all human beings are sinners and their minds are affected by sin, how can the gospel penetrate their darkness? Emil Brunner, who also believed in natural theology, said that the point of

---

40. Berkouwer, *General Revelation*, p. 329.
41. R. C. Sproul, John Gerstner and Arthur Lindsley, *Classical Apologetics* (Grand Rapids: Zondervan, 1984), p. 70.
42. Ibid., p. 72.
43. The Ligonier apologists dedicated their book to Van Til, despite disagreeing with his position, such had been his influence upon them.

contact was the image of God in man, which is twofold: the *formal* image (man as a responsible subject to whom God can speak), and the *material* image (every part affected by sin). For Brunner, the formal image is untouched by the fall and is the point of contact for redeeming grace.

One of the most significant critics of natural theology was Karl Barth, who engaged in a debate on the subject with Emil Brunner.[44] Barth so wanted to stress the uniqueness of the revelation found in Jesus Christ that he would allow no other source of knowledge of God to stand alongside that. Hence he denied the possibility of natural theology. Van Til was also opposed to natural theology due to his fundamental commitment to the notion that, because of the transcendence of God and the noetic effects of sin on the human mind, we can only know God when he reveals himself.

This leads naturally on to the fourth objection to evidentialism, as spelled out by Van Til, namely that evidentialism allowed human beings to judge the truth or falsehood of Christian claims. In other words, it allowed sinners to put God into the balance and make a decision as to whether or not he existed and, if he did, whether or not what he said was true. By doing this, it concedes the Enlightenment view that human beings are autonomous and are the reference point against which everything must be judged. In contrast to this, Van Til insisted that the natural man cannot be seen as an independent being with free will who is able to weigh up the arguments without prejudice or bias. On the contrary, the sinner is a covenant-breaker who has a vested interest in disproving God. He is in rebellion against God and is in no position to act without bias. Van Til was effectively calling for consistency, since we cannot speak about human beings in one way when we do our theology (sinners whose every faculty has been tainted and corrupted by our fallenness) and in another way when we do our apologetics (neutral thinkers who can impartially weigh up the truth).

For Van Til, the ultimate reference point is God (the ontological Trinity) and not man. The key text he used was the fall of humanity in Genesis 3. The first two chapters of the book tell us that God created everything (out of nothing) and that the whole creation was perfectly good but that then the first human beings, Adam and Eve, made a deliberate decision to disobey God. They chose to listen to the voice of the serpent rather than to the voice of God. In making this decision, they asserted their own independence and self-sufficiency. They

---

44. Peter Fraenkel (ed.), *Natural Theology: Comprising 'Nature and Grace' by Professor Dr Emil Brunner and the Reply 'No!' by Dr Karl Barth* (London: Geoffrey Bles: Centenary, 1946).

were saying, in effect, that all of their decisions from that point on would be made on the basis of what *they* wanted, rather than on the basis of what God said. That is to say, they were now looking at the world as if it revolved around them, instead of thinking out of a centre in God. To 'think out of a centre in God' means to have a view of the world which recognizes that God is the creator and sustainer of the whole universe and that everything comes from him and is responsible to him. It is to see everything from God's perspective as revealed to us and to be completely obedient to what he says. This is the way it was in the beginning, as described in the first two chapters of Genesis.

The new situation our first parents created was completely different. They chose to listen not only to God but also to Satan. Having done so, they weighed up what God had said and what Satan had said and then made a decision. In doing so, they were saying something very important. They were saying that God's Word was an opinion they would consider, rather than the final author-ity in all decision-making. In short, they were saying that human beings were capable of deciding whether or not to believe what God said. This was cata-strophic for humanity. The creatures had become so full of their own import-ance that they felt they could put the Creator in his place! Immediately, everything changed. The relationship between God and humanity was broken, Adam and Eve were banished from the presence of God, and God's judgment fell upon them. Because he was the representative of the human race the judg-ment also fell upon every human being born from then until now – except Jesus Christ, whose birth by a virgin sets him apart from those who are 'in Adam'.

For Van Til, the key point was that Eve weighed up the claim and counter-claim of God and the devil and decided she could judge on the basis of facts rather than being. The issue of 'facts' brings us very close to a true under-standing of Van Til. He is quite clear that there are no such things as 'brute facts'; rather, every fact is God-created and God-interpreted. Unbelievers may possess a certain number of facts, but they have no principle of interpretation and therefore no real knowledge. Only when the believer takes the facts do they make sense. Van Til describes the 'facts' possessed by an unbeliever as being like a string of beads that has broken and where you cannot find either end of the string to reconnect them. Thus you have many beads but no way of making them into a necklace. Similarly, unbelievers have many facts but no means of connecting these facts into a coherent world view, because they lack the one piece of information that unites these facts, namely the existence of God and the distinction between the Creator and creation. Unbelievers simply cannot fully comprehend the facts in their possession (1 Cor. 2:14); hence the simplest believer has more real knowledge than the most educated unbeliever!

From that point on until the present, humans have been warped creatures. They have ceased to be truly human because, having been designed to live in fellowship with God, they can find true significance and real meaning only in the context of that relationship. The problem is that, instead of living in total dependence upon God, they have now declared themselves to be independent of him. Humankind was never intended to live like this, and is not equipped to do so.

It is my conviction that, although there is much to be learned from some of the evidentialist writings, Van Til is substantially correct in his analysis of the human condition and in the need to affirm the primacy of God as the one who supernaturally makes himself known, breaking through, by his Spirit, the sinful intransigence and wilful blindness of human beings.

There is a third method of stating and defending the Christian faith that shares some elements of both evidentialism and presuppositionalism. It has come to be known as 'Reformed apologetics' and is associated with the names of two of the most important Christian philosophers of our day, Alvin Plantinga[45] and Nicholas Wolterstorff.[46] This view is based on the notion of 'warranted beliefs' and has significant similarities at points with Scottish common sense realism, developed by Thomas Reid in the late eighteenth century in opposition to the atheistic philosophy of David Hume. This 'Scottish philosophy' had a remarkable influence on the early Princeton theology, through the advocacy of John Witherspoon. The strength of the position advocated by Plantinga and Wolterstorff is that there are certain truths about which there ought to be no dispute and on which all reasonable people are agreed. In other words, there are certain things we know to be true and that simply do not require evidence or argument. It is also argued that evidence from sense perception, which has had such a dominant place in the thinking of post-Enlightenment scholars, is not the only source of true information and knowledge. Indeed, Plantinga follows Calvin in asserting that each human being has a *sensus divinitas*, which brings real knowledge of God and is to be accepted as a warranted belief alongside the evidence from our senses.

---

45. See e.g. Alvin Plantinga, *Warranted Christian Belief* (Oxford: Oxford University Press, 2000); Alvin Plantinga, *God and Other Minds: A Study of the Rational Justification of Belief in God* (Ithaca, N. Y.: Cornell University Press, 1990).
46. See e.g. Nicholas P. Wolterstorff, *Divine Discourse* (Cambridge: Cambridge University Press, 1995); Nicholas P. Wolterstorff and Alvin Plantinga (eds.), *Faith and Rationality: Reason and Belief in God* (Notre Dame, Ind.: University of Notre Dame Press, 1984).

There are strengths in this approach, but most of these strengths fit comfortably with a Van Tilian perspective. In general, I would share the analysis of Reformed apologetics given by John Frame and also Frame's hope of a continuing dialogue between the two positions.[47]

Reconstructing the vocabulary

I have argued, then, that the doctrine of Scripture must be relocated within the theological system, to emphasize that it is an aspect of the work of the Holy Spirit in the context of God's self-revelation. I have further argued that Van Til's presuppositionalist apologetics sits comfortably with this relocation and enables us to answer some of the difficult epistemological questions. We must now move on to consider the vocabulary of this reconstructed doctrine of Scripture.

In spelling out a pneumatological approach to the doctrine of Scripture, I find myself developing a careful vocabulary for the doctrine. First, I affirm that the Holy Spirit is the one responsible for the origin of the Scriptures. He is the one who enabled men to 'speak from God' as he carried them along (2 Pet. 1:21) and he is the one who breathed-out the Scriptures (2 Tim. 3:16). This I call 'divine spiration'. Second, I affirm that the Holy Spirit is the one who enables us to identify the Scriptures as the Word of God, as Calvin expressed it in his notion of the internal testimony of the Holy Spirit. This I call 'recognition'. Third, I affirm that it is the Holy Spirit who gives us understanding of the meaning and significance of the Scriptures, and this I call 'comprehension'. Fourth, I affirm the truth and authority of the Scriptures as this is impressed upon us by the Holy Spirit. In other words, God the Holy Spirit does not simply enable us to recognize the Scriptures and give us understanding of them but also persuades us that in them we hear the authentic voice of God speaking to us; hence they are reliable. For this, I use the word 'infallibility'.

Divine spiration

Since the publication in 1611 of the Authorized (King James) Version of the Bible, the most famous and enduring of the English translations, the word 'inspiration' has generally been used as a translation of the Greek word *theopneustos*, found in 2 Timothy 3:16. The English word 'inspiration' is drawn from

---

47. John M. Frame, *The Doctrine of The Knowledge of God* (Phillipsburg, N. J.: Presbyterian & Reformed, 1987), pp. 382–400.

the Latin word *inspirata*, which was used in the Vulgate translation of the 2 Timothy passage.[48] 'Inspiration' has also become a standard term in theological discussions regarding Scripture. It is very difficult to dislodge a word that has so embedded itself in our theological language and has been invested with such theological content, but the word is problematic and an attempt must be made to do so.

The use of the word 'inspiration' in relation to Scripture is problematic for two reasons. The first problem is that, as a translation of the Greek word *theopneustos*, it is exegetically inaccurate. Following the Authorized (King James) Version, almost all of our English language translations of 2 Timothy 3:16 have routinely rendered *theopneustos* as 'inspired', whereas it literally means 'God-breathed' or 'God-spirited', and the word 'inspiration' (certainly in the modern era) does not adequately and clearly convey this meaning. It was only with the publication of the New International Version of the Bible that 'God-breathed' was used as a translation. This conveys more of the real sense of the term, which is 'expiration' rather than 'inspiration'.

The second reason for saying that the word 'inspiration' is problematic is related to modern English usage. Today, when people say that a poet, an author, a musician or a painter was 'inspired', they mean that there took place a remarkable heightening of that artist's natural powers, enabling the completion of a work of genius. They are rarely suggesting that some kind of divine intervention occurred.[49] Unfortunately, there is a tendency among those who write on the doctrine of the inspiration of Scripture to assume precisely the same meaning when speaking about the authors of Scripture, that is, to think in terms of the writers of Scripture as persons invested with a particular genius, or heightened religious sensitivity or something of the kind. Over against this, we must affirm exegetically that *theopneustos* is not speaking primarily about the authors of Scripture but about the Scriptures themselves. In other words, the claim is not being made that the authors were 'inspired' but rather that the Scriptures were 'God-breathed'. Clearly, these claims are related but are, nevertheless, distinct.

The confusion that has sometimes existed on this matter is exemplified in the writings of William Abraham. Although he has written a great deal on the

---

48. B. B. Warfield says that 'The word "inspire" and its derivatives seem to have come into Middle English from the French' (B. B. Warfield, *The Inspiration and Authority of the Bible* [Philadelphia: Presbyterian & Reformed, 1948], p. 131).

49. See e.g. Timothy Clark, *The Theory of Inspiration: Composition as a Crisis of Subjectivity in Romantic and Post-Romantic Writing* (Manchester: Manchester University Press, 1997).

doctrine of Scripture, much of it profound and helpful, I must take issue with him on this matter of inspiration. Abraham identifies what he perceives to be the problem with some evangelical views on inspiration:

> If there is one mistake in recent theories of inspiration which deserves to be singled out for special attention, that mistake is at root conceptual. Rather than pause to reflect on divine inspiration, Evangelical theologians have built their theories around the idea of divine speaking. This is simply a basic category mistake. It is essential to identify and remove this mistake if there is to be progress or hope for any future account of inspiration.[50]

If inspiration has nothing to do with divine speaking, then how are we to establish what it does mean? Abraham's answer is to begin with the human agent. He argues that many evangelical theologians (especially in the Warfield tradition) have made the mistake of trying to understand inspiration by focusing on God and in particular by focusing on God's speech. This, he argues, is entirely the wrong way to begin.[51] Instead, Abraham looks at the way inspiration is used in human language so that he can then later by analogy determine what it means when God is said to inspire. The problem here is that this is precisely the opposite of good exegesis! Indeed, it may well be a model for how *not* to do theology. Instead of asking what the term means in its original Greek form and in the context in which it appears, Abraham wants to take the modern meaning of the word and then read that back into 2 Timothy. By using this approach, Abraham fails to deal properly with what 2 Timothy 3:16 actually says and means. When Paul says that Scripture is God-breathed, he does not mean that its writers were 'inspired' in the common English use of the term. Abraham uses the illustration of a good teacher inspiring his students and then goes back into the New Testament to 2 Timothy 3:16 and interprets *theopneustos* accordingly, but this is an unacceptable procedure. This becomes obvious when you reach his conclusion:

> What I am suggesting with respect to inspiration is simply this. It is through his revelatory and saving acts as well as through his personal dealings with individuals and groups that God inspired his people to write and collate what we now know as the Bible. Inspiration is not an activity that should be experientially separated

---

50. William J. Abraham, *The Divine Inspiration of Holy Scripture* (Oxford: Oxford University Press, 1981), p. 58.

51. Ibid., p. 62.

from these other acts that God has performed in the past. As a matter of logic, inspiration is a unique activity of God that cannot be defined in terms of his other acts or activity, but as a matter of fact he inspires in, with, and through his special revelatory acts and through his personal guidance of those who wrote and put together the various parts of the Bible. This is the heart of my positive proposal.[52]

To avoid confusion of this kind, I propose that the word 'inspiration' be replaced. The initial thought was that we might use the word 'expiration', since it clearly has the connotation of 'breathing out'. Unfortunately, as a colleague, Dr Alistair Wilson, pointed out, it also has the connotation of a *final* breathing out, indeed a terminal breathing out! The decision to opt for the word 'spiration' was helpfully supported by the *Shorter Oxford English Dictionary*, where the word 'spiration' is defined as 'The creative function of the deity conceived as the action of breathing.'[53] Professor David Wright later expressed the view that an adjective was needed[54] and so I shall use the expression 'divine spiration'.[55] This is, of course, not a novel suggestion, since the word 'spiration' has long been recognized by scholars as a good translation. B. B. Warfield, for example, argued that this was the best translation for *theopneustos*,[56] although he subsequently (like all of the others who have advocated spiration) went on to use 'inspiration' because it was the common currency.

Quite apart from any discussion of the correct English translation for *theopneustos*, however, we must ask what this word conveys (and does not

---

52. Ibid., p. 67.

53. *Shorter Oxford English Dictionary* (Oxford: Clarendon, 1959).

54. In private correspondence, following discussion at the Scottish Evangelical Theology Society conference.

55. I am still pondering the interesting suggestion of my colleague Dr Nick Needham, who says that this expression might have other beneficial consequences by anchoring the work of the Spirit in relation to Scripture in a trinitarian ontology. In trinitarian theology, 'spiration' refers to the action of the Father, who eternally spirates – breathes forth – the Spirit. Could one say that the spiration of Scripture is also an action of the Father through the Spirit? E.g. when we breathe, breath (spirit) is not necessarily all that comes out. Our breath can also form a word. Could it be that the Father breathes out (spirates) the Word through the Breath (Spirit)?

56. Warfield, *Inspiration and Authority*, p. 133.

convey) to the reader. To some extent this depends upon the translation and exegesis of the whole sentence from 2 Timothy 3:16. For example, one possible translation is, 'All inspired Scripture is profitable for . . .' (New English Bible), which could be exegeted to mean that not all Scripture is inspired. Most commentators, however, opt for a translation such as, 'All Scripture is inspired by God and is profitable for . . .'[57] This translation would suggest that the Scriptures have come into existence through the supernatural action of God and that the documents so produced have been given by God for the good of his church in various ways. That still leaves unanswered one further question, namely the composition and extent of the 'Scripture' referred to in the text. There can surely be little doubt that the apostles who wrote the New Testament believed that the Old Testament was the Word of God written (Acts 4:25; 28:25) and that therefore Paul was referring to the Old Testament Scriptures. Given that he has enunciated a principle, however, 'All Scripture is inspired by God', surely the Scriptures then being written by the apostles would also be regarded as inspired? Certainly, Peter does not hesitate to identify the letters of Paul alongside the 'other Scriptures' (2 Pet. 3:16).

It remains a fact, however, that Paul does not explain what he means by his use of the word *theopneustos*. Indeed, it has been argued that he may have coined the word himself, since it does not appear anywhere else in Scripture and the earliest references beyond Scripture are in the second century.[58] How then are we to understand the meaning and significance of this divine spiration of Scripture? B. B. Warfield said that Paul's use of this language conveys the idea that the Scriptures are 'the product of the creative breath of God', albeit, 'without any indication of how God has operated in producing them'.[59] In order to get some indication of how God operated, clearly we must go elsewhere, namely to 2 Peter 1.

In the first eleven verses of 2 Peter 1, the apostle gives a tremendous summary of the key elements of the Christian faith. He speaks of righteousness, faith, grace and peace. He describes Jesus Christ as our God and our Saviour. He speaks about knowledge of God, God's power, God's promises,

---

57. See e.g. I. Howard Marshall, *The Pastoral Epistles*, International Critical Commentary (Edinburgh: T. & T. Clark, 1999), pp. 792–793; and Philip H. Towner, *The Letters to Timothy and Titus*, New International Commentary on the New Testament (Grand Rapids: Eerdmans, 2006), pp. 585–588.

58. Towner, *Letters to Timothy and Titus*, p. 589.

59. Warfield, *Inspiration and Authority*, p. 133.

the Christian life, forgiveness of sins, calling, election, God's eternal kingdom and so on. In verses 12–15, the apostle says that he wants to remind his readers of these matters, although they already know them. He says that he wants to refresh their memories and do everything he possibly can to ensure that the message of the gospel will be firmly planted in their hearts and minds even after he himself has gone. Then, in verses 16–21, he defends his right to speak about these matters with such authority. In particular, he mentions two things: first, the authority he had as an eyewitness of what happened on the mount of transfiguration; second, the authority of the Scriptures whose prophecies foretold Christ. It is in this context, as we saw earlier, that Peter comments on the authors of Scripture, saying that 'men spoke from God as they were carried along by the Holy Spirit' (2 Pet. 1:21).

If we combine, then, what Paul says about the Scriptures (they have been breathed out by God) with what Peter says about the human authors of Scripture (they spoke from God as they were carried along by the Holy Spirit), then we can move to a definition: 'The doctrine of divine spiration (inspiration) is the affirmation that at certain times and in certain places, God the Holy Spirit caused men to write books and his supervisory action was such that although these books are truly the work of human beings, they are also the Word of God. The church, under the guidance of the Holy Spirit, ultimately came to recognize that there are sixty-six books that God caused to be written in this way over a long period of time.'

This was precisely what the apostolic authors claimed for themselves. They knew that they had received revelation from God. In Galatians 1:11–12, Paul says this: 'For I would have you know, brothers, that the gospel that was preached by me is not man's gospel. For I did not receive it from any man, nor was I taught it, but I received it through a revelation of Jesus Christ.' Whatever else this verse means, it surely teaches that the Christian gospel does not have a human origin but a divine origin. In other words, it comes from God. Now it follows from all of this that the Bible has authority. If the people who wrote it were 'carried along' by the Holy Spirit and if it was 'God-breathed', then we must say that it has a unique authority. In order to avoid misunderstanding, however, it is better to reside the authority in God rather than in the Scriptures themselves. We might speak, then, of the authority of God speaking by his Spirit in and through the Scriptures.

Recognition

This brings us to the second suggestion for new vocabulary, namely that we supplement and interpret the word 'illumination' by use of the word 'recognition'. I make this suggestion because the word 'illumination' has sometimes been used in such a way as to imply that the Scriptures need to have light shed upon them before they can be understood. The problem, however, is in the human mind and not in the Scriptures. The Scriptures do not need to be illuminated but rather the human mind, which has been damaged by the noetic effects of sin, needs to be given understanding. Only when the Holy Spirit enables can these spiritual words and spiritual truths be identified as Scripture and properly understood.

It is important that we explain this problem regarding the human mind. If we consider the true condition of humanity, then we shall see the need for the Holy Spirit to enable us to recognize the Scriptures. For example, in Romans 1:18–25, Paul says some startling things. He says that every human being possesses true knowledge of God and that this knowledge is of such clarity that human beings have absolutely no excuse if they deny that they know God. Indeed, he goes so far as to argue that human beings deliberately suppress this knowledge and this truth, because of the innate sinfulness of all fallen creatures. The result of this, he says, is that human beings have exchanged truth for lies and their thinking has become futile. To put it bluntly: they are fools.

The implications of this teaching are of considerable importance. We are being told that all human beings have a true knowledge of God at some level of their being but that they deliberately suppress this knowledge because of their sinful condition. That sinful condition originated in Genesis 3 when our first parents opted to live self-centred rather than God-centred lives. The minds of unregenerate human beings, then, are twisted and perverted. Instead of holding to the truth, they deliberately suppress it, and instead of worshipping and serving God, prefer lies and foolishness. There is, then, according to Paul, a difference between believers and unbelievers when it comes to the mind. Elsewhere, Paul expresses it like this:

> For those who live according to the flesh set their minds on the things of the flesh, but those who live according to the Spirit set their minds on the things of the Spirit. To set the mind on the flesh is death, but to set the mind on the Spirit is life and peace. For the mind that is set on the flesh is hostile to God, for it does not submit to God's law; indeed, it cannot. (Rom. 8:5–7)

That is to say, unbelievers have a 'mindset' opposed to God, which is why Paul can say that 'the god of this world has blinded the minds of the unbelievers, to keep them from seeing the light of the gospel of the glory of Christ, who is the image of God' (2 Cor. 4:4). Only if we recognize the true condition of the human mind can we then properly understand the work of the Holy Spirit in relation to the mind and to the discovery of truth.

One way to approach this more directly is to ask a question about the process by which someone becomes a Christian, in order to see the significance of the mind and the need for it to be acted upon by the Holy Spirit. We can usefully deal with this question with special reference to Colossians 1. Four things in particular in this chapter help us here. First, in verse 5, the gospel is described as 'the word of the truth'. Now that is very significant because it means that the gospel (or good news) is not simply a description of historical events (concerning Jesus of Nazareth), nor is it simply an appeal to believe: it is first and foremost a word of truth.[60] The second thing to notice is in verse 6. Paul tells how the gospel is producing fruit and growing all over the world just as it has also been doing among the Colossians since the day they 'heard it and understood the grace of God in truth'. Paul is saying that the gospel began to do its work among these Colossians when they heard and understood the truth of the gospel. Whatever else we might understand by these words, one thing is clear: in responding to the gospel, we use our minds. The third point follows on directly, at the beginning of verse 7. Speaking of the gospel, Paul says that they 'learned it' from Epaphras. Now that is a somewhat strange way to speak. We often speak about people 'hearing' the gospel, but how often have we ever spoken about someone 'learning' the gospel? Indeed, in some evangelical circles you will hear people say, 'The gospel is caught not taught.' On the basis of this verse in Colossians, we can say that this is not true. The fourth point is found in verse 21. Speaking of what the Colossians were like before they became Christians, Paul says that they were 'alienated' from God and 'hostile in mind'.

When we take these four points together, we may sum them up like this. The gospel of the Lord Jesus Christ is a word of truth that comes to men and women who are enemies of God in their minds. This gospel of truth becomes effectual when it is understood and learned. Thus we can answer the question about the means by which we become Christians by saying that this happens as a direct result of truth being applied to the mind by the Holy Spirit. There are various other passages in the Bible that would support this interpretation of Colossians 1. Most important in this context is Romans 12:2: 'be transformed by the renewal of your mind'. That is the first point of change. Indeed, we can go so far as to say that once the mind has been 'reset' in a Godward direction, it cannot be undone. Thereafter the task is to bring our 'flesh' and our emotions into accord with that new mindset, as Paul implies in Romans 7:25.

---

60. The gospel is also described as 'the word of truth' in Eph. 1:13 and Jas 1:18.

There is a tendency in some Christian circles today to imagine that men and women become Christians as a result of emotional experiences, or because they have been influenced and moved by a testimony, or because they have enjoyed a piece of Christian music, or for one of a hundred other reasons. Ultimately, however, whatever experiences of this nature we might have, to become a Christian it is necessary that truth be applied to the mind. At some point it is necessary that we learn the message of the gospel, understand it, and be persuaded by it. In the last analysis, it is *truth*, not emotion, that makes us Christians. However, none of this argument is intended to suggest that only clever people can become Christians, or that people who have a good mind have a better chance of becoming Christians. In fact, the opposite is probably true, as Paul says in 1 Corinthians 2. The point being made here is that the human mind has been damaged by sin's noetic effects and only when the Holy Spirit acts to renew the mind, enabling us to recognize the truth of God, will we truly become Christians. In other words, it is not the Scriptures that need to be 'illumined'; it is our fallen human minds that need to be renewed by the Holy Spirit to enable us to 'recognize' what is already there in Scripture. The problem lies with us and not with anything lacking in the Scriptures them-selves.

Now I must say that the best writers on the doctrine of illumination have always taken this position and emphasized that the problem of incomprehension relates to the human mind and not to the Scriptures, but many others have not.[61] It would seem reasonable to argue that if we use the word 'recognition', we can deal with some of the confusion and ambiguity that can arise from the word 'illumination'. In order to see the value of the proposal, we must ask the most significant question of all, namely on what basis do we believe that the Scriptures are the Word of God? The answer, following Calvin, is that such belief is possible only by the internal testimony of the Holy Spirit in the life of the believer.[62] In other words, the Holy Spirit enables us to 'recognize' the Scriptures as the Word of God.

Comprehension

This brings us to the third suggestion for additional vocabulary, namely that we supplement and interpret the word 'perspicuity' by use of the word 'comprehension'.

---

61. In my view, much of the difficulty posed by Karl Barth's doctrine of Scripture arises out of a confusion between *theopneustos* and illumination.

62. Calvin, *Institutes* 1.7.1–5.

If illumination as traditionally understood has to do with recognizing the Scriptures as the Word of God, perspicuity has to do with understanding what the Scriptures mean. The problem with the concept of 'perspicuity' is that it can be understood to imply an access to the Scriptures that is entirely human and natural. Now those who first used the expression were making the important point that the Scriptures can be read with profit by any human being, without requiring the aid of a priest or other 'specialist' and that although there is much that is difficult to understand and may require the help of those who have studied the original languages and are trained in exegesis, nevertheless, there is a sense in which the simplest person who can read will be able to discern the gospel in the Scriptures and so find salvation and peace with God. With this use of the word 'perspicuity' I have no problem and my advocacy of the word 'comprehension' is not intended to undermine this core point in any way. Rather, my intention in using 'comprehension' is to underline the fact that only God the Holy Spirit can give us understanding (comprehension) of the Scriptures.

The same Holy Spirit who gives us 'recognition' that the Scriptures are what they claim to be, also communicates the meaning of the Scriptures to us, such that we have 'comprehension'. In this way, God the Holy Spirit enables us to understand the meaning of the Scriptures, through the enlightening of our minds. This notion of the human mind receiving enlightening from the Holy Spirit is found in many places. For example, this is precisely the point Paul was making in 1 Corinthians 2:11–16:

> For who knows a person's thoughts except the spirit of that person, which is in him? So also no one comprehends the thoughts of God except the Spirit of God. Now we have received not the spirit of the world, but the Spirit who is from God, that we might understand the things freely given us by God. And we impart this in words not taught by human wisdom but taught by the Spirit, interpreting spiritual truths to those who are spiritual.
>
> The natural person does not accept the things of the Spirit of God, for they are folly to him, and he is not able to understand them because they are spiritually discerned. The spiritual person judges all things, but is himself to be judged by no one. 'For who has understood the mind of the Lord so as to instruct him?' But we have the mind of Christ.

This is a remarkable passage that has important implications for theology and for theologians. It teaches us that understanding the things of God is a God-given ability and not a natural human ability. The same idea is found in Jesus' answer to the disciples' question as to why he spoke in parables. He replied:

> To you it has been given to know the secrets of the kingdom of heaven, but to them
> it has not been given. For to the one who has, more will be given, and he will have an
> abundance, but from the one who has not, even what he has will be taken away. This
> is why I speak to them in parables, because seeing they do not see, and hearing they
> do not hear, nor do they understand. (Matt. 13:11–13)

Many attempts have been made to undermine the clear meaning of this text because the common wisdom is that Jesus spoke in parables in order to make himself clear, to be more easily understood. It is pointed out that people can understand stories better than long propositional narratives and so Jesus used this as an educational tool. This, however, is not what Jesus actually said! He said that he spoke in parables to conceal (and not to reveal) his message. Only if we have a theology that gives a significant place to the ministry of the Holy Spirit in providing 'comprehension' of the Scriptures shall we be comfortable with these words of Jesus.

There is no doubt that someone who is not a Christian can read and intellectually engage with the words of Scripture, but it is also true that such a person cannot properly understand the Scriptures without the work of the Holy Spirit. That is why, at Caesarea Philippi, when Jesus asked his disciples who they believed him to be and Peter identified him as 'the Christ, the Son of the living God', Jesus immediately said, 'Blessed are you, Simon Bar-Jonah! For flesh and blood has not revealed this to you, but my Father who is in heaven' (Matt. 16:16–17). Similarly, when Paul and his companions shared the gospel with Lydia outside the town of Philippi, Luke tells us that 'The Lord opened her heart to pay attention to what was said by Paul' (Acts 16:14). In other words, it was not simply a matter of human acceptance of the message; it was necessary that God the Holy Spirit should 'open her heart'. There is also the interesting occasion when Paul and Barnabas were preaching the gospel and some of the Gentiles became Christians. Luke tells us, 'and as many as were appointed to eternal life believed' (Acts 13:48). Notice, it is not simply those who believed but those who were 'appointed', surely emphasizing that God the Holy Spirit, who effectually calls, gives comprehension.

Infallibility

The final suggestion in respect of vocabulary is that we should opt for the word 'infallibility' as over against the word 'inerrancy'. This is not new language, because the word 'infallibility' has regularly been used in speaking of the Scriptures. In recent years, however, there has been a growing dominance of the use of the word 'inerrancy' (a word rarely used in Europe) and this, in some of its forms, has represented a turn towards a somewhat mechanical and even rationalistic approach to Scripture, basing its authority on a set of inerrant manuscripts. The argument for 'infallibility' is that the final authority for the Christian is the authority of God speaking in and through his Word and that the Holy Spirit infallibly uses God's Word to achieve all he intends to achieve. It is, therefore, a more dynamic (or organic) and less mechanical view of authority. It also avoids a number of serious problems related to the word 'inerrancy', as we shall see.

In choosing 'infallibility' over against 'inerrancy', I am advocating an equally 'high' but yet somewhat different theology of Scripture. Since this is one of the principal objectives of the book, I shall devote the next three chapters to the subject. In the next chapter, I shall explain the development of liberal theology out of its roots in the Enlightenment and also note the main opponents of this theological perspective. Then, in the next chapter, I shall trace the origins of the inerrantist position. I shall then go on in the following chapter to offer a European alternative to the American inerrantist position.

3. THE ENLIGHTENMENT AND LIBERAL THEOLOGY

Introduction

Any discussion of the idea of 'inerrancy' must be set in the context of the Enlightenment and the resulting liberal theology, since it was liberal theology's rejection of the older orthodoxy that prompted an evangelical response and the development of the inerrantist position. In this chapter, we shall examine the doctrine of Scripture that emerged from liberal theology and see two of the main responses to that position. In this way, we shall identify the three main dialogue partners in the modern debate concerning inerrancy: liberal theology, neo-orthodoxy and conservative evangelicalism. Then, in the next chapter, we shall consider the development of the inerrantist position out of its origins in fundamentalism.

The Enlightenment

We must now pause and note that the orthodox doctrine of Scripture, set in the context of an understanding of God's self-revelation, remained largely unchallenged for around 1,700 years of Christian history. That, however, is no longer the case. Most theologians in the modern period have rejected this classic expression of the doctrine. There can be little argument but that an anti-supernaturalist position has long been the prevailing view within the academy.

How did this change take place? To understand this, we must go back to the Enlightenment of the eighteenth century. Much was good about the Enlightenment, notably the desire for freedom from oppression and ignorance and the desire to think rationally. In many ways, it carried forward the progress made by the humanists, who laid the foundation for modern scholarship. Essentially, however, the Enlightenment led to the secularization of society because it could find no place for the kind of God described in the Scriptures, namely a God who created all things and who holds all things in being, a God who speaks and acts.

At the heart of the Enlightenment were two key elements, an affirmation of human autonomy and an affirmation of the final authority of reason. Both of these factors militated against the orthodox Christian doctrine of revelation. After all, if reason is the final authority, then no appeal can be made to a Word purporting to have come from a divine being; and if human beings are autonomous, then they must decide for themselves what to believe without any interference from God, church or Bible. No wonder, then, that Barth could characterize the Enlightenment as 'a system founded upon the presupposition of faith in the omnipotence of human ability'.

To understand the significance of the Enlightenment and the genius of its main philosopher, Immanuel Kant, we must recognize that he brought together into a new synthesis the two opposing schools of philosophy current at the time, empiricism and rationalism. Empiricism argued that all knowledge comes about by sense perception and that it is not possible to obtain knowledge in any other way. This became a crucial element in modern scientific methodology, whereby truth is obtained through experiment, followed by logical deduction from the evidence produced by the experiment. The three most famous empiricist philosophers were the Englishman John Locke, the Irish bishop George Berkeley and the Scottish sceptic David Hume. Hume was clearly the most radical of the empiricists. He argued that all talk of God, life after death, the soul and so on is totally meaningless because it is not based on sense perception. If I cannot see, hear or touch God, then it is meaningless to talk about the existence of such a being. Those who took empiricism most seriously seemed almost to question whether any object had a real existence. For example, if I see something I describe as a tree, it produces a number of 'sensations': I can touch it, I can perhaps smell its blossoms and, if it has fruit, I can taste it. The difficult question became, how do I know that the tree is still there when I am not there to perceive it? Clearly, I must make an assumption or a deduction. Bishop Berkeley solved this problem by saying that it was still there because God was perceiving it! Similarly, Hume questioned the whole notion of causation, asking whether we could really speak about cause and effect. The common example used in this discussion is of a snooker ball. If I strike a white snooker ball with a cue and it runs into a red snooker ball I might observe that the red one immediately takes off and goes into the pocket in the corner. I might observe that every time a white ball hits a red ball, the red ball moves away. If, however, I then say that the white ball 'causes' the red ball to move by striking it, the consistent empiricist would say that I am making an assumption, one not justified by the evidence.

Rationalism, on the other hand, argued that all knowledge comes about by reasoning from certain general principles, or self-evident truths. The three most significant philosophers in this school were Descartes, Spinoza and Leibniz, of whom Descartes was probably the most important. He believed that the empiricist notions of observation and experience could not be the basis for real knowledge because they were uncertain and even deceptive. He began with his famous dictum *cogito ergo sum* (I think therefore I am) and tried to deduce everything from that (to him) self-evident truth. For the rationalist, mathematics is the most precise form of thought, and the rationalist philosopher looked forward to the day when the whole universe would be understood completely in mathematical terms, as a huge, complex machine. In this philosophical system, God was often reduced to a part of an argument, something necessary to prove something else.

Kant could see that there was some truth both in rationalism and in empiricism, but also that there were problems in each system. His solution, a new theory of knowledge, involved a fusion of the two. The rationalists were saying that the human mind is born with certain self-evident truths written upon it, whereas the empiricists (especially Locke) were saying that the human mind is like a blank page (*tabula rasa*), only written upon as we experience various things. Now Kant had been trained in the rationalist school of thought and was committed to the autonomy of human beings and to the supremacy of reason, but he could also see that the empiricists had a point. All of our knowledge is indeed derived from experience. His criticism of empiricism, however, was more subtle. He could not accept that the mind was a blank page as Locke suggested. The mind, as Kant believed, played a part in the reception of knowledge because it processed the facts gained in experience according to its own inbuilt concepts. In other words, the mind is not a blank page being written on, but a part of the process of reception. Kant decided, then, that he must examine the part the mind plays in processing the facts of experience. In short, he embarked on a critical analysis of the place of the mind in knowledge. He concluded that it was possible to make the link between experience and reason that both the rationalist and the empiricist found to be impossible. The human mind provides the missing link. The human mind, in fact, provides objectivity.[1]

Kant tried to bring Christianity into line with his thinking, but did so in a way that seriously damaged it. He argued that there were two realms, the phenomenal realm and the noumenal realm. The phenomenal realm is the 'real' world, the world of sense experience, whereas the noumenal world is entirely separate – a world in which the normal rules of sense experience and rational deduction do not apply. In seeking to secure a place for religious experience, he thus stripped Christianity of its supernatural elements, including the idea of faith and of a personal God, and reduced it largely to a religion of self-help. The result is a non-supernatural religion that bears little or no relation to biblical Christianity and that becomes essentially a system of ethics.[2]

Few would deny that Kant's work transformed the philosophical world, and therefore one must either come to terms with his conclusions or demonstrate that he was mistaken.

Liberal theology

The Enlightenment having taken place, some Christian theologians responded to its concerns by seeking to bring Christian theology into line with the philosophy, science and overall world view of the Enlightenment. Those who did so developed a school of theology that came to be known as 'liberal theology', which had its origins in Germany. The Christian theologians involved felt keenly the challenge of three factors their predecessors had never faced. First, they were faced with Kant's philosophy and they believed his conclusions to be so well established that it would be suicidal to continue to advocate a Christianity that did not take account of his concerns. Second, they were faced with the rapid scientific advancement then taking place, within a Newtonian framework, which indicated that we live in a closed, causal universe where the

1. See Immanuel Kant, *The Critique of Pure Reason* (Cambridge: Cambridge University Press, 1999); Immanuel Kant, *Critique of Practical Reason* (New York: Liberal Arts, 1956); and Immanuel Kant, *Critique of Judgment* (Mineola, N. Y.: Dover, 2005).
2. See Immanuel Kant, *Religion within the Limits of Reason Alone* (New York: Harper & Row, 1960); and Immanuel Kant, *Groundwork of the Metaphysics of Morals* (Cambridge: Cambridge University Press, 1997).

supernatural and the miraculous have no place. Third, they were faced with the rapidly developing 'higher critical' school within German biblical studies, which questioned earlier assumptions about the nature of Scripture. All of this helped to drive the movement forward. Thus there began a whole-sale reconstruction of Christianity. The first to attempt this was Friedrich Schleiermacher, whom many regard as the greatest Protestant theologian since Calvin.

Schleiermacher largely accepted the criticisms Kant made of religion and so was concerned to seek another way to provide a foundation for religious claims. In the event, he broke entirely new ground and said that the heart of religion is not to be found in dogma, or reason but in experience, feeling and intuition. This was a new idea, although to some extent it can be seen in the seventeenth-century Pietism to which Schleiermacher owed a debt by his upbringing. He spoke of a 'feeling of total dependence' that, in other places, he called 'God consciousness'. In his reaction against Kant, Schleiermacher was anxious to found his faith upon something other than propositional truth. For him, doctrine is secondary; religious experience is primary. Thus, for Schleiermacher, theology was no more and no less than an attempt to put religious experience and feeling into words. We do not believe in God because his existence can be proved; rather, we believe in God because of this feeling of absolute dependence. Everything was worked out from this basic princi-ple. Indeed, Schleiermacher was probably the first major figure in the Protestant tradition to attempt a complete theological reconstruction of Christianity. In his two most famous books, he seeks to apply this basic prin-ciple. In the first volume, *On Religion: Speeches to its Cultured Despisers*,[3] he deals with religion in general. In that early book, Schleiermacher was attempting to give a defence of Christianity in a post-Enlightenment world. His later (and classic) volume is called *The Christian Faith*,[4] originally published in 1822, in which he tries to apply all he had learned to an exposition and defence of Christianity.

According to Schleiermacher, all religions share in this feeling of absolute dependence, but Christianity is the highest form of religion because of Jesus Christ. Each of us has a 'God consciousness' but this is impaired in various ways because of our sin. Jesus Christ, however, had a perfect 'God con-sciousness', and because of this he had a special relationship to God. We are

3. Friedrich Schleiermacher, *On Religion: Speeches to its Cultured Despisers* (Cambridge: Cambridge University Press, 1996).
4. Friedrich Schleiermacher, *The Christian Faith* (Edinburgh: T. & T. Clark, 1960).

now redeemed by belonging to the community he founded. This means, of course, that Jesus was not God incarnate but a man who was so close to God, so utterly dependent upon him, that his God consciousness was perfect. It is perhaps important to say that when Schleiermacher used the term 'feeling', he was not simply thinking about emotion. He believed that through 'feeling' you could obtain real knowledge, and have a genuine insight into reality. The religious self-consciousness is aware of God, but you cannot know much about this God as he is in himself, since these aspects of God are not disclosed in our 'feeling of dependence'. As Schleiermacher said, 'All attributes which we ascribe to God are to be taken as denoting not something special in God, but only something special in the manner in which the feeling of absolute dependence is to be related to him.'[5] In this theology, the Bible has authority but not as part of God's self-revelation or as a source of divine truth. Rather, its authority derives from its contribution to the shaping of God consciousness.

There were, of course, others who subsequently added their voices to that of Schleiermacher in this project of restating Christianity, including Albrecht Ritschl, Adolf Harnack and Wilhelm Hermann. The most significant of these was Albrecht Ritschl. Indeed, many would argue that he, rather than Schleiermacher, was the true founder of liberal theology. Ritschl rejected metaphysical knowledge of God. In other words, he argued that we cannot know God as he is in and of himself; we can know him only through the community of faith and through our experience in the church.[6] He was quite convinced that, from earliest times, Christian theology had been damaged by a dependence upon Greek philosophy, and he was concerned to reinterpret it so as to remove this influence. In many ways he continued what Schleiermacher had begun, although at certain major points he distanced himself from Schleiermacher. He followed Schleiermacher both in drawing clear lines between philosophy and theology and in largely accepting and affirming Kant's philosophical conclusions. Also, like Schleiermacher, he began with the believer and with what religious statements mean for the believer rather than beginning with revelation. Contrary to Schleiermacher, however, he rejected any pietistic or mystical individualism

---

5. Ibid., p. 194.

6. For a fuller account of his position see Albrecht Ritschl, *Justification and Reconciliation* (Edinburgh: T. & T. Clark, 1900). My colleague Dr Nick Needham has pointed out that this is similar to the Eastern 'apophatic' view, which is not dependent upon Enlightenment presuppositions.

whereby we claim to have direct knowledge of God through a relationship with him. Ritschl made the church the place where justification and reconciliation take place rather than the human heart. He also taught that Jesus Christ's great work was to create the church or, rather, to inaugurate the kingdom of God.

For Ritschl, all Christian doctrines are simply 'value judgments'. What he is getting at here is that doctrines do not convey any truth about reality, simply about what that reality means to us. In other words, to talk about Christ having two natures or being of one substance with the Father and the Spirit in trinity does not really tell us anything true or factual about Jesus, but is a reflection of what he means to us. Hence we must go behind these doctrines to the historical facts of Christ's life and ministry.

Several scholars developed the work of Ritschl, some of whom were more sympathetic to his key arguments than others. One who was less sympathetic, but perhaps more consistent than others, was Ernst Troeltsch, a theologian, historian and philosopher. He taught theology in Heidelberg and Bonn, and philosophy in Berlin. He also served for a time as minister for education in the German government. Perhaps the best reason for mentioning Troeltsch in a study of early liberal theology is to emphasize that there were different strands running through the movement and that one important strand taught that Christianity was only one religion among others. It might be better in some respects than others, but essentially it was only one valid expression of religion among other valid expressions. Troeltsch was of this school. He did try to argue that Christianity was the highest form of religion, but even weakened on this in his later work. He denied that Christianity was unique and insisted that genuine religion and divine revelation were possible in other religions. Troeltsch belonged to the 'history of religions' school, and applied W. Dilthey's philosophy of history to Christianity. In terms of our present study, we should particularly note one key element in his thinking, namely his denial of the reliability of the historical accounts of the miraculous elements in the Bible.

With Schleiermacher and Ritschl, then, there began a movement known as liberal theology (or liberal Protestantism) that increasingly questioned the older orthodoxy. The miraculous elements in the Bible were treated with doubt and even scepticism, the so-called Greek philosophical influences were removed and Christianity became an ethical religion with little or no possibility of real personal knowledge of God.

The doctrine of Scripture that arose from this movement of liberal theology marked a radical departure from everything the church had previously believed. The Scriptures are to be understood simply as historical human documents, which help us because they have arisen within the faith community of which we are a later part. It is helpful, even instructive, for us to know what Jews and Christians of an earlier generation believed, although we are by no means bound to accept their views. Indeed, every generation must engage in theological work (as the writers of Scripture did) reflecting upon our own religious experience. What we must not do, however, is to imagine that there was any kind of supernatural activity that led to the writing of these ancient documents. The notion that they came into being as the direct result of the supernatural action of a personal God is to be rejected. Nor must we invest them with divine qualities or hold them to be unique – other religions also have their 'Scriptures'. Above all, we must recognize that the only authority they have in the church is the authority of tradition. That is to say, we may highly value their insights and their religious genius without thereby assuming that we are obliged to agree with them on everything. Liberal theologians argued that much of what has been included as Scripture is flawed and mistaken, as we can see more clearly from our more mature scientific and philosophical perspectives. For example, we can safely discard much that reflects the writers' own historical and religious context and their lack of knowledge. Indeed, many of their views are 'primitive' and even 'immoral', such as the view that God would command them to destroy their enemies.

It was argued that we cannot identify the Scriptures as God's Word because they are human documents, and to do so is bibliolatry. Kevin Vanhoozer takes a different view:

> Those who affirm biblical infallibility are often charged with holding a quasi-magical view of the Bible as a sort of talisman that reveals the secrets of the universe. The Scripture principle, it is true, can degenerate into a species of bibliolatry. However, I shall contend that identifying the Scriptures as the Word of God need not result in bibliolatry, so long as God's communicative acts are not mistaken for the divine being itself. The Word of God is God in communicative act, and there is no reason that some communicative acts cannot be verbal. This implies that the dichotomy between propositional and personal revelation is not as hard and fast as almost a century of debate has implied.[7]

Even today, decades after liberal theology began its terminal decline, many hold to broadly the same position concerning Scripture. This can be exemplified

---

7. Kevin J. Vanhoozer, *First Theology* (Leicester: Apollos, 2002), p. 131.

by the work of John Barton.[8] Barton's *People of the Book? The Authority of the Bible in Christianity* argues for the importance of biblical criticism and for a non-fundamentalist approach to the Bible. Coming from a liberal tradition of biblical interpretation, Barton is clear that there are irreconcilable contradictions in Scripture that no amount of careful harmonizing can gainsay.[9] He also seems to take delight in provocative language, arguing, for example, that Paul's interest in the Old Testament 'seems at best intermittent and casual'[10] and that, in the modern world, it is not possible to hold to a high view of Scripture. He says that the Enlightenment is the dividing line between biblicism and a more modern critical theology.[11]

He has scant regard for the notion of prophecy or fulfilment[12] and presents various arguments against the conservative position.[13] He also discusses canonical criticism,[14] but his conclusion is fairly negative: 'It seems to me that any satisfactory discussion of the canon or the canonical principle must do justice to both sides of this opposition, if it is not to be anachronistic. In my judgment modern "canonical" approaches fail in this respect.'[15] Barton seeks to avoid the canonical debate by arguing that the 'rule of faith' is the final authority, rather than Scripture. He quotes Lessing to the effect that 'the Church in the first couple of centuries spoke more of the "canon of truth" or the "rule of faith" than of the canon of Scripture. This rather than Scripture itself was the ultimate "canon" according to which all teaching had to be assessed.'[16] Once this concept of the rule of faith has been established, the

---

8. We might also have looked at the writings of another Oxford scholar, James Barr. Barr's principal writings on Scripture have been intended to demonstrate that what he calls a 'fundamentalist' approach to the Scriptures is misguided, although he clearly includes the views of conservative evangelicals in his strictures. He writes on this matter with a certain ferocity that belies, or more likely is explained by, his own earlier commitment to the conservative evangelical position.

9. John Barton, *People of the Book? The Authority of the Bible in Christianity* (London: SPCK, 1988), p. 5.

10. Ibid., p. 6.

11. Ibid., p. 12.

12. Ibid., p. 15.

13. Ibid., p. 19.

14. Ibid., pp. 27–28.

15. Ibid., p. 30.

16. Ibid.

Bible does have a role to play: 'As a guide to faith the canon of Scripture, accepted as equally authoritative in all its parts, is useless. But *once given* the church's rule of faith, the books of the Bible exercise an extremely powerful check on that rule by providing a record of the roots of the Judaeo-Christian tradition.'[17]

This does, of course, change the significance of the arguments about the canon:

> Within such a scheme of thought, what is assumed is not that all the books of Scripture cohere strongly in the sense that they form a single 'work', like a well-constructed novel by a single author, but that they are all written from within a genuine encounter with God. Their canonicity is not a fact about their internal structure or about their relationship with each other, but about their correspondence to an external norm, the faith of the Church.[18]

Barton does want to affirm some form of inspiration, however, and speaks positively about Austin Farrer's Bampton Lectures, noting that Farrer manages to give a non-fundamentalist account of the inspiration of Scripture that yet is based 'on an utter conviction of the supernatural character of Scripture'.[19] Barton himself wants to argue for the importance of the Bible, not as some final unquestionable authority for decision-making, but as one of the earliest witnesses to the events concerning Jesus.[20] The Bible's authority, then, is not that of a collection of books or oracles that have come to us from God and must be obeyed, but rather, its authority is like the words of a trusted friend.[21]

Ultimately, for Barton, the Bible is a human book in which human beings reflect upon their experiences of God. To say more than this is to 'set it on a pedestal that it does not need'.[22] Nor does the Bible determine what we ought to believe. Barton is clear that 'the exposition of the Bible cannot in itself produce theological truth: the resolution of truth-questions raised by the Bible cannot be settled by appeal to the Bible'.[23] On a more positive note, Barton

---

17. Ibid., p. 41.
18. Ibid., p. 31.
19. Ibid., p. 36.
20. Ibid., p. 40.
21. Ibid., p. 45.
22. Ibid., p. 46.
23. Ibid., p. 54.

argues that the Bible illuminates the mind and heart, despite its inadequacy for the tasks allocated to it by fundamentalists. It is not a means of primary revelation, which 'lies before and outside the text of Scripture', but is an important witness to the knowledge of God and has an important place in the life of the church, especially in worship.[24]

Above all, Barton wants us to focus on Christ, not the Bible, although he affirms the need for the Bible in its capacity as providing the documentary evidence for the origins of Christianity.[25] He is, however, quite dismissive of some Protestant views on Scripture: 'In turning *sola scriptura* from a symbol by which the God-given character of the gospel is defended into a literal and positive statement about where its heart can be found, the Protestant churches sold their birthright for a mess of hermeneutics.'[26]

At the end, he affirms again the priority of the gospel: 'Central to my own thinking about the authority of the Bible is the conviction that we can say nothing worthwhile about the Bible except by beginning with the Christian gospel that existed before there ever was a Bible and could survive if every Bible was destroyed.'[27]

Barton's view is somewhat more nuanced than some of the earlier liberal theologians and, like Farrer, he does want to use the language of inspiration, yet he remains on the side of those who see the Bible primarily as a human book reflecting the spiritual experiences of a community, rather than seeing it as having come from God through human authorship.

The legacy of liberal theology has been highly destructive of orthodox Christianity. Key elements of biblical Christianity have been questioned or denied and creedal affirmations such as the virgin birth, the incarnation and the resurrection have been rejected. This has led in turn to the devastation of the church in the West, where these views have been most strongly prominent. In many places, congregations and even denominations have been divided, between those who accept the Scriptures as having come from God through human authorship and those who see the Bible as simply a human book reflecting the spiritual experiences of a community. Even in those places where no division has occurred, it can be argued that the spiritual lives of many have been damaged. After all, if there is no supernatural being who created all things and who came to this earth in the person of his Son, was born of a

---

24. Ibid., p. 60.
25. Ibid., p. 83.
26. Ibid., p. 86.
27. Ibid., p. 89.

virgin, died on a cross and was raised from the dead, then the essential core of salvation is gone. At best, we have a self-help religion of good works.

The response to liberal theology

Liberal theology has had, then, an enormous impact on Christian theology, and although there may not be many today who hold precisely to the views of Schleiermacher, Ritschl or Hermann, there have been many schools of thought in modern theology which show that they have inherited the same Enlightenment world view and come to many of the same conclusions. Indeed, some of the mid-twentieth-century movements in theology went much further in their abandonment of the orthodoxy of the church's creeds and confessions.

Although the remnants of the old liberal theology still exist today, many theologians who were brought up in this tradition have made significant moves in a different direction. This latter group includes those who have followed in the tradition of Karl Barth and other neo-orthodox scholars, as well as those, like Hans Frei, who have advocated narrative theology, or like Brevard Childs who has developed canonical theology. It also includes those who have been involved in a resurgence of confessional and evangelical views.

This change has come about because the three main factors that drove Schleiermacher, Ritschl and the others towards liberal theology have been largely answered. On the Enlightenment, Colin Gunton and others have recognized that this was the point when things went wrong for Christian theology, and have returned to that point in intellectual history and sought to rethink everything differently. On science, T. F. Torrance has brilliantly demonstrated that a liberal theology built on convictions about a closed, causal Newtonian cosmology is quite inadequate in the light of an Einsteinian cosmology, which describes an open and even expanding universe. On higher-critical scholarship, serious questions have been raised about its apparently firm conclusions, and there has been a return to a more positive and constructive type of biblical studies, from Adolf Schlatter onwards.

I am not going to trace all of the strands of thought that came out of liberal theology. Instead, since the purpose of this chapter is to set the scene for the debate concerning inerrancy, we shall confine ourselves to observing the two main responses to liberal theology in the early years of the twentieth century. These are neo-orthodoxy and conservative evangelicalism. Strikingly, these movements were led by two men who had been hugely influenced by the liberal theologian Wilhelm Hermann, namely Karl Barth and J. Gresham Machen.

Neo-orthodoxy

In order to explain some of the core teaching of neo-orthodoxy we shall look at its origins in the life and ministry of Karl Barth, then its doctrine of Scripture as expounded by J. K. S. Reid and finally its view of Kantian philosophy as expounded by T. F. Torrance.

Karl Barth

Karl Barth, as a young pastor in Safenwil in Switzerland, became the leading opponent of liberal theology, despite the fact that he had been trained in it, his most significant teacher having been Wilhelm Hermann. A combination of factors led him to this position. First, a dissatisfaction with the ethics (particularly the war ethics) of liberal theology; second, a growing recognition that liberal theology had capitulated before the philosophy of the Enlightenment; and third, the fact that he found himself with little or no message to preach Sunday by Sunday because the Bible had been so emptied of content by the higher-critical scholarship that was a key element of liberal theology. This was an important turning point for theology. As Hans Frei said, 'No more crucial event has taken place in modern Protestant theology than Karl Barth's break with liberalism. It was the most significant single impetus to the subsequent theological generation's conception of its task.'[28]

Barth first of all published a commentary on Romans that, in both form and content, expressed a direct challenge to liberal theology.[29] Instead of giving over most of the text to critical and contextual questions, as had become the norm, Barth genuinely sought to understand what Paul was saying and to understand its significance. Barth was then called to teach theology in the university of Göttingen, which gave him time to develop his thinking and to carry the work a stage further. Indeed, one of the things he did was to write another, completely different commentary on Romans in 1921. A comparison of these two commentaries shows how much Barth was wrestling to find a new way. What happened as a result was that radical changes began to take place in the school of thought he had come to represent and that was becoming known as 'dialectical theology' or 'neo-orthodoxy'. Barth began to see that his notion of a God who was 'wholly other' owed a great deal to Kant and was not as valuable a concept as it had first appeared. At this point, Barth began to turn to

---

28. Hans Frei, 'The Doctrine of Revelation in the Thought of Karl Barth, 1909 to 1922' (PhD diss., Yale University, 1965), p. iii.

29. Karl Barth, *The Epistle to the Romans* (Oxford: Oxford University Press, 1975).

more orthodox writings from the post-Reformation Lutheran and Calvinist schools. This led him to a more serious understanding of 'revelation', which henceforth becomes a key element in his thought. As Alasdair Heron says, liberal theology had reduced theology to anthropology, had failed to take seriously the reality of God and the need for revelation, had not accepted the authority of the Bible as a vehicle for God's word and had not taken seriously the encounter between time and eternity. Heron goes on to say this: 'Dialectical Theology thus set out to reverse the approach, and in particular to emphasise, first, the "Godness of God"; second, the reality of the Word of God in Jesus Christ; third, the impossibility of building theology itself on any other foundation.'[30]

In all of this thinking, Barth developed his doctrine of Scripture.[31] He spoke about the threefold aspect of the Word of God (following Calvin) with Jesus as the *living* Word of God, the Bible as the *written* Word of God and *preaching* or *witnessing* as the third form of the Word of God. Although accepting this tripartite division, Barth wanted to argue that when we speak about the Word of God, we are primarily speaking about Jesus. This is natural enough because of his concentration on the person of Christ. It is no exaggeration to say that Barth's whole theology is based on a Christological method, that is, a 'Christ-centred' theology. This means that he regards the Scriptures as a witness to the Word of God. He is normally characterized as saying that the Bible becomes the Word of God in our existential encounter with the person of Jesus Christ. Thus the Bible is not objectively the Word of God; it becomes the Word of God when God speaks to me through it.

We must be careful, however, not to accept too easily a quick evangelical summary of Barth's position, without careful study and reflection. Even his chapter on Scripture just cited has to be read in a wider context.[32] It is notoriously easy to read one section of Barth and to assume that one understands his view on a particular subject only to turn to another section of the *Church*

---

30. Alasdair I. C. Heron, *A Century of Protestant Theology* (Guildford: Lutterworth, 1980), p. 79.

31. Karl Barth, *Church Dogmatics*, vol. 1/2: *The Doctrine of The Word of God* (Edinburgh: T. & T. Clark, 1956), pp. 457–740.

32. In this context, Geoffrey Bromiley warns us against reading Barth's chapter on Holy Scripture (ch. 19) out of its context, since 'The mistake of isolation can lead only to an incomplete and misleading understanding and evaluation' (Geoffrey W. Bromiley, *Introduction to the Theology of Karl Barth* [Edinburgh: T. & T. Clark, 1979], p. 34).

Dogmatics and find the subject examined from a different perspective that sheds new light on the whole matter. I say this because there are those, like Bruce McCormack, who present Barth's doctrine of Scripture in a somewhat different light.[33]

J. K. S. Reid

One of the most neglected of modern theologians is J. K. S. Reid, and yet his book on the doctrine of Scripture, published in the 1950s, is perhaps the clearest and most cogent presentation of a neo-orthodox position.[34] Here is a scholar who shares Barth's view on the relationship between Scripture and the Word of God.[35] His primary concern is to ask questions about the nature of Scripture, an understanding of which is vital, he says, 'if it is to be both norm and nourishment for men's faith'.[36] This, then, is no ivory tower academic, asking purely intellectual questions. Here is a scholar who is also a churchman, a man of faith, someone concerned that the Bible should feed souls.

In seeking to identify the nature of Scripture, Reid is anxious to avoid two positions he believes to be in error. On the one hand, he is anxious to avoid the liberal dismissal of Scripture. On the other hand, however, he warns against 'bibliolatry', which he identifies as having appeared at different times in church history but perhaps especially in post-Reformation Protestant orthodoxy. He writes, 'there appears over the years a recurrent movement from living authority to literal authority'.[37] In this movement, he identifies a 'rigid torpor' that takes the place of a 'living voice'.[38] In particular, he is concerned by 'those who today subscribe to biblical infallibility in "fundamentalist" terms'.[39] He is referring to those who affirm biblical inerrancy.

Interestingly, Professor Reid argues that this doctrine of inerrancy, in the way it is expressed today, is an entirely new theological position. He is willing

---

33. Bruce L. McCormack, 'The Being of Holy Scripture Is in Becoming: Karl Barth in Conversation with American Evangelical Criticism', in V. Bacote, L. C. Miguelez and D. L. Okholm (eds.), *Evangelicals and Scripture: Tradition, Authority and Hermeneutics* (Downers Grove: IVP, 2004), pp. 55–75.

34. J. K. S. Reid, *The Authority of Scripture: A Study of the Reformation and Post-Reformation Understanding of the Bible* (London: Methuen, 1957).

35. Ibid., p. 278.

36. Ibid., p. 8.

37. Ibid., p. 25.

38. Ibid.

39. Ibid., p. 27.

to agree that throughout the centuries many held to the position of verbal inspiration, but notes (with supporting quotations from Gore and Hebert) that the older form of verbal inerrancy was combined with an allegorism that the modern inerrantists have replaced with an inflexible literalism.[40] He writes:

> In earlier ages, a view of the Bible was held that possessed enough suppleness to accommodate such critical discrepancies as were discovered, and still to retain the authority of the Bible. In the later period, the Bible was regarded in terms of a type of literal inerrancy which, when the discoveries were remade and extended, made it impossible for biblical authority to survive. A view of the Bible was held which no longer had the resilience necessary to meet the fresh challenge, and authority seemed to suffer a mortal blow. If the authority of the Bible be construed in the sense that every isolated word of Holy Scripture is inerrant, to call in question of even one of these points is enough to shatter that authority.[41]

He argues that neither Luther nor Calvin were subject to either of these errors. Rather, they interpreted 'the authority of the Bible in a living way, not as the deposit of faith to be assented to, but as the means through which God makes his Word heard in the present day'.[42] He is conscious that many have identified Calvin as holding to verbal inerrancy, but suggests this is only partly true: 'One cannot deny that out of the available material a formidable case for holding Calvin to be a literalist can be constructed. But when this has been done, it is still possible to doubt whether the real Calvin has been discerned or his intention rightly construed.'[43] Noting that Calvin sometimes expresses himself in ways that would not indicate a commitment to verbal inerrancy, he concludes, 'Two kinds of expression have to be accommodated; and the view that Calvin does not hold to verbal inspiration accommodates them more easily than the view that he does.'[44] Reid argues that, for Calvin, the Word of God has authority because it is God speaking.[45]

Reid says there are two reasons for refuting the view that Calvin believed in verbal inspiration, and both of them relate to the relationship between the

---

40. Ibid.

41. Ibid.

42. Ibid., p. 26.

43. Ibid., pp. 35–36. This notion of the 'real' Calvin is one that we also see in Karl Barth, T. F. Torrance, D. G. Bloesch and others.

44. Reid, *Authority of Scripture*, p. 36.

45. Ibid., p. 47.

Word and the Spirit. He writes, 'The refutation rests rather on Calvin's expressed view that there is no identity of Spirit and Word, and on his statement that the Word must be supplemented by the operation of the Spirit before becoming effective for faith and salvation.'[46] The first reason involves a particular view of inspiration and the second a particular understanding of the internal testimony of the Holy Spirit.

On the first of these issues, Reid notes that Calvin, does not 'identify the Holy Spirit with the Word of God, or for that matter lock the Holy Spirit up within Scripture. The two are not only distinguishable in thought, but separate in reality,'[47] concluding that 'If this separation be recognised, it is impossible to impose upon Calvin a doctrine of verbal infallibility and inerrancy.'[48] This matter of the relationship between the Word of God and the Holy Spirit occasions a quotation from Reid that summarizes his overall position:

> The Word does not become authoritative and win acceptance with men by incorporating the Holy Spirit in itself, or by receiving the stamp of the Holy Spirit upon itself. It becomes authoritative and is received, when, by the operation of the Holy Spirit, it is made the Word of the living God and the living Word of God. It is this and no other thing that vivifies.[49]

Having defined Calvin's position, Reid attempts to show that scholasticism (both Lutheran and Calvinist), which followed the magisterial Reformers, departed from the earlier doctrine of Scripture at two key points: 'It failed to maintain such a high freedom over against the formulations of the Reformers; and, even more fatally, it failed to carry over the essentially dynamic view of Scripture which the Reformers held.'[50] Reid sums up the difference between the position held by Luther and Calvin as over against the position of those who followed:

> Luther stands at a cross-roads, and from the point he occupied at least two paths lead forward. One is that which he himself and also Calvin followed, according to which the Bible is a living authority making itself felt and heard in religious experience. The

---

46. Ibid., p. 48.
47. Ibid., p. 47.
48. Ibid.
49. Ibid., p. 51.
50. Ibid., p. 59.

other is the path followed by Protestant scholasticism, which, holding no less that the Bible is an inspired book, regarded it as a fixed and external standard and textbook of what may be believed.[51]

Luther is said to have had a much clearer understanding of Scripture than those who followed because he 'brings subject and object into a living relationship'.[52] This notion of the living relationship becomes a recurring theme in the book. Reid goes further and says that 'For Luther, Scripture is not the Word, but only witness to the Word, and it is from Him whom it conveys that it derives the authority it enjoys.'[53] This can be viewed as one example of the attempt by Reid and other neo-orthodox theologians to see in Luther and Calvin elements of the later Barthian theology. One interesting aspect of Reid's argument is where he compares the Lutheran and Reformed confessional statements and demonstrates that the doctrine of Scripture is much less prominent in the Lutheran statements. He concludes, 'The Calvinistic tradition gives Holy Scripture a more explicitly prominent place; the treatment of Scripture is more detailed; and it is possible to trace some development towards greater literal rigidity.'[54] Nevertheless, he concludes that the developing orthodoxy of the two traditions came together later.

It is when he comes to examine that later orthodox consensus that Reid is at his most critical, quoting approvingly the famous comment from Brunner that 'The age of Orthodoxy appears like a frozen waterfall – mighty shapes of movement, but no movement.'[55] Continuing his defence of Luther and Calvin, he argues that they 'left doors open which they did not enter. It is these alternative doors that are now used. The paths to which they lead are followed to very different conclusions.'[56] He says that as Protestant Orthodoxy developed, Scripture 'came to be credited with an authority of the same kind as the Church had formerly wielded', an authority 'of an external and objective kind'.[57] Thus 'The distinction between Scripture and the Word of God, which Luther maintained but so often by his own utterances imperilled, is now lost,

---

51. Ibid., p. 61.
52. Ibid., p. 71.
53. Ibid., p. 72.
54. Ibid., p. 76.
55. Ibid., pp. 77–78.
56. Ibid., p. 78.
57. Ibid., p. 82.

and the two are regarded as identical.'[58] Not only so but 'Orthodoxy, attempting with right to exclude the dependence of the inspiration of Scripture upon
the church or upon the individual believer, falls into the trap of making
Scripture self-contained. The sovereign action of God in making Scripture the
vehicle and occasion of His Word is excluded.'[59]

We can note a number of recurring theses in Reid's book. First, Calvin
and the other Reformers held a doctrine of Scripture that was flexible
and dynamic, emphasizing Scripture as the means by which human beings
encounter God, whereas the Protestant scholastics reduced this to a literalist and rigid inerrantist position.[60] Second, it is vital to have a view of
Scripture that involves a living relationship between subject and object.
Third, we must constantly emphasize the word 'witness' in relation to the
Scriptures.

T. F. Torrance

Those within the neo-orthodox tradition recognized that the Enlightenment
marked the beginning of the new world view that led to liberal theology,
and so they tackled it head on. One of the most significant assaults on the
Enlightenment world view came from T. F. Torrance, who attacked its dualism
and also its dependence upon a Newtonian scientific paradigm.

In responding to the Enlightenment and the impact it has had on theology,
T. F. Torrance sums up his main concerns thus:

> The problem that now faces us in contemporary theology is this: while scientists have
> moved on, far beyond the narrow mechanistic determinisms of the Laplacians or the
> Marxists, to a profounder and more unitary grasp of the intelligible connections in
> the contingent order of the universe, theology tends, for the most part, to remain
> stuck in obscurantist modes of thought that have their roots in the radical dualisms
> of the past. And the so-called liberal theology that plies its free-thinking within the
> carefully guarded autonomous status of man's religious and moral experience easily

---

58. Ibid.

59. Ibid., p. 83.

60. The idea that Protestant scholasticism completely changed the view of the doctrine
of Scripture as held by the Reformers is assumed but not proven. Indeed, there are
virtually no references to support this view, a view common among neo-orthodox
scholars. The work of Richard Muller has effectively demonstrated the weakness
and inadequacy of this view. See Muller, *Post-Reformation Reformed Dogmatics*, vol. 2,
pp. 86–96.

slips into empty humanist subjectivism, even when eked out by some kind of mystical transcendentalism – it is evidently the least able to establish intelligible connections with natural science and to share in a common advance to a deeper and more unitary understanding of the universe of space and time as the orderly creation of the one Triune God.[61]

T. F. Torrance directs his criticisms at Kant from the vantage point of the relationship between theology and science, to which he has devoted his life's work. His primary thesis is that much modern theological methodology is still based on Kantian and post-Kantian dualism, having completely ignored the transformation in the methodology of modern physics due to the work of Einstein. Torrance sees no disagreement between theology and science, holding that truth is always a unity, this belief being based on the Christian doctrine of creation. Disputes between theology and science can ultimately be traced back to the use of a Kantian dualistic methodology, and hence the disagreement is conceptual and not actual. The relationship with science is one of dialogue, and

> This dialogue with pure science can do theology nothing but good, for it will help theologians to clarify their fundamental methods in the light of their own peculiar subject-matter, and to wrestle again with the implacable objectivity of the Word of God until they learn to distinguish objective realities more clearly from their own subjective states.[62]

Torrance develops this thesis by noting that the base concept in pre-Einsteinian physics was the idea of the container universe, that is, the notion of space as the infinite receptacle of all things. This notion had come out of the Renaissance, had been taken up to some extent by Galileo and was incorporated into the structures of classical physics by Newton.

> Thus over against Descartes's view of space as extension in which he modified the Aristotelian concept of the interdependence of container and contained matter through his idea of the coordinate system, and over against the thoroughly relational view of space advocated by Leibniz and Huygens in which they stood

---

61. Thomas F. Torrance, *The Ground and Grammar of Theology* (Belfast: Christian Journals, 1980), p. 20.
62. Thomas F. Torrance, *Theology in Reconstruction* (Grand Rapids: Eerdmans, 1965), p. 20.

closer to certain aspects of Platonic and Patristic thought, Newton separated space from what happened in it, and put forward the idea of an infinite receptacle, formed by time as well as space, which he held to be the container of all creaturely being.[63]

Here, then, was developed a dualism wherein space and time were viewed as concepts separate from the material world. For Newton himself this infinity was really God, and hence infinite space and eternal time were regarded as his attributes. As Torrance notes, however, 'this joining together of God and the world by giving them space and time in common led finally to their separation'.[64]

One of the important differences between Newton and Einstein in this regard was that Newton took the Aristotelian notion of looking at everything as if the reference point was a point of absolute rest, whereas Einstein's theory of relativity conceived of motion itself as a reference point. This dualism was gradually built into the fabric of theology and made the relationship between Christianity and history difficult. Thus D. F. Strauss and later Bultmann argued that the mythological must be removed from the kerygmatic based upon their understanding of history. Torrance responds, 'it is high time that it was made clear that this concept of mythology rests upon the axiomatic assumption of a radical dichotomy between phenomenon and idea which is as impossible for Christianity as it is for modern science'.[65]

It is in this context, and with this background, that Torrance develops his critique of Kant. The dualism posited by Kant between phenomena and noumena plays an important part in anchoring the Newtonian physics in philosophy. Since phenomena are the only things we can know, and since it is the a priori concepts of the human mind that arrange and systematize these phenomena, 'we must regard things as they are in themselves as remaining quite unknowable. In other words, what Kant did was to apply to the human mind itself the receptacle notion of space which conditions and makes possible our knowledge of nature.'[66]

Torrance argues that this involves making God unknowable, since Kant's dualism will allow such knowing to be a matter of 'faith' only. Taking this to its logical conclusion he writes:

---

63. Thomas F. Torrance, *Space, Time and Incarnation* (Oxford: Oxford University Press, 1969), pp. 37–38.

64. Ibid., p. 38.

65. Ibid., p. 43.

66. Ibid.

If space and time are a priori forms of man's sensory perception then the point of
absolute rest is transferred to a centre in man himself. His one fixed point is his self-
understanding. Theologically this must mean that there can be no God for man
outside of himself or independent of his consciousness, no divine Constant invariant
with human determinations and valuations. Then the only God man can or will have
is that which he postulates in his need and morally appropriates for himself.[67]

Modern science, however, has moved on from this dualism and rejected
both the science of Newton and the philosophy of Kant.

Einstein, following out a line of thought from four-dimensional geometry, found he
had to reject the notion of absolute space and time both as taught by Kant, for whom
they were a priori forms of intuition outside the range of experience, and as taught
by Newton, for whom they formed an inertial system independent of material events
contained in them but acting on them and conditioning our knowledge of the
universe. This has had the effect of shattering the receptacle idea and of undermining
the radical dualism to which it had given rise in modern philosophy and theology as
well as science.[68]

It is Torrance's conviction that theological understanding has been so con-
ditioned by Kantian dualism that we have often had more of a 'deistic' picture
of the relation of God to the universe than a specifically 'Christian theistic'
picture. He further argues that although Newtonian physics has been universally rejected in favour of Einstein, theological science has not made the parallel transition in its methodology. Torrance expands this critique somewhat in
an essay entitled 'Influence of Reformed Theology on Scientific Method',[69]
wherein he agrees with Kant that the study of science involves the bringing of
questions to nature and the eliciting of replies, and that indeed it is true that
we must impose hypothetical structures as a means of this empirical testing,
but there he concludes his agreement. Kant, he says, 'went on to convert this
into a general principle and to elaborate it in his doctrine of a permanent structure of categories of the understanding'.[70] This complaint is similar to Van
Til's notion of the autonomous man as the ultimate point of reference, but is
more related to methodology than epistemology.

---

67. Ibid., p. 44.
68. Ibid., p. 58.
69. T. F. Torrance, *Theology in Reconstruction*, pp. 62–75.
70. Ibid., p. 71.

Torrance argues that this leads to the view that we do not discover reality but rather 'create' it. He illustrates this point by showing that many scientists are of the persuasion that reality takes shape under the 'creative efforts of scientific knowledge'.[71] He also affirms that reality changes all the time under such activity. Torrance accepts that there is some truth in the assertion that science is creative and not simply confined to the pastime of discovery, but his critique is unaltered and he suggests that it is the task of Reformed theology to challenge these scientists. He writes:

> The question Reformed theology must ask these natural scientists is whether they are not projecting their own ontological constructions into nature and identifying them with ontic structures in reality, and whether they do not thus make the fundamental mistake of thinking that they can offer in theoretical statements an account of how their theoretical statements are related to being.[72]

From this critical analysis Torrance moves on to develop a constructive epistemology not based on Kantian dualism. He believes that there was a corresponding move in philosophy to the move Einstein made from the Newtonian concept of rest as a point of reference to the notion of relativity. This philosophical redirection (which was an explicit rejection of Kant) began with Kierkegaard, who refused to contemplate the Truth from a point of rest but took 'a step forward in which he allowed his reason to move along with the movement of the Truth in order to acquire the mode of rationality for apprehending Truth that moves and acts upon us in history'.[73]

This method, which Torrance gives the name 'kinetic thinking', plays a key role in his theological reconstruction. It is not really necessary to discuss this further here except to say that it is most significant. Torrance insists that our methodology (and hence our epistemology) must be based on truth. This involves the acceptance of a scientific framework of thinking and, to some extent, the use of its intellectual tools. It does not mean, however, that we simply accept terminology because it is modern or because it is scientific; rather, Christian theology has its own contribution to make in that we must critique modern science from the standpoint of God and his Word. Holding these things in balance, he concludes, 'Only if theology is prepared, face to face with God in his revelation, constantly to repent of false habits of mind, and to adopt

---

71. Ibid.

72. Ibid.

73. Ibid., p. 73.

modes of rationality that actually correspond with the nature of its objectively given reality, can it be established firmly on its own foundations.'[74]

The starting point in epistemology for Torrance is not ourselves and our questions, but knowledge of God, knowledge that is both actual and objective. He says, 'We have to remind ourselves unceasingly that in our knowing of God, God always comes first, that in a genuine theology we do not think out of a centre in ourselves but out of a centre in God and his activity of grace towards us.'[75]

The only real dissimilarity between theology and the other sciences is on the matter of the object. God is not an object to be studied; rather, he is an acting subject. Thus all our knowledge must be spoken of in the overall context of sovereign, revealed grace. For Torrance this means that the only truly scientific theology is Reformed theology. Knowledge of God comes by revelation, and the epitome of this revelation was the incarnation. Thus Christological theology is true theology, and Christocentricity must be a characteristic of every attempt in the search for knowledge. This key role of revelation defines all else, and so he rejects the possibility of any anthropological approach to God, since our knowledge of God is related to God's revelation of himself and not to our seeking after him. Thus analogical language is not acceptable; that is, we do not say 'God' by saying 'man' in a loud voice, as Paul Althaus has said. Torrance is moving towards a definition of all this when he says:

> In scientific theology we begin with the actual knowledge of God, and seek to test and clarify this knowledge by inquiring carefully into the relation between our knowing of God and God himself in his being and nature. Then in the light of this clarification we seek to be more and more open and ready for God so that we may respond faithfully and truly to all that he declares and discloses to us of himself. It is through this disciplined obedience of our mind to God as he gives himself to be known by us that we advance in knowledge of him.[76]

This knowledge he takes to be rational knowledge, which he understands in terms of our capacity for objectivity. Further, this knowledge is not 'special'; rather, we are using the word in precisely the same way as we do in all other branches of academia.

---

74. Ibid., p. 75.

75. Ibid., p. 9.

76. Thomas F. Torrance, *Theological Science* (Oxford: Oxford University Press, 1969), p. 9.

Conservative evangelicalism

In order to present conservative evangelicalism's response to liberal theology, we consider first the contribution of J. Gresham Machen and then, second, Cornelius Van Til's analysis of Kantian philosophy.

J. Gresham Machen

If neo-orthodoxy represents one response to liberal theology, another response came from the conservative evangelical side, in the person of a professor at Princeton Theological Seminary, J. Gresham Machen. Machen had spent some time in Germany and came under the influence of Wilhelm Hermann. Indeed, Machen underwent a theological crisis where he began to question the Princetonian theological viewpoint in which he had been trained, and came close to turning towards Hermann's liberal perspective.[77] Later, having returned to his theological roots with a new conviction, he published a book called *Christianity and Liberalism*.[78]

In this book, Machen sets out to identify and explain the nature of liberal theology in a way that would show how different it is from historic, orthodox Christianity. His concern is not simply academic; rather, he has a passionate concern for the whole church of his day, which he believed was in danger of succumbing to this new theology and losing the gospel itself. His principal argument throughout the book is that liberalism is not a form of Christianity but is, in fact, an entirely different religion. For this reason it cannot be permitted to coexist in the church with evangelicalism and must be named for what it is, an enemy of biblical Christianity. In making his case, Machen notes that one of the key marks of liberal theology is its antagonism towards doctrine. In liberal theology, Christianity has to do with feeling, action, religious experience or whatever, but not with doctrine. It was often said that doctrine is simply a reflection of experience and therefore different doctrines, even apparently contradictory doctrines, might coexist as the different expressions of different people's experience. This leads to a pluralism in which many different creeds, religions and belief systems are held to be compatible. Machen takes the opposite view and writes, 'According to the Christian conception, a creed is not a mere expression of Christian experience, but on the contrary it is a setting forth of those facts upon which

---

77. See the biographical sketch of this crisis in his intellectual development: Terry A. Chrisope, *Toward a Sure Faith: J. Gresham Machen and the Dilemma of Biblical Criticism, 1881–1915* (Fearn: Christian Focus, 2000).

78. J. Gresham Machen, *Christianity and Liberalism* (Grand Rapids: Eerdmans, 1923).

experience is based.'[79] Machen drives this criticism forward when he argues that liberal theology, instead of speaking in doctrinal terms about what God has done in Christ and then calling forth a response, becomes entirely a matter of action. He puts it like this, 'Here is found the most fundamental difference between liberalism and Christianity – liberalism is altogether in the imperative mood, while Christianity begins with a triumphant indicative; liberalism appeals to man's will, while Christianity announces first, a gracious act of God.'[80]

Machen goes on to argue that it is in their doctrines of God and humanity that the liberal theologians demonstrate how far they have moved from orthodoxy. One of the most persistent errors of liberal theology, he argues, is a vague but persistent notion of the universal fatherhood of God and the brotherhood of man. Machen points out that the Bible knows nothing of such a God and writes:

> It is very strange how those who accept only the universal fatherhood of God as the sum and substance of religion can regard themselves as Christians or can appeal to Jesus of Nazareth. For the plain fact is that this modern doctrine of the universal fatherhood of God formed no part whatever of Jesus' teaching.[81]

Rather, argues Machen, the Scriptures teach us we become God's children only when we are adopted into his family by an act of his grace. Machen goes on to stress a further disparity between liberal theology and orthodox Christianity, namely in the rejection of the transcendence of God. He actually accuses many liberal theologians of having become pantheists.[82] The liberal view of man is also faulty, says Machen. He describes the contrast in stark terms: 'According to the Bible, man is a sinner under the just condemnation of God; according to modern liberalism there is really no such thing as sin. At the very root of the modern liberal movement is the loss of the consciousness of sin.'[83] Rather than seeing man as a sinner, entirely cut off from God and in need of forgiveness and reconciliation, liberal theology has a doctrine of man that is radically different. Man is really quite good and there is a 'satisfaction' with human goodness.[84]

---

79. Ibid., p. 19.
80. Ibid., p. 47.
81. Ibid., p. 59.
82. Ibid., p. 63.
83. Ibid., p. 64.
84. Ibid.

Liberal theology is characterized best, however, by its attitude to the Bible, and it is here that Machen directs the main force of his attack. He portrays liberal theology as asserting that the Bible is a human book with many errors. Over against this he claims that 'According to the Christian view, the Bible contains an account of a revelation from God to man, which is found nowhere else.'[85] Machen responded to liberal theology's view of Scripture by demonstrating the cogency of the orthodox position and by seeking to undermine the positing of Christian experience as a criterion for truth as over against Scripture. He summed up his position thus: 'It is no wonder, then, that liberalism is totally different from Christianity, for the foundation is different. Christianity is founded upon the Bible. It bases upon the Bible both its thinking and its life. Liberalism on the other hand is founded upon the shifting emotions of sinful men.'[86]

Perhaps the most striking criticism Machen makes of liberal theology comes when he refers to the fact that in liberal theology Christ is often portrayed not as a Saviour but as an example. He argues that by taking such a position liberalism lives on in the days between the cross and the resurrection. Jesus, instead of a risen Lord, becomes a blessed memory to inspire us, and his teaching becomes ethical instruction – Christianity is shorn of its significance. Machen puts very clearly this argument that sees Jesus as more than just an example:

> Jesus was not for Paul merely an example for faith; He was primarily the object of faith. The religion of Paul did not consist in having faith in God like the faith which Jesus had in God; it consisted rather in having faith in *Jesus* . . . The plain fact is that imitation of Jesus, important though it was for Paul, was swallowed up by something far more important still. Not the example of Jesus, but the redeeming work of Jesus, was the primary thing for Paul.[87]

In all of this, Machen was concerned about the tendency of liberal theology to regard Jesus as simply the first Christian. Whatever else the New Testament teaches, however, it does not teach that Jesus was a Christian. Machen sums up his argument thus: 'There is a profound difference, then, in the attitude assumed by modern liberalism and by Christianity toward Jesus the Lord. Liberalism regards him as an Example and Guide; Christianity, as a Saviour:

---

85. Ibid., p. 69.
86. Ibid., p. 79.
87. Ibid., p. 81.

liberalism makes him an example for faith; Christianity, the object of faith.'[88]
This being the case, it is no wonder that Machen concludes his book by arguing
for the necessity of individual salvation and the importance of the church as
the community of those who have been saved by God's grace.

Cornelius Van Til

Just as those like T. F. Torrance in the neo-orthodox tradition have challenged
the world view of the Enlightenment, so too have theologians in the conservative evangelical tradition. We shall consider one of these, Cornelius Van Til.
Although Van Til and Torrance come from quite different theological perspectives within the broad Reformed tradition, Van Til a conservative evangelical and Torrance a Barthian (although he himself prefers to be called an
Athanasian), it is striking to note a number of similarities. Both rejected
Kantian dualism, both rejected natural theology and both expressed a strong
allegiance to Calvin. In this chapter, however, we are concerned to see how
they challenged the Enlightenment consensus.

Van Til begins the critique of Kant by assessing his position with regard to
empiricism and rationalism. He writes:

> We can perhaps best express the crux of what Kant tried to contribute to the process
> of antitheistic thought by saying that he represents the third and last method of
> Platonic reasoning. Plato's last method of reasoning was the result of an attempt to
> combine his first and second methods of reasoning. Similarly, Empiricism tried to
> interpret reality in terms of the sense world alone, and Rationalism tried to interpret
> reality in terms of the world of ideas alone, while Kant attempted to effect a
> combination of the two.[89]

Kant is here seen to be attempting an interpretation of reality in terms of a
mixture of temporal and eternal categories. In defence of this conclusion, Van
Til notes, 'That Kant does as a matter of fact try to interpret reality by a mixture
of categories is evident from that which forms the very heart of his position,
namely, that the union of the a posteriori and a priori elements of thought are
found in the human mind.'[90] Van Til accepts Kant's critique of empiricism and
rationalism, that is, we cannot separate the facts of the universe from the mind

---

88. Ibid., pp. 95–96.

89. Cornelius Van Til, 'Volume 2 – A Survey of Christian Epistemology' (unpublished
    class syllabus) (den Dulk, 1969), pp. 106–107.

90. Ibid., p. 107.

of man, but his disagreement lies in his conviction that the mind of man should never have been considered in separation from the mind of God. In other words, we can accept the 'Copernican revolution' effected by Kant in terms of his rescue of philosophy from the scepticism of Hume, but he did not go far enough and retained the concept of man as the ultimate reference point. Van Til concludes:

> As Kant maintained that all the troubles of Empiricism and Rationalism were due to a false separation of the subject and the object of knowledge, so we would maintain that all the antinomies of antitheistic reasoning are due to a false separation of man from God. If it were not for sin man would never have thought of his knowledge as otherwise than representative of the knowledge that God has of himself and of man and his world.[91]

The primary critique Van Til makes of Kant is the same as his critique of most philosophy and some theology; that is, it posits the autonomy of man and the primacy of reason as being the frame of reference for all thought. In opposition to this, as we have seen, Van Til argues that our point (or frame) of reference for thought must be the ontological trinity, and in particular the self-identifying Christ of Reformation theology. Van Til believes that the ontological question must be asked prior to the epistemological question: 'As Christians we cannot begin by speculating about knowledge by itself. We cannot ask *how* we know without at the same time asking what we know.'[92]

This decision is based on the belief that as Christians we must take our ontology and epistemology from the Bible, and the God revealed there is such that his nature is the ultimate reference point and the beginning of all things. Three statements taken together will enable us to understand this ontological starting point better. First, 'God is absolute personality and therefore absolute individuality. He exists necessarily. He has no non-being over against himself in comparison with which he defines himself; he is internally self-defined.'[93] Second, 'The persons of the Trinity are mutually exhaustive of one another. The Son and the Spirit are ontologically on a par with the Father.'[94] Third, 'In God's being there are no particulars not related to the universal and there is nothing universal that is not fully expressed in the particulars.'[95]

---

91. Ibid., p. 109.
92. Van Til, *Defense of the Faith*, p. 32.
93. Ibid., p. 25.
94. Ibid.
95. Ibid., p. 26.

To put it another way, God is the only court of appeal in the question of knowledge, being the only independent and self-existent dialectical relationship to man, but rather is externally existing. Our being depends upon his being, but his being is necessary being. Another important point here is that we begin with the ontological trinity before moving on to a consideration of the economical trinity. Being comes before function; that is, truth claims about the nature of God are logically prior to questions about his action.

If this is all true, however, then where do we begin? Those who deny transcendence do so in order to forge a frame of reference for 'God talk' with non-Christian humans. If we assert transcendence, then what is the common ground with those who do not believe from which we can move towards Christian theism? In other words, what is the point of contact? The answer must be that there can be no point of contact because our theory of humanity stands in contradistinction to that of the non-Christian.

It must be said at this point that the position just taken is the position of a consistent Calvinist and not the position of all Christians. As we saw earlier, Roman Catholic and Arminian theologians argue that there is a point of contact with the 'natural man', and that point of contact is the truth of natural theology. More specifically, many Christian theologians hold to the idea of a person's freedom to which God must appeal in order to win over that person. This concept of freedom, however, involves a doctrine of humanity that Van Til is totally unable to accept. He comments, 'The idea of freedom, as entertained by Roman theology, is based upon man's being metaphysically distinct from "god".'[96]

This again brings us back to the crucial difference between a consistent Calvinist and all other forms of Christian philosophy. If a person is held to be autonomous, then it is impossible to speak of such a God as is revealed in the Judaeo-Christian tradition. The thesis must be posited that we cannot, on the one hand, hold to Van Til's doctrine of God and yet, on the other hand, view a person as the ultimate judge or reference point. In Van Til's words, 'The revelation of a self-sufficient God can have no meaning for a mind that thinks of itself as ultimately autonomous.'[97]

This rejection of any point of contact in the natural man is not to suggest that there can be no contact, and it is here that we must bring in the doctrine of the fall. The 'normal' situation is always to be regarded as that of Adam prior to the fall. Man was created perfect by God and this perfection extended

---

96. Ibid., p. 88.
97. Ibid., p. 89.

to the knowledge situation. I am not, however, saying that Adam's knowledge was comprehensive, since that applies only to God. Being made in the image of God meant that Adam's knowledge was true, therein consisting the likeness of God (or part of it). But that likeness did not extend to transcendence, and therefore his knowledge was not comprehensive. Once again, we have come to a clear disagreement between Christian and non-Christian epistemology, since it is only Christian epistemology that does not posit the ideal of comprehensive knowledge.

When Adam 'fell' and disobeyed God, this innate knowledge was tainted. In introducing the notion of 'sin', it must be borne in mind that sin concerns the ethical and not the metaphysical realm. To put it another way, humanity's breach with God is moral and not ontological. Hence Van Til can say:

> We know that sin is an attempt on the part of man to cut himself loose from God. But this breaking loose from God could, in the nature of the case, not be metaphysical; if it were, man himself would be destroyed and God's purpose with man would be frustrated. Sin is therefore a breaking loose from God ethically and not metaphysically. Sin is the creature's enmity and rebellion against God but is not an escape from creaturehood.[98]

With regard to the question of knowledge, the fall signified the beginning of the present period wherein humans attempt to interpret everything with reference to themselves and not to God. This cataclysmic revolution in the frame of reference cannot be overestimated. Of man, from this juncture forward, Van Til can say, 'The assumption of all his future interpretation was the self-sufficiency of intra-cosmical relationships.'[99]

Van Til has done a great deal of work on Genesis 1 – 3 in terms of philosophical interpretation, and this is illustrated by his discussion of the position of Eve. We have already noted that the ontological question must be asked prior to the espistemological question and that the reversal of this is sin, but Eve neglected the logical priority. Van Til writes:

> God claimed that he was the Creator. He claimed that his Being was ultimate while Satan's being was created and therefore dependent upon God's being. Satan said in effect that she should pay no attention to this problem of being. He told her she should decide the question 'How do we know?' without asking the

---

98. Ibid., p. 46.
99. Ibid., p. 47.

question 'What do we know?' He said she should be neutral with respect to his interpretation of God's interpretation of what would take place if she ate of the forbidden tree. Eve did ignore the question of being in answering the question of knowledge. She said she would gather the opinions of as many as she could find with a reputation for having knowledge and then give the various views presented a fair hearing.[100]

Having begun by noting the fall, we can now see where the means of contact lies. Because of the fall and the doctrine of autonomous man that followed, this has been located in the ultimacy of man, but Van Til wants to argue that man's mind is derivative. This would mean that his self-consciousness depends upon God-consciousness; hence only when man is considered in this relationship can we proceed. At this stage Paul's argument in Romans 1:18–19 comes into its own. Humans, even after the fall, have an inherent awareness of God. Calvin, in the first few chapters of the *Institutes* makes this a keynote of his theology, and Van Til follows suit. The knowledge of God in every person is sufficient to leave him or her without excuse before God. Humans sinfully suppress this knowledge although they can never efface it. The illustration given of this is as follows: 'The natural man is such a one as constantly throws water on a fire he cannot quench.'[101]

The means of contact with the natural man, then, is this sense of deity that underlies his own notion of self-conscious autonomy. The critique of Roman Catholic and Arminian theology is that they are not prepared to be so radical. Van Til compares the problem to that of internal cancer. The Roman Catholic and the Arminian theologian are like the surgeon who wants to be kind and helpful, giving the patient various medications and all the while assuring him that deep down he is all right, and that the problem is only on the surface. The consistent Calvinist, on the other hand, is likened to the honest surgeon who tells the patient that he needs internal surgery and who proceeds to tackle the problem at the root.

This is also where we see the doctrine of total depravity in its true perspective. By allowing the natural man to assume his own premises and then placing Christian premises on the top, we are completely failing to take issue where it matters. This is precisely the significance of transcendence. Theologians who deny transcendence appear to be saying nothing that non-Christians could not also say. Hence Van Til's radical critique of theology

---

100. Ibid., p. 34.
101. Ibid., p. 92.

built on the foundation of the autonomous human, the 'natural man'. Concerning this compromising type of theology he writes, 'If the natural man is given permission to draw the floor-plan for a house and is allowed to build the first storey of the house in accordance with his own blueprint, the Christian cannot escape being controlled in a large measure by the same blueprint when he wants to take over the building of the second storey of the house.'[102]

On the question of theistic evidences Van Til is in agreement with Kant. The total negation of all univocal use of such arguments for God's existence must be pressed. As Van Til notes, however, such arguments do not destroy the analogical use of theistic arguments. The discussion of this leads Van Til into one of the most crucial issues at stake, and leads him to point out a grave inconsistency in Kant. Kant's theory that there is a noumenal realm 'above' is contradictory. Many theologians have not seen such a contradiction in Kant's dualism, being content to leave the phenomenal realm to Kant so long as he is prepared to leave the noumenal realm to them. The contradiction, however, stands: on the basis of this noumenal–phenomenal dualism Kant cannot have any true knowledge even of the phenomenal realm, because, having accepted the existence of a noumenal realm, there is no logical argument for saying that something in the noumenal realm might not effect something in the phenomenal realm (except Kant's statement to this effect!).

On this subject Van Til writes:

> Take for a moment the phenomenon of Jesus walking on earth. If the orthodox Christian view is correct there was in Jesus a combination of the phenomenal and the noumenal. Yet Kant would have to maintain that Jesus was exclusively phenomenal. Thus he would be denying the contact of the noumenal with the phenomenal . . . To be consistent he would therefore have to deny the existence of the noumenal world or he would have to give up his insistence that we can be sure that we have true knowledge of the phenomenal world without reference to the noumenal world.[103]

It is with this criticism that we see the challenge of Kant's position to biblical theology. I could discuss further Van Til's critique of Kant in many areas, but to move away from this central area of the autonomy of man and its significance for theology would be to broaden the argument too far.

---

102. Ibid., p. 111.

103. Van Til, 'Christian Epistemology', p. 110.

Conclusion

In this chapter we have seen how the Enlightenment philosophy created the movement of liberal theology with its rejection of the traditional doctrine of Scripture. This in turn led two groups of Protestant scholars to oppose liberal theology, namely neo-orthodoxy and conservative evangelicalism. As we now turn more directly to the discussion of inerrancy, we shall see that these are the three main parties to the debate.

4. FUNDAMENTALISM AND INERRANCY

Introduction

Having set the context by looking at the liberal theology that arose from the Enlightenment and the neo-orthodox and conservative evangelical responses to that liberal theology, we must now turn to the issue of 'inerrancy'. In this chapter I shall do three things. First, I shall examine the origins of the belief in the inerrancy of Scripture, particularly in the context of fundamentalism and its opposition to liberal theology. Second, I shall take note of those evangelicals who oppose the inerrantist position, highlighting the fact that the debate on this subject in the United States has been polarized between 'inerrantists' and 'errantists'. Third, I shall highlight the main arguments against the inerrantist view.

In the next chapter, I shall draw attention to an evangelical alternative to inerrancy, which enables us to hold a high view of Scripture while at the same time avoiding the need to demonstrate (or assume) the scientific accuracy of the *autographa*, as is required by the word 'inerrancy'. In other words, I shall argue that evangelicals ought to abandon the word 'inerrancy' and use language that is more biblically accurate and theologically constructive.

Warfield and Hodge

Classic expression was given to the evangelical doctrine of Scripture by B. B. Warfield and A. A. Hodge, professors at Princeton Theological Seminary, in an article entitled 'Inspiration', first published in 1881.[1] In that 1881 article, Hodge and Warfield gave expression to the doctrine of inerrancy, although without using that word. As Roger Nicole points out, 'the words *inerrant* and *inerrancy* do not occur, although the terms *errorless* and *without error* are repeatedly used by both writers and the whole intent of the article is to make it clear that the superintendence of God in Scripture guarantees the errorless infallibility of all scriptural affirmations'.[2] They argued that the *autographa*, that is, the original manuscripts of the biblical books as penned by the authors, were entirely without error.

Hodge and Warfield did not imagine that they were saying anything new, merely spelling out the orthodox doctrine of Scripture in order to resist the encroaches of the developing liberal theology. As far as they were concerned, this had always been the position of Reformed theologians and indeed of the whole Christian church, until relatively recently. The historian Mark Noll agrees:

> Most Christians in most churches since the founding of Christianity have believed in the inerrancy of the Bible. Or at least they have believed that the Scriptures are inspired by God, and so are the words of eternal life. The term *inerrancy* was not common until the nineteenth century. But the conviction that God communicates in Scripture a revelation of himself and of his deeds, and that this revelation is entirely truthful, has always been the common belief of most Catholics, most Protestants, most Orthodox, and even most of the sects of the fringe of Christianity.[3]

---

1. A. A. Hodge and B. B. Warfield, 'Inspiration', *Presbyterian Review* 2 (1881), pp. 225–260. The article is more explicit than, but not contrary to, the views earlier expressed by Charles Hodge in his own article of the same name: Charles Hodge, 'Inspiration', *Biblical Repertory and Princeton Review* 29 (1857), pp. 660–698. The Hodge and Warfield article was edited and republished by Roger R. Nicole: A. A. Hodge and B. B. Warfield, *Inspiration* (Grand Rapids: Baker, 1979). This edition contains a number of useful bibliographical and other appendices.
2. A. A. Hodge and Warfield, *Inspiration*, p. xiv.
3. Mark Noll, 'A Brief History of Inerrancy, Mostly in America', in *The Proceedings of the Conference on Biblical Inerrancy 1987* (Nashville: Broadman, 1987), pp. 9–10.

Warfield went on to write a great deal on the doctrine of Scripture.[4] Indeed, the subject was of primary concern to him, not least because of the battles raging within the Presbyterian Church over this very issue.[5] In particular, he responded to those who argued for a 'Limited Inspiration' view, notably Henry Preserved Smith, who was found guilty of heresy because of his views on Scripture, which he made public in defence of Charles Briggs.[6] It also became a distinguishing mark of the theological position held by those who taught at Princeton Theological Seminary.[7]

Warfield was undoubtedly a spiritual and theological giant whose work on Scripture is very important. The published collection of his writings on the subject provides a clear indication of his views on most of the controversial areas.[8] His general position on the doctrine of Scripture places him in the line

------

4. The first volume of the Oxford edition of Warfield's collected writings and the first volume of the later Presbyterian & Reformed edition of his collected writings were both devoted to the doctrine of Scripture: B. B. Warfield, *Revelation and Inspiration* (New York: Oxford University Press, 1927); B. B. Warfield, *The Inspiration and Authority of the Bible* (Philadelphia: Presbyterian & Reformed, 1948). For a complete list of Warfield's writings see John E. Meeter and Roger R. Nicole, *A Bibliography of Benjamin Breckinridge Warfield, 1851–1921* (Nutley, N. J.: Presbyterian & Reformed, 1974).

5. Professor Charles Briggs of Union Theological Seminary, New York, who was found guilty of heresy due to his denial of the doctrine of the inerrancy of Scripture and suspended from the ministry of the Presbyterian Church in 1893, was co-editor with Warfield of the *Presbyterian Review*. For an analysis of the Briggs case see Lefferts A. Loetscher, *The Broadening Church* (Philadelphia: University of Pennsylvania Press, 1954), pp. 48–62.

6. See Henry Preserved Smith, *Inspiration and Inerrancy: A History and a Defense* (Cincinnati: Robert Clarke, 1893). Warfield's response to Smith came the following year: B. B. Warfield, 'Professor Henry Preserved Smith, on Inspiration', *Presbyterian and Reformed Review* (January 1894), pp. 600–653. Warfield's article was later republished, with an introduction by J. Marcellus Kik: B. B. Warfield, *Limited Inspiration* (Philadelphia: Presbyterian & Reformed, 1962).

7. Mark Noll (ed.), *The Princeton Defense of Plenary Verbal Inspiration* (New York: Garland, 1988).

8. In addition, some scholars have given serious attention to his writings on this subject and sought to expound his position in more detail. See e.g. John J. Markarian, 'The Calvinistic Concept of the Biblical Revelation in the Theology of B. B. Warfield' (PhD diss., Drew University, 1963).

of orthodox Christianity. Noting that the 'religion of the Bible is a frankly super-natural religion',[9] he affirmed the reality of revelation, wherein God makes himself known to human beings. He supported this belief with a detailed analysis of the various modes of revelation found in Scripture.[10] It is not possible to understand his doctrine of the inspiration of the Scriptures without this background of his view of revelation. On the matter of inspiration, he accepted the received teaching of the church, which, despite the confusion of his own day, he asserted had always been the position of the church, providing evidence from the Fathers and from the creeds and confessions.[11] He was not, however, satisfied to accept the position simply on the basis of the church's authority, and in a well-known article demonstrated that the inspiration of the Scriptures was clearly taught by the Scriptures themselves.[12] As one of the leading scholars of his day, who had a wide knowledge of the developing German higher-critical theology, he was aware of the problems many scholars had in accepting the inspiration of the Scriptures and he addressed these carefully, especially in so far as they related to the disputes within the church.[13] Nevertheless, he argued for the maintenance of a 'high' view of Scripture's inspiration and authority, holding the line against the encroaching liberal theology. His work is of such quality and detail that he has left the church in his debt.

Although his general position is one that all evangelicals can appreciate, the specific issue of inerrancy became controversial. Indeed, there were some who rejected this doctrine of inerrancy, despite being very close to Warfield on most other issues. As we shall see later, this was the position taken by the Scottish theologian James Orr and the Dutch theologians Abraham Kuyper and Herman Bavinck.

Fundamentalism

Warfield and Hodge developed their view of the inerrancy of Scripture in the context of opposition to the developing liberal theology of the nineteenth century. They were not alone in these concerns, however, being only one strand in a large and significant protest movement that arose at the beginning of the

---

9. Warfield, *Inspiration and Authority*, p. 71.
10. Ibid., pp. 83–96.
11. Ibid., pp. 107–112.
12. Ibid., pp. 131–166.
13. Ibid., pp. 169–226.

twentieth century, which came to be called 'fundamentalism'. In order to provide a historical context for our examination of the concept of the inerrancy of Scripture, it is useful to trace the roots of fundamentalism and to indicate the differences between fundamentalism and the later neo-evangelicalism.

The Fundamentals

In 1909, Lyman Stewart, an oil millionaire from Southern California, with the help of his brother Milton, commissioned the publication of a series of volumes to articulate and defend the fundamental doctrines of the Christian faith. Ultimately, this involved the publication of twelve paperback volumes, published between 1910 and 1915.[14]

Having commissioned these volumes, the two brothers then paid for them to be sent out to those they considered to be in positions of influence. George Marsden notes, 'They financed free distribution to every pastor, missionary, theological professor, theological student, YMCA and YWCA secretary, college professor, Sunday school superintendent, and religious editor in the English-speaking world, and sent out some three million individual volumes in all.'[15] R. A. Torrey, the third Executive Secretary of the committee charged with the responsibility of carrying out the commission to publish *The Fundamentals*, tells us that some of the individual volumes went to as many as 300,000 people, but that by 1917 many of them had gone out of print and, there being still a demand for them, a new edition was published.[16]

Each volume contained a number of articles, by different writers, from various parts of the English-speaking world. Some of the writers were distinguished scholars, such as B. B. Warfield and Charles R. Erdman,[17] professors

---

14. A. C. Dixon, L. Meyer and R. A. Torrey (eds.), *The Fundamentals: A Testimony to the Truth*, 12 vols. (Chicago: privately printed and distributed, 1910–15).

15. George M. Marsden, *Fundamentalism and American Culture: The Shaping of Twentieth Century Evangelicalism: 1870–1925* (New York: Oxford University Press, 1980), p. 119.

16. R. A. Torrey, *The Fundamentals* (Grand Rapids: Baker, 1970), p. 5. This four-volume edition is a reprint 'without alteration or abridgment from the original, four-volume edition issued by the Bible Institute of Los Angeles in 1917'. Torrey tells us that all of the articles in the original twelve-volume work were reproduced in this four-volume edition, 'with the exception of a very few that did not seem to be in exact keeping with the original purpose of The Fundamentals'. The references below are to this 1970 reprint.

17. Warfield wrote one article: B. B. Warfield, 'The Deity of Christ', in Torrey, *Fundamentals*, vol. 2, pp. 239–246; Erdman wrote several, including the following:

at Princeton Theological Seminary, and James Orr, Professor at the United Free Church College in Glasgow, Scotland.[18] Some of the other writers were relatively unknown.[19] Several of the articles were taken from the writings of authors who had lived in earlier days, such as Thomas Boston[20] and Bishop J. C. Ryle.[21] A very high percentage of the articles dealt with the doctrine of Scripture in general and with the so-called 'higher critics' in particular.

The evangelicals who wrote the articles in *The Fundamentals* were united in their conviction that God had inspired the Bible, which therefore had full authority, although they would have disagreed on other matters, given the range of theological perspectives among them, including Reformed, dispensationalist and Arminian. Even on the doctrine of Scripture, the authors ranged from those who 'tended to drift towards the dictation theory'[22] to those who were unhappy with any doctrine of inerrancy.[23] These differences did not impact on *The Fundamentals*, however, and have to be established from the authors' other writings.

Fundamentalists

The publication of *The Fundamentals* was followed by the World Conference on Christian Fundamentals. This took place in 1919 in Philadelphia and resulted

---

Charles R. Erdman, 'The Holy Spirit and the Sons of God', in Torrey, *Fundamentals*, vol. 2, pp. 338–352; Charles R. Erdman, 'The Church and Socialism', in Torrey, *Fundamentals*, vol. 4, pp. 97–108; and Charles R. Erdman, 'The Coming of Christ', in Torrey, *Fundamentals*, vol. 4, pp. 301–313.

18. Orr wrote a number of articles, including the following: James Orr, 'The Holy Spirit and Modern Negations', in Torrey, *Fundamentals*, vol. 1, pp. 94–110; James Orr, 'The Early Narratives of Genesis', in Torrey, *Fundamentals*, vol. 1, pp. 228–240; James Orr, 'Science and Christian Faith', in Torrey, *Fundamentals*, vol. 1, pp. 334–347; and James Orr, 'The Virgin Birth of Christ', in Torrey, *Fundamentals*, vol. 2, pp. 247–260.

19. Or even unidentified, such as the article entitled 'Evolutionism in the Pulpit', where the author is identified merely as 'By an Occupant of the Pew': Torrey, *Fundamentals*, vol. 4, pp. 88–96.

20. Thomas Boston, 'The Nature of Regeneration', in Torrey, *Fundamentals*, vol. 3, pp. 128–132.

21. J. C. Ryle, 'The True Church', in Torrey, *Fundamentals*, vol. 3, pp. 315–319.

22. Marsden, *Fundamentalism*, p. 122.

23. As I have already noted, there was a difference of opinion on this matter between B. B. Warfield and James Orr, two of the contributors to *The Fundamentals*.

in the formation of 'The World's Christian Fundamentals Association'. Harold B. Kuhn notes that

> the organisation required of its members adherence to nine points of doctrine, namely: (1) the inspiration and inerrancy of Scripture, (2) the Trinity, (3) the deity and virgin birth of Christ, (4) the creation and fall of man, (5) a substitutionary atonement, (6) the bodily resurrection, (7) the regeneration of believers, (8) the personal and imminent return of Christ, and (9) the resurrection and final assignment of all men to eternal blessedness or eternal woe.[24]

Bruce Shelley tells us that it was not long before the word 'fundamentalist' was created. He writes, 'By 1918 the term "fundamentals" had become common usage, but "fundamentalist" and "fundamentalism" were coined in 1920 by Curtis Lee Laws, Baptist editor of the *Watchman-Examiner*.'[25] As a direct result of this, there arose among the Baptists in America a group calling themselves 'fundamentalists'. For our purposes, it is important to note that, at this stage, 'fundamentalist' was a title some evangelical Christians took for themselves as a positive identification with the 'fundamentals' of the faith. It was not a pejorative term applied to them by others, as it would later be.

Fundamentalism was and is primarily an American movement and its history has been well documented.[26] It did affect other countries, notably the UK, but never in the same way and certainly not to the same extent.

---

24. Harold B. Kuhn, 'Fundamentalism', in E. F. Harrison (ed.), *Baker's Dictionary of Theology* (Grand Rapids: Baker, 1960), pp. 233–234.

25. Bruce Shelley, 'Fundamentalism', in J. D. Douglas (ed.), *The New International Dictionary of the Christian Church* (Grand Rapids: Zondervan, 1974), pp. 396–397.

26. For an overview of the rise and development of fundamentalism see the following: Stewart G. Cole, *The History of Fundamentalism* (Westport, Conn.: Greenwood, 1931); Norman F. Furniss, *The Fundamentalist Controversy, 1918–1931* (Hamden, Conn.: Archon, 1954); Louis Gasper, *The Fundamentalist Movement* (The Hague: Mouton, 1963); Ernest R. Sandeen, *The Roots of Fundamentalism: British and American Millenarianism 1800–1930* (Chicago: University of Chicago Press, 1970); George W. Dollar, *A History of Fundamentalism in America* (Greenville, S. C.: Bob Jones University Press, 1973); C. Allyn Russell, *Voices of American Fundamentalism: Seven Biographical Studies* (Philadelphia: Westminster, 1976); Nancy Tatom Ammerman, *Bible Believers: Fundamentalists in the Modern World* (New Brunswick: Rutgers University Press, 1987); and Mark Ellingsen, *The Evangelical Movement: Growth, Impact, Controversy, Dialog* (Minneapolis: Augsburg, 1988).

Characteristics of fundamentalism

As time went on, however, fundamentalism began to develop certain characteristics that distinguished it from the mainstream of the evangelical movement, not least a strong emphasis on premillennial eschatology, within the broader context of dispensational theology. Indeed, Ernest Sandeen sees this emphasis, which he traces to the English Brethren writer J. N. Darby, as the main identifying feature of the movement.[27] This aspect of fundamentalism was strengthened by the increasing use of the Scofield Reference Bible.[28]

Fundamentalism was also affected by the revivalist movement, not least among those who had been brought to faith in Christ through the Moody and Sankey campaigns. In addition, there was an increasingly separatist mentality, including a gradual withdrawal from mainstream schools and theological colleges when it became apparent that theological liberalism had affected the teaching in those mainstream schools. As a social phenomenon, the movement adopted certain cultural distinctives: fundamentalists did not dance or drink or smoke or go to the cinema and so on. Above all, there was an increasing anti-intellectual thrust to the movement, with the complete rejection of any form of biblical or textual criticism. There was also serious concentration on one issue, namely the campaign to ensure that the case for biological evolution was not permitted to be taught in the public schools. This led to the infamous trial in 1925, when John T. Scopes, a schoolteacher in Dayton, Tennessee, was found guilty of teaching evolution.[29] This became a cause célèbre and leading figures rallied to support both prosecution and defence. The national and international coverage of the case was astonishing, but ultimately did not help the cause of fundamentalism. As Louis Gasper noted, 'This farcical episode, as it turned out to be, attracted the attention of the nation and other parts of the world, but it did not seem to have helped the fundamentalists to any great extent, even though Scopes was found guilty.'[30]

Fundamentalism and politics

In its later development, fundamentalism also had a political side. Indeed, it can be argued that this was what ultimately led to the formation of the 'New

---

27. Sandeen, *Roots of Fundamentalism.*
28. C. I. Scofield (ed.), *The Scofield Reference Bible* (New York: Oxford University Press, 1909). A later edition was published as C. I. Scofield (ed.), *The New Scofield Reference Bible* (New York: Oxford University Press, 1967).
29. For an account of the controversy see Furniss, *Fundamentalist Controversy*, pp. 3 ff.
30. Gasper, *Fundamentalist Movement*, p. 14.

Religious Right'. This pro-America, anti-communist force was normally Republican in its sentiments but was taken seriously by both main political parties, not least when independents like Pat Robertson were put forward as presidential candidates by the fundamentalists themselves.[31]

It was perhaps unlikely that fundamentalists would become involved in politics. Two sociologists, Robert C. Liebman and Robert Wuthnow, edited a symposium on the 'New Religious Right'.[32] They begin their introduction to the book with these striking words:

> Scarcely anyone expected it. For more than 50 years evangelicals kept studiously aloof from American politics. They sang hymns and tended to souls, but left the burdens of legislation and social policy to their more worldly counterparts in the Protestant mainstream. From time to time an occasional voice broke the self-imposed silence – Carl McIntyre striking out at the liberal establishment or Billy James Hargis stirring up anti-Communist fears. But these were the exceptions and even fellow fundamentalists tended to regard them with suspicion. Politics was an evil of the flesh, an exercise in futility. Only repentance and salvation could bring genuine renewal. That evangelicals might emerge as a political force seemed dubious at best. They were, by all indications, a declining remnant, destined to survive only by withdrawing from active confrontation with the secular age. Like Prohibition and creationism, evangelicals appeared to be more a vestige of the past than a vital dimension of the present. That their own pastors would lead a political movement seemed out of the question.[33]

---

31. It is important, however, to recognize that the 'New Religious Right' is only one expression of the ongoing relationship between American Christianity and politics. William Martin, in a book written to accompany a television series documenting the 'New Religious Right', argues that the Puritan legacy, not least in its understanding of the relationship between church and state and its consciousness of human sin, provides the background against which all such movements are to be understood. He writes, 'This combination of covenantal thinking, conviction of divine mission, and profound awareness of human fallibility have marked American political institutions and movements from the Mayflower Compact to the Declaration of Independence and the Constitution, through the New Deal and New Frontier and Great Society, to the rise of the Moral Majority and the Christian Coalition and the construction of the Republican Party's 1994 Contract with America' (William Martin, *With God on Our Side: The Rise of the Religious Right in America* [New York: Broadway, 1996], p. 2).

32. Robert C. Liebman and Robert Wuthnow (eds.), *The New Christian Right: Mobilization and Legitimation* (New York: Aldine, 1983).

33. Ibid., p. 1.

The 'New Religious Right' has become such a noteworthy movement that it has attracted significant academic attention. A number of important books and symposia have been published, both sympathetic and unsympathetic, from a popular perspective,[34] and from a more academic perspective.[35] Perhaps the best volume from a broadly sympathetic position is the symposium edited by Richard John Neuhaus, now Editor in Chief of *First Things* but who, at that time, was Director of the Rockford Institute Center on Religion and Society in New York City, and Michael Cromartie, Director of Protestant Studies at the Ethics and Public Policy Center in Washington. Their book seeks to define the differences between fundamentalists and evangelicals and to identify their respective concerns.[36] Neuhaus is well known for his concern about the 'Naked Public Square', where religion is excluded from political and social debate, and the book argues strongly for an involvement of Christians in the formation of public policy. After some introductory essays that set the historical context, including chapters by Neuhaus himself and by George Marsden, there are chapters written by evangelicals and fundamentalists themselves, including Carl F. H. Henry, Jerry Falwell, Charles W. Colson and Jim Wallis. Finally, there are essays by a number of leading American intellectuals, including Martin E. Marty and Harvey Cox. For a more critically objective academic treatment, see the work of the British sociologist Steve Bruce.[37] Bruce surveys a significant ten-year period in the history of the 'New Religious Right' and identifies what he regards as the factors that led to the demise of the movement, or at least to a lessening of its influence on American politics.

Fundamentalism and Scripture

Having outlined something of the character of fundamentalism as a movement, we must now focus on the fundamentalist doctrine of Scripture. We noted earlier that, among the writers of *The Fundamentals*, there was a range of opinion on the doctrine of Scripture. Ultimately, this was resolved and the

---

34. Robert Zwier, *Born-Again Politics: The New Christian Right in America* (Downers Grove: IVP, 1982).

35. Melvin I. Urofsky and Martha May (eds.), *The New Christian Right: Political and Social Issues* (New York: Garland, 1996).

36. Richard John Neuhaus and Michael Cromartie (eds.), *Piety and Politics: Evangelicals and Fundamentalists Confront the World* (Washington, D. C.: Ethics and Public Policy Center, 1987).

37. Steve Bruce, *The Rise and Fall of the New Christian Right: Conservative Protestant Politics in America 1978–1988* (Oxford: Clarendon, 1988).

fundamentalists took their stand on the doctrine of inerrancy, thus excluding even some contributors to *The Fundamentals*, such as James Orr, who could not accept this position. Among those who held to the doctrine of the inerrancy of Scripture, however, there were also differences that soon came to light. Some continued to express the doctrine of inerrancy in a way that suggested the 'dictation' theory and rejected any possibility of biblical or textual criticism. Others could not accept this view. Ultimately, this disagreement led to a parting of the ways between those who continued to call themselves 'fundamentalists' and those who began to define themselves as 'neo-evangelicals'. I shall deal first with the fundamentalists and then turn to the neo-evangelicals.

As indicated above, both fundamentalists and most other evangelicals shared the commitment to biblical inerrancy. Many of the fundamentalists defined and used this term in precisely the same way as the later neo-evangelicals, and indeed both groups followed the lead of the Princeton theologians. On this matter, at least, there was agreement among evangelicals. Where the fundamentalist doctrine of Scripture developed some uniqueness, however, was in the matter of textual criticism. In an overreaction to the higher-critical movement, which stemmed mostly from German liberal theology, many fundamentalists argued that no form of textual criticism was acceptable.[38] This, of course, caused many problems in developing a doctrine of Scripture. Which text of Scripture are we to use? Which Hebrew and Greek manuscripts are to be the basis for translations of the Scriptures into English and other languages? The fundamentalists normally resolved this question by arguing that the Authorized (King James) Version (KJV), is the only one that should be used and rejected any findings of textual criticism that questioned the accuracy of the text used by the KJV translators. This argument is still maintained by many fundamentalists today.

Two different but related arguments were put forward in support of this position. The first argument was that God acted supernaturally in and through the 1611 translators, so as to keep them from all error and hence to guarantee the virtual inerrancy of the KJV. Those who held to this position argued that no other English translations are either possible or desirable because God had given his church, once for all, an inerrant English Bible. The second argument, seeking to defend itself against apparently arbitrary claims concerning the superiority and indeed finality of the KJV, insisted that it was not the KJV itself that was providentially preserved in an inerrant condition but rather the Hebrew and Greek manuscripts that provided the basis for this translation.

---

38. Although some accepted 'lower criticism', not least in their arguments in favour of the Textus Receptus.

These manuscripts came to be called the Textus Receptus or 'Received Text', the early printer Elzevir having used the phrase to advertise and commend his edition. Those who hold to this position are prepared to accept that modern translations of the Bible into English are permissable, so long as the Textus Receptus is the manuscript basis for any new translation.

The most significant early defender of one ancient text against the modern textual critics was John William Burgon, in the late nineteenth century.[39] He advocated the Byzantine texts, although he is often mistakenly quoted by those who favour the Textus Receptus, in support of their position. Modern defences of the Textus Receptus range from fairly academic studies such as those by Wilbur Pickering[40] and Ted Letis[41] to some very intemperate, popular material, which shows no willingness to engage in any serious manner with the textual arguments and is severely discourteous to any Christian taking another position.[42] Much of the modern work defending the KJV and the Textus Receptus has been published or promoted by the Trinitarian Bible Society. There have been a number of responses to the fundamentalists. Perhaps the best two volumes of response in terms of accessibility have been those written by James White[43] and by D. A. Carson.[44] The whole issue of evangelical scholarship in relation to the Bible, especially but not exclusively in America, has been well documented by Mark Noll.[45]

---

39. John William Burgon, *The Revision Revised* (London: John Murray, 1883).

40. Wilbur N. Pickering, *The Identity of the New Testament Text* (Nashville: Nelson, 1977); updated version available free online at <http://www.revisedstandard.net/text/WNP/>, accessed 31 May 2007.

41. T. P. Letis (ed.), *The Majority Text: Essays and Reviews in the Continuing Debate* (Philadelphia: Institute for Renaissance and Reformation Biblical Studies, 1987).

42. See e.g. Peter Ruchman, *Why I Believe the King James Version Is the Word of God* (Pensacola: Bible Baptist Bookstore, 1988); and Gail Riplinger, *New Age Bible Versions* (Munroe Falls, Ohio: A. V., 1993).

43. James R. White, *The King James Only Controversy: Can You Trust the Modern Translations?* (Minneapolis: Bethany House, 1995). White is particularly good at explaining the key issues to the reader with no technical background. He also responds very well to the extremists, particularly to Ruchman and Riplinger.

44. D. A. Carson, *The King James Version Debate: A Plea for Realism* (Grand Rapids: Baker, 1979). This is an excellent introduction to the nature and significance of biblical textual criticism and the principles of translation.

45. Mark Noll, *Between Faith and Criticism: Evangelicals, Scholarship and the Bible in America* (San Francisco: Harper & Row, 1986).

Departure from fundamentalism

As a result of the theological, sociological, political, separatist and anti-intellectual factors noted above, by the 1950s the word 'fundamentalist' had come to be identified with a particularly narrow form of evangelical Christianity. As a result of this rather negative image and particularly because of the view of Scripture adopted by those within the fundamentalist movement, certain evangelicals who shared the essential concerns highlighted in *The Fundamentals* no longer wanted to be identified as 'fundamentalists'. They believed that the name had been hijacked by a group of people who were theologically narrow, socially exclusivist and politically extremist. Those who took this view coined for themselves the name 'neo-evangelical'. This group included such distinguished evangelical leaders as Carl F. H. Henry, Harold John Ockenga, E. J. Carnell and Billy Graham. They founded a new magazine called *Christianity Today* and sought to develop an evangelicalism that was, among other things, more intellectually respectable.[46] They also founded Fuller Seminary.[47] Ultimately, this group simply became known as 'evangelicals'.[48]

The crucial point for this study, however, is that the new evangelical movement, as represented by Henry, Graham and others, did not abandon use of the word 'inerrancy'. Despite their rejection of the anti-intellectual attitude of fundamentalism and despite their affirmation of the importance of biblical scholarship, including textual scholarship, they retained the same commitment to inerrancy as the fundamentalists. The inerrancy of Scripture remained a key concept in binding together those who were opposed to various strands of post-Enlightenment liberal theology. Both evangelicals

---

46. Carl F. H. Henry, *The Uneasy Conscience of Modern Fundamentalism* (Grand Rapids: Eerdmans, 1947).

47. George M. Marsden, *Reforming Fundamentalism: Fuller Seminary and the New Evangelicalism* (Grand Rapids: Eerdmans, 1987).

48. It should be noted in passing that, despite the clear difference between fundamentalism and evangelicalism, at least as characterized by scholars like Carl Henry, E. J. Carnell and others, the word 'fundamentalist' is still used to refer to evangelical Christianity in general, even where none of the social, political, cultural, theological and anti-intellectual elements of fundamentalism exist. It is in this sense that the word is used by James Barr, himself a former evangelical. This demonstrates either an ignorance of the difference between fundamentalism and evangelism or a quite cynical disregard for the facts. In either case, it is entirely inappropriate to use the word 'fundamentalist' to refer to evangelicals.

and fundamentalists held to this doctrine, although they expressed it in different ways. Inerrancy is still a key word today in identifying a community of believers and scholars who share a world view where the teaching of Scripture is the final determining factor in all of our theological, ecclesiastical and personal decision-making.[49]

The modern inerrancy debate

Although there was common cause between most fundamentalists and evangelicals concerning their affirmation of the inerrancy of Scripture, there were always some who resisted this view. More recently, however, the opposition to inerrancy among evangelicals has been more sustained and more closely argued. This opposition has focused on Warfield's claim that the doctrine of inerrancy has always been the position held by the church. It has been argued that, far from being the historic position of the Reformed church, inerrancy was, in fact, a creation of Warfield's or that of his contemporaries. Professor Ernest Sandeen, for example, argued strongly that inerrancy originated with Warfield and certain other nineteenth-century theologians.[50]

The most significant proponent of this view has been Jack Rogers. In his doctoral thesis, written under the supervision of G. C. Berkouwer, he argued that the Westminster Confession of Faith ought not to be interpreted as teaching the doctrine of inerrancy.[51] This was followed by a much more sustained attack on the doctrine of inerrancy, from a historical basis, in a book co-written with Donald McKim.[52] In this book they argued there could be traced a 'Central Christian Tradition' concerning the doctrine of Scripture that all major theologians held, including the early church Fathers and the Reformers, which was contrary to the notion of inerrancy. This 'Central Christian Tradition' stands between the extremes of rationalism and mysticism, which

---

49. E.g. an affirmation of belief in inerrancy is required for membership in the Evangelical Theological Society in the USA.

50. Ernest R. Sandeen, 'The Princeton Theology: One Source of Biblical Literalism in American Protestantism', *Church History* 31 (1962), pp. 307–321 Also, Sandeen, *Roots of Fundamentalism*.

51. Jack B. Rogers, *Scripture in the Westminster Confession: A Problem of Historical Interpretation for American Presbyterianism* (Grand Rapids: Eerdmans, 1967).

52. Jack B. Rogers and Donald K. McKim, *The Authority and Interpretation of the Bible: An Historical Approach* (New York: Harper & Row, 1979).

have been seen in every age of the church. In this 'Central Christian Tradition', the Bible is to be accepted by faith and not by rational proofs; it is not to be regarded as authoritative in matters of science or on other subjects, but rather as a means of salvation. As Donald Bloesch has expressed it, 'Scriptural inerrancy can be affirmed if it means the conformity of what is written to the dictates of the Spirit regarding the will and purpose of God. But it cannot be held if it is taken to mean the conformity of everything that is written in Scripture to the facts of world history and science.'[53] The Bible must be viewed also in terms of the concept of 'accommodation', that is, the affirmation that God has spoken to us in ways we as sinful human beings can understand. Therefore, to 'erect a standard of modern, technical precision in language as the hallmark of biblical authority was totally foreign to the foundation shared by the early church'.[54]

Rogers and McKim argued that Barth, Berkouwer and the 1967 confession produced by the United Presbyterian Church in the USA are the true representatives of this 'Central Christian Tradition' and therefore the true successors of Calvin and the Reformed tradition. Their principal argument is that, in the nineteenth century, Princeton Theological Seminary developed the doctrine of the inerrancy of Scripture. It did so, we are told, because of two underlying causes. First, because it used Francis Turretin's *Institutio Theologiae Elencticae* as its textbook in systematic theology; and second, because the philosophical basis for its theology was the Scottish philosophy called 'common sense realism'.[55]

Specifically rejecting the doctrine of inerrancy as taught by Hodge and Warfield, they write:

> If evangelicalism is to be a creative and renewing force in American life, it must
> come to historical clarity concerning the authority and interpretation of the Bible.
> Until now, the heavy hand of the Princeton theology has prevented that from
> happening. Because of its pervasive influence in American evangelical theology,
> few have dared to challenge the Princeton theology's post-Reformation scholastic
> theory concerning the Bible. Those who self-consciously hold to the old Princeton
> position continue to assert that it is the historic Christian, and Reformed, approach.
> The large majority of evangelicals are far from the Princeton position in their actual

---

53. Donald G. Bloesch, *Holy Scripture: Revelation, Inspiration and Interpretation* (Downers Grove: IVP, 1994), p. 107.

54. Rogers and McKim, *Authority and Interpretation*, p. xxii.

55. Ibid., p. xvii.

use of Scripture. Most thoughtful evangelicals, for example, accept the usefulness
of responsible biblical criticism. But because they have no alternative theory, they·
continue to hold to the Hodge-Warfield apologetic, which was designed to deny any
scholarly contextual study. Evangelicals are often reminded of the dangers of liberal
subjectivism. In a sincere desire to avoid that extreme, they claim the rationalistic
scholasticism of old Princeton as their theory, even though their practice is far
from it.[56]

It would be too much of a diversion at this point to bring a counter-
argument to this view of Warfield's scholarship. Simply let it be said that the
suggestion that Warfield, of all people, was against scholarly contextual study
is an astonishing claim given his continued and vigorous engagement with the
scholarship of his day and his promotion of solid academic study of the
Scriptures.

The Rogers and McKim view has been challenged by those evangelicals
who are committed to the doctrine of inerrancy.[57] The most significant
volume published in response came from John Woodbridge.[58] He argues
against the Rogers and McKim proposal on two grounds. First, he says that
Rogers and McKim have partly misunderstood and partly misrepresented the
history of the doctrine of biblical authority. His historical analysis is very persuasive and in those places where he demonstrates that Rogers and McKim
have quoted inaccurately, incompletely or out of context, his points are well
made.

His second main argument is that Rogers and McKim, far from putting
forward the historic Reformed position, were rather proponents of a particular theological perspective, namely the theology of Berkouwer. On this point,
Woodbridge writes:

Nevertheless, it is not an adequate survey of the history of biblical authority. Rather
it constitutes a revisionist piece of literature that apparently attempts to interpret the

56. Ibid., pp. 460–461.
57. Randall H. Balmer, 'The Princetonians and Scripture: A Reconsideration',
    Westminster Theological Journal 44 (1982), pp. 352–365. See also John D. Woodbridge·
    and Randall H. Balmer, 'The Princetonians and Biblical Authority: An Assessment
    of the Ernest Sandeen Proposal', in D. A. Carson and J. D. Woodbridge (eds.),
    Scripture and Truth (Leicester: IVP, 1983), pp. 251–279.
58. John D. Woodbridge, *Biblical Authority: A Critique of the Rogers/McKim Proposal*
    (Grand Rapids: Zondervan, 1982).

history of biblical authority with the categories of the later Berkouwer. Because
those categories do not find antecedents in large tracts of the history of the
Christian churches, Rogers and McKim's own proposal becomes forced and not
very reliable.[59]

Interestingly, Donald Bloesch, although sharing much in common with
Rogers and McKim in terms of his understanding of Scripture, supports
Woodbridge's analysis of the history of the doctrine. He writes:

> Contrary to what is commonly believed in liberal and neo-orthodox circles, there is a
> long tradition in the church that represents the teaching of Scripture as being without
> error. References to the Scriptures as *inerrabilis* are to be found in Augustine, Aquinas
> and Duns Scotus. The adjective *infallibilis* was applied to Scripture by John Wycliffe
> and Jean de Gerson. Luther and Calvin described the Bible as being infallible and
> without error. Calvin referred to the Bible as 'the unerring rule' for faith and practice.
> The word *inerrancy* first became current in English in the middle and later nineteenth
> century. It was first generally used by Roman Catholics and then by conservative
> Presbyterians.[60]

Bloesch deals in some detail with the Rogers and McKim debate with John
Woodbridge.[61] While finding some helpful material in Rogers and McKim he
criticizes them at several points:

> While I readily grant that scriptural infallibility can legitimately be described in
> functional terms, is one being faithful to the biblical perspective by thinking of
> infallibility exclusively in these terms? Besides infallibly directing us to Christ,
> does not Scripture provide infallible information concerning the will and
> purpose of God as supremely manifested in Christ? The Bible not only directs us
> to truth but also speaks truth. It not only points to truth but also communicates
> truth.
>
> Rogers and McKim remind us that the Reformers had an instrumental view of
> scriptural authority in that they saw Scripture as the instrument of the Spirit of God.
> But Scripture could be the ongoing instrument of God's Spirit only because the Spirit
> was the ultimate author of Scripture. Our two authors sometimes give the impression
> that the Bible is an inspiring but not an inspired book.

---

59. Ibid., p. 151.
60. Bloesch, *Holy Scripture*, pp. 33–34.
61. Ibid., pp. 131–140.

In contradistinction to Rogers and McKim and perhaps also to the later Berkouwer, I see the Bible as having an ontological as well as a functional authority. It not only brings sinners the saving message of redemption by the action of the Spirit, but its writing is filled and penetrated by the presence of the Spirit. The light that shines through Scripture is also the light that made possible the production of the canon of Scripture.[62]

One of the aspects of the Rogers and McKim proposal that Woodbridge did not deal with in any great detail was the argument that the Princeton theologians developed a doctrine of the inerrancy of Scripture because, *inter alia*, they built their theology on common sense realism, the philosophy of Thomas Reid (1710–96).[63] There is no doubt that the Princetonians were indebted to common sense realism and used it as a basis for some of their thinking.[64] Were Rogers and McKim correct, however, in arguing that it played a major part in determining their theological system and, more specifically, in providing the basis for their doctrine of inerrancy?

Dr J. Ligon Duncan has responded to this argument and demonstrated cogently that it is not substantial.[65] Interestingly, he demonstrated that common sense realism was also the philosophical basis for the theologians at Yale, Harvard and Andover, who certainly did not teach inerrancy.[66] He also

---

62. Ibid., pp. 132–133.

63. For a detailed study of common sense realism see S. A. Grave, *The Scottish Philosophy of Common Sense* (Oxford: Clarendon, 1960).

64. See Paul Helm, 'Thomas Reid, Common Sense and Calvinism', in II. Hart, J. Van Der Hoeven and N. Wolterstorff (eds.), *Rationality in the Calvinian Tradition* (Lanham, Md.: University Press of America, 1983), pp. 71–89. For the impact of this philosophy on one Princetonian see James McCosh, *The Scottish Philosophy* (New York: Charles Scribner's Sons, 1890).

65. J. Ligon Duncan III, 'Common Sense and American Presbyterianism: An Evaluation of the Impact of Scottish Realism on Princeton and the South' (MA thesis, Covenant Theological Seminary, 1987). Compare another article in this area: D. Clair Davis, 'Princeton and Inerrancy: The Nineteenth Century Philosophical Background of Contemporary Concerns', in J. D. Hannah (ed.), *Inerrancy and the Church* (Chicago: Moody, 1984), pp. 359–378.

66. This is to say nothing of the fact that some common sense realists were not Protestants at all. See e.g. the fascinating study comparing Thomas Reid and the French Jesuit philosopher Claude Buffier: Louise Marcil-Lacoste, *Claude Buffier and Thomas Reid, Two Common Sense Philosophers* (Montreal: McGill-Queen's University Press, 1982).

pointed out that Thomas Reid himself was a 'Moderate' Church of Scotland minister who would have had little sympathy for the Princeton school of theology.[67] Duncan examines four nineteenth-century American Presbyterians: two Princeton theologians, Charles Hodge and B. B. Warfield, and two southern Presbyterian theologians, Robert Lewis Dabney and James Henley Thornwell, all of whom believed in the inerrancy of Scripture. His intention was to examine what influence common sense realism had upon their theology. He concluded that common sense realism cannot be regarded as the source of the doctrine of biblical inerrancy. He writes, 'Common Sense Philosophy's greatest contributions to nineteenth century American Presbyterianism were in language, epistemology, apologetics, and methodology. At the same time, Realism contributed little to their theology or their view of Scripture.'[68]

Duncan sets his response to Rogers and McKim in the overall context of this examination of these four Presbyterian theologians. He outlines nine propositions, drawn from Rogers and McKim, in relation to the influence of common sense realism on Princeton theology in general and the doctrine of inerrancy in particular.[69] Having concluded his case studies of the four theologians, he responds to the nine propositions point by point.[70] He then concludes that

> Almost all the problems in the Rogers and McKim interpretation of Common Sense's influence at Princeton can be traced to their unhistorical approach to the subject. They are not primarily interested in understanding Common Sense Philosophy's influence, but in securing a polemic against the Princeton doctrine of Scripture. This deficient approach is reflected in some of the characteristics of Rogers and McKim's analysis.[71]

---

67. Of course, the fact that common sense realism fed other systems of thought does not prevent it from being a substantial influence on Princeton. Also, the fact that Reid was not an evangelical is not a conclusive argument against his influencing evangelicals. It could reasonably be argued that, although common sense realism does not inevitably lead to inerrancy, inerrancy requires a base in common sense realism.

68. Duncan, 'Common Sense', p. 109.

69. Ibid., p. 21.

70. Ibid., pp. 109–113.

71. Ibid., p. 113.

It was precisely to answer the Rogers and McKim proposal and similar questions that the International Council on Biblical Inerrancy was set up. In October 1978, under the auspices of the Council, 300 theologians and church leaders met at Chicago to affirm their position. They produced The Chicago Statement on Biblical Inerrancy,[72] and that statement remains today the position held by many evangelicals. The strength of the statement was that it not only said what its authors believed about inerrancy but also noted what they did not believe, in a series of Articles of Affirmation and Denial.[73]

Of course, many different arguments are put forward in favour of the term 'inerrancy', depending upon whether one believes that the doctrine of inerrancy is directly taught in Scripture, or whether it is a necessary implicate and consequence of believing that the Scriptures are God-breathed. Inerrantists themselves can be divided into three groups. First, there are those whom we might call 'fundamentalist inerrantists', who reject all textual criticism, are largely anti-academic, sometimes tend towards dictation theories and usually argue that the King James Version of the Bible is the only legitimate version. Second, there are those whom we might call 'Textus Receptus inerrantists', who offer a detailed textual argument in favour of the view that the *autographa* are accurately represented by (and only by) the so-called Textus Receptus.[74] Third, there are those whom we might call 'Chicago inerrantists', being those who can affirm the Chicago Statement on Biblical Inerrancy as explained above.

In my view, the position held by the fundamentalist inerrantists is not tenable. We cannot bury our heads in the sand and ignore the fact that the Bibles we use are translations based on Hebrew, Greek and Aramaic texts, and that these texts themselves vary considerably. For example, no two manuscripts of the New Testament, of which we have around 5,000, are identical. Scholars are forced to compare texts and decide on the 'best and most probable' reading. The fundamentalist inerrantist often gives the impression that the

---

72. The Chicago Statement is found in various publications, including J. I. Packer, *God Has Spoken*, rev. ed. (London: Hodder & Stoughton, 1979), pp. 139–155.

73. The Evangelical Theological Society has now adopted the Chicago Statement as the definitive interpretation of what is meant by the word 'inerrancy' in its doctrinal basis.

74. See e.g. Letis, *Majority Text*; and T. P. Letis, *The Ecclesiastical Text: Text Criticism, Biblical Authority and the Popular Mind* (Philadelphia: Institute for Renaissance and Reformation Biblical Studies, 2000).

Bible fell down from heaven intact and that no textual criticism is or has been necessary.

Another problem with the fundamentalist inerrantist is a tendency to choose a position because it is convenient, rather than because it is demonstrably true. For example, it is certainly true that the hypothesis of an inerrant KJV makes life easier for the believer. That, of course, does not mean it is true! Some of the epistemological arguments seem to be based on the following doubtful logic: 'Without inerrant truth we can never have certainty; it is vital that we have certainty; therefore, our English translation of the Bible must be inerrant.' This argument falls down when we recognize that it is grounded upon our need for certainty rather than upon anything God has revealed. In any case, why should it be that one seventeenth-century translation of the Bible, into one European language, by a group of Anglican scholars should somehow be the only inerrant text of the Bible available to humanity? Further, why should it be the case that only the manuscripts available to those scholars at that time and in that place were supernaturally preserved by God in an inerrant condition?

For similar reasons, I am not persuaded by the Textus Receptus inerrantists. The idea that only one manuscript tradition is authentic and that all of the other manuscripts are inauthentic does not stand up to close scrutiny and is very difficult to sustain. The scholarly debate on these issues is much more complex than some of the Textus Receptus inerrantists allow, and the literature is both important and demanding.[75]

The most significant argument for inerrancy, in my view, comes from the Chicago inerrantists. This group defines inerrancy with extreme care and make clear what they *do not* mean as well as what they *do* mean when using the term. In their statements and in the books sponsored by the International Council on Biblical Inerrancy, they argue for inerrancy from Scripture, from church history and on the basis of philosophical, apologetic arguments. Above all, they argue that, since Scripture has its origin in

---

75. Two standard introductions to the discipline are Kurt Aland and Barbara Aland, *The Text of the New Testament: An Introduction to the Critical Editions and to the Theory and Practice of Modern Textual Criticism* (Grand Rapids: Eerdmans, 1989); and Bruce M. Metzger, *The Text of the New Testament: Its Transmission, Corruption and Restoration* (New York: Oxford University Press, 1992). See also the important *festschrift* for Bruce Metzger: Bart D. Ehrman and Michael W. Holmes (eds.), *The Text of the New Testament in Contemporary Research: Essays on the Status Quaestionis* (Grand Rapids: Eerdmans, 1995).

God and since God's character is such that he cannot lie, Scripture must be inerrant.

Arguments against inerrancy

Most biblical scholars reject the inerrantist position for one reason or another. These scholars are essentially divided into three main groups, although naturally there are variations on a theme and not everyone will fit neatly into one or other of these groups.

First, there are those who hold to the 'critical paradigm' and who believe that the 'assured results' of higher-critical study of the Bible, that is to say, the actual phenomena of the texts, their origin and transmission make it intellectually impossible to hold to inerrancy. In this category, we have most biblical scholars of the past hundred years, including C. H. Dodd, Rudolf Bultmann and others. Such scholars would normally dismiss inerrantists as obscurantists or fundamentalists. I reject the views of this group on the doctrine of Scripture, believing that their argument is based on outdated and inadequate Enlightenment presuppositions of the kind I dealt with earlier. In short, their critical approach to Scripture is not well founded and is now widely regarded as theologically bankrupt. A brief survey of books on the doctrine of Scripture published since the 1980s demonstrates clearly that the old nineteenth- and early twentieth-century liberal theology is in its last, dying gasps and that we are now in a new era. Even those writers on the doctrine of Scripture who would not share the evangelical view propounded in this book, are much closer to the 'critical paradigm' position than to the old liberal theology.[76]

Second, there are evangelical scholars who are happy to affirm their belief in the authority of Scripture and who would hold to a 'high' view of Scripture but who would, nevertheless, not be prepared to use the word 'inerrancy'. In this category, as we have seen, we have such scholars as G. C. Berkouwer and Donald G. Bloesch. Scholars in this category reject the concept of inerrancy, believing that, although the Scriptures can be relied upon in matters of doctrine and

---

76. E.g. Francis Watson, *Text, Church and World: Biblical Interpretation in Theological Perspective* (Edinburgh: T. & T. Clark, 1994); Colin E. Gunton, *A Brief Theology of Revelation* (Edinburgh: T. & T. Clark, 1995); Carl E. Braaten and Robert W. Jenson (eds.), *Reclaiming the Bible for the Church* (Grand Rapids: Eerdmans, 1995); and Walter Brueggemann, *The Book That Breathes New Life: Scriptural Authority and Biblical Theology* (Minneapolis: Fortress Press, 2005).

ethics, there are mistakes in matters of history, science and so on, even in the *autographa*. As we shall see later, the problem with this position is the difficulty of maintaining a distinction between form and content, or between those parts of Scripture without error and those not.

Third, there are evangelicals who are unhappy with the term 'inerrancy' but who nevertheless also reject the notion of 'errancy', believing that they are being presented with a false dichotomy. Those in this group would disagree with Norman Geisler, who argues that all scholars are either 'inerrantists' or 'errantists'. They would argue that 'inerrancy' is not a biblical word, that it is not required by any of the confessions of faith stemming from the Reformation and that it is of relatively recent origin, without the weight of church history behind it. They would also argue that it is mistaken theologically. The strongest proponents of this position are James Orr and Herman Bavinck, although a good case can be made for saying that it is consistent with the view of Calvin. It is this third position for which I shall be arguing in the next chapter. Before that, let us begin by considering three arguments against the inerrantist position.

Definition of terms

The first argument against inerrancy, at a very preliminary level, concerns the definition of terms. After all, if it took the International Council on Biblical Inerrancy around twelve pages to define and explain their use of the word 'inerrancy' in the famous Chicago Statement, then surely there must be a better word we could use? Any word that requires so much definition, qualification, affirmation and denial must surely have questions raised as to its value. Not only so, but the definition itself in many ways empties the word of its content. For example, if numbers can be inaccurate but not affect the claim to inerrancy, then when is an error an error? One gains the clear impression that no matter what objection might be brought against the inerrantist position, it would simply be argued that this is an exception quite permissable within the terms of the definition. As I. Howard Marshall says, 'It is worth asking whether "inerrant" is really the most appropriate word to use to describe Scripture. It needs so much qualification, even by its defenders, that it is in danger of dying the death of a thousand qualifications.'[77] Could it be argued that, in their determined and legitimate defence against liberal theology and in their attempts to support Warfield's position, those who prepared the Chicago

---

77. I. Howard Marshall, *Biblical Inspiration* (London: Hodder & Stoughton, 1982), pp. 72–73.

Statement were determined to continue to use a word that, if they had been starting with a clean sheet of paper, they would not have used?

One example of the lengths to which inerrantists will go to in order to defend their use of the word is found in Norman Geisler's *Inerrancy*, sponsored by the International Council on Biblical Inerrancy.[78] The issue addressed was a problem related to genealogies. The question was this: 'If one of the compilers of Kings or Chronicles quoted a pre-existing genealogy that had an error in it, are we to assume that God supernaturally enabled the Chronicler to identify the mistake and correct it; or could it be that what was quoted in error is of no consequence in the purpose of God for that particular portion of Scripture?' One of the contributors to the volume, Paul Feinberg, is prepared to accept that these discrepancies exist, yet offers a way of still holding to inerrancy.

In asserting that inerrancy is related to Scripture's intention, Feinberg speaks of the distinction

> between *historical* or *descriptive* authority and *normative* authority. Historical or descriptive authority applies equally to every word of an inerrant Bible. It merely means that whatever was said or done was in fact said or done. No judgment is passed as to whether it should or should not have been said or done. Normative authority, on the other hand, not only means that what was said or done was actually so but also that it should or should not have been said or done.[79]

To support this argument, he provides a quotation from John Gerstner:

> Suppose they [the biblical writers] did think of a three-storied universe, which was the common opinion in their day, the Bible does not err unless it teaches such as a divine revelation of truth. In fact, by showing that the writers may have personally entertained ideas now antiquated it reveals its own historical authenticity, without its normative authenticity suffering.[80]

Feinberg goes on to make the point even more boldly:

> The point to be made here is that we cannot preclude in advance the possibility that some of the historically or descriptively authoritative material may contain errors.

---

78. Norman L. Geisler (ed.), *Inerrancy* (Grand Rapids: Zondervan, 1979).
79. Ibid., pp. 297–298.
80. Ibid., p. 298.

This does not, however, admit errors into what I have called the *teaching of Scripture*. At the same time great caution must be used in invoking this solution, since it is fraught with hazards.[81]

In a footnote at the end of this comment Feinberg says:

I wish to emphasize that before such a case could be claimed two things must be shown. First, we must show that something is simply affirmed and, second, that it is false. I do not assert that any such cases do in fact exist, only that such a possibility *could* be compatible with a doctrine of inerrancy. Given what the Bible teaches about itself, *if* such an error *were found*, then such an explanation would be necessary. I seriously doubt that this kind of solution is necessary.[82]

A couple of pages later, in a discussion about the problems posed to inerrancy by modern science, he repeats the solution: 'Let me again state the possibility that certain alleged scientific problems may be accounted for in the distinction between descriptive or historical authority and normative authority.'[83]

Reminiscent of James Orr's comments about possible errors in pre-existing source material (genealogies etc.) used by the biblical writers, Feinberg surprisingly argues that '*Inerrancy does not demand the infallibility or inerrancy of the non-inspired sources used by biblical writers.*' And again:

The definition and doctrine of inerrancy here advocated does not rule out a priori the possibility, or even probability, that sources are cited with historical and descriptive authority but not normative authority. That is, the errors that these noninspired sources contain are accurately recorded, since Scripture's intention is not to approve those errors as true.[84]

Let us be clear about what is being said here. Feinberg is arguing that if the Chronicler quoted correctly the genealogy he had before him as he wrote, although it may have been mistaken, nevertheless his accuracy in copying the original before him is sufficient to ensure 'historical' inerrancy, despite the mistake in the genealogy. It is argued that this is similar to the accurate

---

81. Ibid.
82. Ibid., p. 472.
83. Ibid., p. 300.
84. Ibid., p. 302.

recording by the Gospel writers of the words of the Pharisees, even where what they said was untrue. This does seem to me like special pleading. Indeed, it seems to me that this argument drives a coach and horses through the concept of inerrancy.

The autographa

The second argument against inerrancy concerns the emphasis placed on the *autographa* by those in the Warfield tradition. If textual inerrancy is so vital to the doctrine of Scripture, why did God not preserve the *autographa* or precise copies of the same? Indeed, if inerrancy only applies to the *autographa* (which we do not possess), then surely it is a somewhat pointless affirmation? Everyone accepts that there are errors in the extant manuscripts and translations. What is the point of insisting that there once existed (very briefly) perfect versions of these texts, if we no longer possess them? Those who emphasize the inerrancy of the *autographa* are thus faced with a difficult question: 'What was the point of God acting supernaturally to provide an inerrant text providentially if it ceased to be inerrant as soon as the first or second copy was made?' If God could act with such sovereign overruling providence to ensure that the text was absolutely perfect when it left the hand of the author, why did he not preserve it for us, if an inerrant text is so vital to the life of the church? In any case, can all the problems of apparent contradiction, textual variants and so on be traced to the copying of manuscripts and therefore solved by reference to inerrant *autographa*? It is certainly convenient to hypothesize about perfect, inerrant originals, but what does that say about the actual texts we possess? In any case, what do we mean by *autographa*? Even if we affirm that Moses was the author of Deuteronomy, he clearly did not write the last chapter containing the account of his death! In that case at least, an editor or scribe added something. Could not other books have received similar treatment? If so, which is the autographic text? Could further changes have been made to Deuteronomy much later? If so, do these scribal additions or emendations affect the status of these books as Scripture? What is the relationship between the autographic text and the versions admitted to the canon? As these questions demonstrate, a simple appeal to *autographa*, as made by some scholars, does not solve all of the difficulties.

One example of this argument comes from Greg Bahnsen, who insists that we must hold to inerrancy because God's veracity is at stake:

> Only with an inerrant autograph can we avoid attributing error to the God of truth. An error in the original would be attributable to God Himself, because He, in the pages of Scripture, takes responsibility for the very words of the biblical authors.

Errors in copies, however, are the sole responsibility of the scribes involved, in which case God's veracity is not impugned.[85]

This is a curious argument, which implies that God has no further interest in, nor control over, the biblical texts after the *autographa* have been produced.

Bahnsen even tries to insist that this is the view of Scripture itself. He asserts that

> the Bible evidences a pervasive concern to *tether current copies to the autographical text*. There is, as one would expect, no explicit biblical teaching regarding the autographa and copies of them, but the point being made is still abundantly illustrated in the course of Scripture's teaching and statements.[86]

It is difficult to see any evidence for this assertion and I am not at all persuaded by the references he presents in the pages following.

He returns to this issue later, when he writes:

> We can admit . . . that God did not keep the copyists from error and that nevertheless the church has grown and survived with an errant text, but to infer from these facts that an inerrant autograph was not vital to God or necessary for us would be to commit the fallacy of hasty generalization. The importance of original inerrancy is that it enables us to confess consistently the truthfulness of God Himself. We thereby can avoid saying that the one who calls Himself 'the Truth' made errors and was false in his statements.[87]

Despite this, Bahnsen quotes approvingly from Warfield to the effect that present translations are 'adequate' for the needs of God's people.[88] He goes on to say that, when Scripture itself makes reference to extant copies of Scripture, 'What we primarily learn is that these nonautographical manuscripts were deemed adequate to perform the purposes for which God originally gave the Scriptures.'[89] This concept of 'adequacy' is important and can be affirmed even by those who would not use the word 'inerrancy', but he makes little of it.

---

85. Ibid., p. 179.

86. Ibid., p. 161.

87. Ibid., p. 181.

88. Ibid., p. 156.

89. Ibid., p. 159.

In responding to the question as to why God did not preserve the *autographa* if they are so important, Bahnsen admits that we do not know and says that we must 'turn away from such questions, which presume to have an a priori idea of what to expect from God'.[90] Is it not the case, however, that his own case for inerrancy depends upon an a priori commitment, namely that if God 'inspired' Scripture, therefore it must be inerrant because of his character?

Bahnsen, like some other inerrantists, often makes extreme claims for his position. For example, he argues that assurance of salvation is dependent upon inerrancy:

> This doctrine of scriptural inerrancy, whether presented in the pages of the Bible itself, in church confessions, or by stalwart theologians, is never an academic curiosity or aside; it goes to the very heart of the trustworthiness and truth of the life-giving message of the gospel found in God's written Word. If the Bible is not wholly true, then our assurance of salvation has no dependable and divine warrant; it rests rather on the minimal and fallible authority of men.[91]

In the same volume, Henry Krabbendam, in an essay comparing Warfield and Berkouwer, speaks in even sharper terms against those who will not affirm inerrancy. He regards Berkouwer's later position as being based on an 'apostate methodology'. Indeed, he goes so far as to say that 'The rejection of biblical inerrancy may very well imply lack of heart commitment to God.'[92] He even concludes by calling non-inerrantists to repentance:

> In short, one's rejection of biblical inerrancy appears to indicate the rebellion of his heart or to be bound up with a deficiency in his life. To call the matter of biblical inerrancy, therefore, an epistemological problem does not deal with the fundamental issue. Berkouwer and his followers are in the grip of a dialectic that arises from apostasy and can arise *only* from apostasy. This is the transcendental root of the structure of modern theology, the thought of the later Berkouwer, and the wholesale rejection of biblical inerrancy.[93]

Such extreme language does nothing to further the discussion and is casually dismissive of evangelical Christians who have honestly come to a different

---

90. Ibid., p. 182.
91. Ibid., p. 154.
92. Ibid., p. 445.
93. Ibid., p. 446.

view. Such comments also give the impression that the divine action is all that matters. G. C. Berkouwer gave a different perspective when he wrote, 'The human element of Scripture does not receive the attention it deserves if certainty of faith can only be grounded in the divine testimony, for then it can no longer be maintained that God's Word came to us in the form of human witness.'[94] Or, as he went on to express the same point, 'We may not risk tarnishing the mystery of Scripture by disqualifying the God-ordained way in which it came to us.'[95] This is the same point made by Herman Ridderbos, who calls us to recognize the human authorship of Scripture, while not neglecting the divine speaking. He writes, 'But divine inspiration does not necessarily mean that the men who spoke and wrote under inspiration were temporarily stripped of their limitations in knowledge, memory, language, and capability of expressing themselves, as specific human beings in a certain period of history.'[96]

Textual issues

The third argument against inerrancy concerns how we deal with textual issues such as apparent conflicts and contradictions. As I noted earlier, it is often the desire for epistemic certainty that drives this concern for inerrancy. The argument is sometimes presented thus: if we find that there is a contradiction between two biblical passages, or if one name in a genealogy in Chronicles is inaccurate, then how can we be sure about what the Scriptures say about the resurrection? Inerrantists will typically reply in one of two ways. Either they will argue that this is only an antimony, an apparent but not real contradiction, or they will argue that if we had the *autographa* we would see that the problem does not exist there, only in errant manuscripts, because of errors in the copying over the centuries.

Such issues are not so easily dealt with, however, perhaps especially in relation to the Synoptics. I. Howard Marshall provides a very good example of the problem:

> In the story of Jairus as recorded by Matthew it is simply said that when Jairus first met Jesus he told him that his daughter was dead (Matt. 9:18). According to Mark and Luke, however, the daughter was merely on the point of death at the beginning of

---

94. G. C. Berkouwer, *Holy Scripture* (Grand Rapids: Eerdmans, 1975), p. 18.

95. Ibid., p. 19.

96. Herman Ridderbos, *Studies in Scripture and Its Authority* (Grand Rapids: Eerdmans, 1978), p. 25.

the story and it was only later – after the incident of the woman with the haemorrhage – that Jairus and Jesus learned that she had actually died (Mark 5:35 f.; Luke 8:49 f.). There is a clear contradiction between the initial words of Jairus as recorded by Matthew and the other Evangelists. We can, of course, explain the contradiction quite easily and acceptably by saying that Matthew, whose general policy was to tell stories about Jesus in fewer words than Mark, has abbreviated the story and given the general sense of what happened without going into details. But the fact still remains that Matthew has attributed to Jairus words which he did not actually say at the time stated.[97]

Herman Ridderbos points out similar problems in the different versions of the Lord's Prayer and the Beatiutudes.[98] Must we assume that problems like this did not exist in the *autographa* or that explanations can be forthcoming for all of them? It is also surely the case that the amount of time required to defend the inerrancy of biblical statements that appear to be in conflict with each other or with other well-established facts is neither justified nor profitable. After all, if God is able to use the errant copies (manuscripts, translations, editions) that we do have, in order to do his work, why invest so much theological capital in hypothetical originals we do not have?

The rationalist implication

The basic error of the inerrantists is to insist that the inerrancy of the *autographa* is a direct implication of the biblical doctrine of inspiration (or divine spiration). In order to defend this implication, the inerrantists make an unwarranted assumption about God. The assumption is that, given the nature and character of God, the only kind of Scripture he could 'breathe out' was Scripture that is textually inerrant. If there was even one mistake in the *autographa*, then God cannot have been the author, because he is incapable of error.

Notice, the argument is not that God, being all powerful, is *able* to deliver a perfectly inerrant autographic text. On that matter there is no disagreement between us, since I am happy to affirm God's sovereign power. Rather, the argument of the inerrantists is that God is *unable* to produce anything other than an inerrant autographic text. In other words, I agree with the inerrantists

---

97. Marshall, *Biblical Inspiration*, p. 61.

98. Ridderbos, *Studies in Scripture*, pp. 26–27.

that God *could* have brought into being inerrant autographic texts, had he chosen to do so, but I reject their argument that he *must* have acted in this way. This implication, which moves from inspiration to inerrancy, with its underlying assumption about the nature and character of God, has many weaknesses, as I shall seek to prove. First, I shall demonstrate that inerrancy is, at best, an implication rather than a biblical doctrine. Second, I shall demonstrate that it is rationalist. Then, third, I shall demonstrate that the underlying assumption underestimates God and undermines the significance of the human authors of Scripture.

Inerrancy not a biblical doctrine

Let me begin by noting the core argument of the inerrantists: God chose to give us the Scriptures through the writers he chose. They spoke directly from him, being under the direct influence of the Holy Spirit. This ensured that the resultant text could be said to be 'God-breathed'. Since God is perfect and does not mislead us and since God is all-powerful and able to do all things, it is inconceivable that he would allow mistakes in this process of Scripture-production. In short, since God is God, we must assume that the Scriptures he gave us are inerrant in every respect.

One can see the logic of this progression from biblical proposition (Scripture is God-breathed) to implication (therefore Scripture must be inerrant) by means of a conviction about the nature and character of God (he is perfect and therefore does not lie or mislead). Nevertheless, this inerrantist conviction that the doctrine of the divine spiration of Scripture implies inerrancy is the weak point in their argument. The divine spiration of the Scriptures is undoubtedly a biblical doctrine. The apostles clearly teach that God 'breathed out' the Scriptures and that their authors wrote as they were 'carried along by the Holy Spirit', but nowhere in Scripture itself is there a claim to the kind of *autographic* inerrancy Warfield taught. Those who advocate inerrancy might well (and do) argue that it is a legitimate and natural implication of the doctrine of divine spiration, but they cannot argue that inerrancy is itself taught in Scripture.

The clearest argument in favour of the view that inerrancy is not itself a biblical doctrine comes from the pen of Carl Henry, paradoxically one of the strongest advocates of inerrancy, as evidenced by his massive, six-volume work, *God, Revelation and Authority*.[99] Henry was very unhappy with the publication of Harold Lindsell's *The Battle for the Bible* because it appeared to call in

---

99. Carl F. H. Henry, *God, Revelation and Authority*, 6 vols. (Carlisle: Paternoster, 1999).

question the reality of the Christian profession of those who denied inerrancy. Henry insisted that many evangelical Christians rejected inerrancy and that their Christian profession should not be called in question. He believed that those evangelicals who rejected inerrancy were wrong, but he believed them to be Christians.[100] He took this position because he recognized that inerrancy is not a biblical doctrine but an implication drawn from another biblical doctrine (inspiration). It was an implication Henry himself accepted and for which he argued strongly. He recognized, however, that other evangelicals did not accept the implication and, since it was an implication and not itself a biblical doctrine, it could not be insisted upon as a test of Christian discipleship.

If we accept this argument that inerrancy, properly understood, is not a biblical doctrine but rather an implication from another doctrine, then it is reasonable to ask if it is a legitimate implication. My argument is that it is not a legitimate implication and, further, that this implication was not drawn by some of the best Reformed scholars. Rather, I shall argue that this supposed implication (inerrancy) is a rationalistic nineteenth-century response to the developing liberal theology, based on a particularly high view of the notion of scientific accuracy.

The assumption is rationalist

Even the most doughty defenders of inerrancy are prepared to recognize that the Princetonians and their theological successors sometimes succumbed to rationalism. For example, J. I. Packer accuses A. A. Hodge and Louis Berkhof of rationalism in their formulations of the doctrine of the atonement. He argues that in their resistance to Socinian views, they fell into the trap of arguing in the same way as their opponents. As Packer says, 'in their zeal to show themselves rational, they became rationalistic'.[101] The argument I present here is that this same rationalism affected their formulation of the doctrine of Scripture.

The rationalism of Warfield and others was understandable in an age when a fast-developing scientific world view, based on the prevailing Enlightenment

---

100. I am grateful to George Coon, whose paper 'Is Inerrancy Enough . . . or too Much? A Consideration of Carl Henry's Position', delivered at the annual meeting of the Evangelical Theological Society in 2005, helped me to understand Henry's position.

101. J. I. Packer, 'What Did the Cross Achieve? The Logic of Penal Substitution', *Tyndale Bulletin* 25 (1974), pp. 4–5.

philosophy, challenged a pre-scientific world view. Like most of their con-temporaries, the Princetonians had a very high view of the achievements of modern science, to the point where Charles Hodge adopted a highly ques-tionable theological method and Warfield's view of science as 'true truth' led him to become a theistic evolutionist.

In the inerrantist argument, truth is largely viewed in propositional terms and theological method is conceived of in scientific terms. Thus the impres-sion is often given that the whole Bible can be reduced to a set of propositions that can then be demonstrated to be 'true'. This then leads to a theological methodology based on a scientific method, such as that of Charles Hodge, to which I have just made reference. Based on the view that theology is a science, Hodge defines his method thus:

> In every science there are two factors: facts and ideas; or, facts and the mind . . .
> The Bible is no more a system of theology, than nature is a system of chemistry or
> mechanics. We find in nature the facts which the chemist or the mechanical
> philosopher has to examine, and from them ascertain the laws by which they are
> determined. So the Bible contains the truths which the theologian has to collect,
> authenticate, arrange, and exhibit in their internal relation to each other. This
> constitutes the difference between biblical and systematic theology. The office of
> the former is to ascertain and state the facts of Scripture. The office of the latter is
> to take those facts, determine their relation to each other and to other cognate
> truths, as well as to vindicate them and show their harmony and consistency.[102]

This explanation of theological method is founded on the notion that Scripture can be reduced to a set of 'facts' or 'propositions', which are then collected and arranged into a systematic theology.[103] This rationalist approach, however well intentioned, actually undermines the authority of the Scriptures. Rather, we must insist that the Scriptures are the Word of the living God who uses them to address us, save us, challenge us, teach us, encourage us, feed us and much more. To reduce the Scriptures to a set of 'facts' for the theologian, who must then 'arrange and exhibit' them, is to change the Scriptures from

---

102. Charles Hodge, *Systematic Theology*, vol. 1 (London: James Clarke, 1960), pp. 1–2. Many evangelical scholars today follow this method (e.g. Wayne Grudem).

103. This method, as used by Hodge, has been rightly criticized by Kevin Vanhoozer: Kevin J. Vanhoozer, 'On the Very Idea of a Theological System: An Essay in Aid of Triangulating Scripture, Church and World', in A. T. B. McGowan (ed.), *Always Reforming: Explorations in Systematic Theology* (Leicester: IVP, 2006), pp. 136–138.

their true nature as the Word of God into something cold and clinical, which *we* possess and which *we* manipulate. The best of the inerrantists take into account the genres of Scripture but many do not. In these latter cases, everything tends to be flattened and reduced to a set of propositions that are then deemed to be inerrant.

This is not to deny that the task of the theologian is to study the Scriptures and to communicate their message in a coherent and ordered manner. Nor is it to deny that the theologian is engaged in an intellectual process, with appropriate use of logic and reason. It is to deny, however, that the Scriptures can ever become mere data to be processed by the theologian, rather than the means by which God confronts and communicates with us.

We must recognize, of course, that there is an extreme on the other side also. Some have so emphasized the 'personal' nature of God's revelation that they hardly seem able to accept the notion of propositional revelation at all. Kevin Vanhoozer helpfully guides us through this minefield, rejecting the dichotomy between personal and propositional and demonstrating the usefulness of such concepts as speech-acts in helping us to avoid these extreme positions.[104] He is supported in this by the helpful work of his doctoral student, Timothy Ward.[105]

During the period of Hodge and Warfield, science developed at an astonishing pace, with remarkable and beneficial results, not least in human biology and in medicine. Science soon became the model for all academic work and 'scientific accuracy' became the standard against which all other truth claims was judged. Could things be 'proved' scientifically? If not, then the reality of the truth claims was called into question. No wonder, then, that in this context the Princetonians were determined to ensure that their theological method and their argumentation were truly 'scientific'. Unfortunately, this led to the rationalistic approach that, as we saw, Packer identifies in their view of the atonement. We can see the same rationalism in their doctrine of Scripture. Their reasoning was essentially simple: in order to develop a solid epistemology, we must have propositional truth that can be guaranteed with scientific accuracy. We must then handle that truth by using a scientific method. The result is thus a belief in the inerrancy of the *autographa* and a theological method that reduces Scripture to a set of propositions under the theologian's control.

---

104. Kevin J. Vanhoozer, *First Theology* (Leicester: Apollos, 2002), pp. 127–158.
105. Timothy Ward, *Word and Supplement: Speech Acts, Biblical Texts, and the Sufficiency of Scripture* (Oxford: Oxford University Press, 2002).

The assumption underestimates God and undermines the human authors

Perhaps the most striking problem with the rationalistic implication concerning inerrancy is that it limits God. It assumes that God can only act in a way that conforms to our expectations, based on our human assessment of his character. It assumes that whatever God does must conform to the canons of human reason. It also assumes that our desire for epistemological certainty must be satisfied and that it can be satisfied only through the receiving from God of inerrant autographic texts.

In opposition to these inerrantist assumptions, we must surely argue that God is free to act according to his will. With this in mind, we might suggest an alternative view: God the Holy Spirit breathed out the Scriptures. The instruments of this divine spiration were certain human beings. The resulting Scriptures are as God intended them to be. Having chosen, however, to use human beings rather than a more direct approach (e.g. writing the words supernaturally on stone without human involvement, as with the Ten Commandments), God did not overrule their humanity. This explains, for example, the discrepancies between the Gospels. Nevertheless, this is not a problem because God, by his Holy Spirit, has ensured that the Scriptures in their final canonical form are as he intended them to be and hence is able to use them to achieve his purpose.

Surely this scenario is at least as likely as the argument that God chose the method of inerrant *autographa*? It is also much more persuasive than the 'errantist' view, that God acted supernaturally to ensure that the theological, religious and ethical parts of Scripture can be relied upon but not the sections dealing with geography, history and science!

If it is argued that God could not possibly have acted in this way, based on the same analysis of his character that led to the inerrantist implication in the first place, then we could ask about God's use of preachers. How can anyone be saved without a preacher (Rom. 10:14)? Yet no-one argues that these preachers are inerrant, nor that they are kept supernaturally from all mistakes. No-one doubts that God is able to communicate his Word through his preachers and that he does not need them to be perfect for this communication to take place. Some might argue that preaching is different from the Word of God, but that is not the Reformation position. As we shall see at greater length in chapter 7, the Second Helvetic Confession says, 'The preaching of the Word of God is the Word of God.' If God can effectively communicate and act savingly through the imperfect human beings who are called to preach his gospel, why is it necessary to argue that the authors of Scripture were supernaturally kept from even the slightest discrepancy?

In other words, we must not tell God what the Bible ought to be like, based on our views of what God could and could not do. Ridderbos is very helpful here when he writes:

> The fact is that the infallibility of Scripture has in many respects a character other than that which a theoretical concept of inspiration or infallibility, detached from its purpose and empirical reality, would like to demand. One must be careful when reasoning about what is and what is not possible under inspiration by God. Here too the freedom of the Spirit must be honored; and we shall first have to trace the courses of the Spirit in reverence, rather than come at once to overconfident pronouncements, however proper our intentions.[106]

We might sum this up by saying that the *autographa* (if we could view them) might very well look just like our existing manuscripts, including all of the difficulties, synoptic issues, discrepancies and apparent contradictions, because that is what God intended. In other words, God chose to use human authors and although he spoke through them and ensured that they communicated his Word, he did not overrule their humanness. The inerrantists run the danger of so denying the humanness of the authors of the Scriptures that they fall into a 'dictation theory' of Scripture, a theory that, in their better moments, most inerrantists would deny.

Rejecting the incarnational model

Having argued that we must take seriously the fact that the Scriptures were written by human beings, with all that this implies, I must offer a word of caution. We have noted that some inerrantists, while paying lip service to the place of the human authors, often speak in ways that undermine that affirmation. At the same time, however, other inerrantists seek to give a full and proper place to the human authorship of Scripture but do so by adopting an inappropriate theological model. The model to which I am referring is the incarnational model for understanding the nature of Scripture. This model is increasingly used by inerrantists. The argument goes as follows: 'Just as Jesus Christ had both a divine nature and a human nature, so Scripture has both a divine nature and a human nature.'

---

106. Ridderbos, *Studies in Scripture*, p. 28.

One presentation of this argument comes in the recently published book on Scripture by Peter Enns.[107] It is a significant book, in that he forces evangelicals to take seriously what biblical scholars have had to deal with for years, in terms of the ancient Near Eastern background to biblical passages. His analysis of the problems facing evangelical biblical scholars is very perceptive and he certainly raises a number of issues that will require a careful scholarly response by anyone who objects to the way in which he has dealt with these matters. The problem is not with his analysis, however; rather, it is with his solution. By using the incarnational analogy to solve some of the difficulties he has identified, he has created even bigger problems. He rightly wants to emphasize the humanness of Scripture but does not require an incarnational analogy to do so. After all, there can be no hypostatic union between the divine and the human aspects of Scripture and, even if it is taken simply as a metaphor, it is open to misunderstanding.

There are two major problems in using this incarnational analogy to speak of Scripture. First, the concept is not taught in the Scriptures themselves. Second, only God is divine and therefore only God can have a divine nature. The most fundamental of these problems, of course, is the second one. How can the Scriptures have a divine nature, since only God is divine? Notice, I am not denying that the Scriptures (like human beings) can share some of the divine attributes. For example, the Scriptures are holy. This is different, however, from arguing that they have a divine nature, like Christ. In 1954, T. F. Torrance wrote a review of B. B. Warfield's then recently republished *Inspiration and Authority of the Bible*. After speaking very highly of Warfield and of his status as one of the truly great Reformed theologians, Torrance expressed his problem with Warfield's notion of the relationship between the divine and the human in Scripture. In particular, he said that for Warfield's position on Scripture to be correct, there would have to have been an incarnation of the Holy Spirit.[108]

Herman Bavinck, too, was well aware of the problem involved in affirming a view of Scripture that seems to make it into a divine book. He refers to Tholuck, who tells of one Nitzsche in Gotha who 'wrote a dissertation on the question of whether Holy Scripture itself was God'.[109] This might seem a

---

107. Peter Enns, *Inspiration and Incarnation* (Grand Rapids: Baker, 2005).

108. Thomas F. Torrance, 'Review: The Inspiration and Authority of the Bible. By B. B. Warfield', *Scottish Journal of Theology* 7 (1954), pp. 104–108.

109. Herman Bavinck, *Reformed Dogmatics*, vol. 1: *Prolegomena* (Grand Rapids: Baker, 2003), p. 416.

strange view, similar to arguments about angels on pin ends, but there is a vital theological point at stake here, namely that only God can have a divine nature. As I argued before, Scripture can share certain divine attributes but it cannot have a divine nature, because it is not God.

Much as I appreciate Enns's concern to open up the debate concerning the humanity of Scripture and the need to study Scripture in its ancient contexts, the dangers in using the analogy are too great. John Webster sums up the position well:

> Like any extension of the notion of incarnation (in ecclesiology or ethics, for example) the result can be Christologically disastrous, in that it may threaten the uniqueness of the Word's becoming flesh by making 'incarnation' a general principle or characteristic of divine action in, through or under creaturely reality. But the Word made flesh and the scriptural word are in no way equivalent realities. Moreover, the application of an analogy from the hypostatic union can scarcely avoid divinising the Bible by claiming some sort of ontological identity between the biblical texts and the self-communication of God.[110]

Conclusion

The inerrantist position was created in the heat of battle. Liberal theology was on the march and evangelicals struggled to find ways of defending a high view of Scripture. Unfortunately, in the heat of battle a hardening of positions often takes place, where people are forced into more and more extreme statements by their opponents, afraid to give any quarter lest the battle be lost. This is, I believe, what happened in the debate over the doctrine of Scripture. As we stop and reflect on this and seek to reconstruct our evangelical doctrine of Scripture, we must remember two vital things. First, we must not give to the Scriptures a place they do not give to themselves; and second, we must not attribute to the Scriptures a nature and character they do not claim for themselves.

The Scriptures are human documents, written by human beings, with all this entails. At the same time, however, these documents were 'breathed out' by God. We must hold these truths in tandem, not emphasizing one over against the other. The inerrantists so emphasize God's action that the authors often

---

110. John Webster, *Holy Scripture: A Dogmatic Sketch* (Cambridge: Cambridge University Press, 2003), pp. 22–23.

become mere ciphers, whereas the old liberals so emphasized the human side that the Scriptures lost their place of authority in the church. We must seek to restore the balance. The Scriptures were written by men but their origin, purpose, meaning and interpretation are to be found in the God who spoke through men who were 'carried along by the Holy Spirit'.

It is surely possible to say that the Scriptures are human documents, produced by human beings, which nevertheless have come to us from God. It is surely not necessary to invest them with divine qualities in order that they should fulfil their God-given purposes. Just as God uses preachers, sacraments and other instruments, so he uses Scriptures. This is precisely the position that some of the best Reformed theologians have advocated, and to two of them we now turn.

5. INFALLIBILITY: AN EVANGELICAL ALTERNATIVE

Introduction

In the previous chapter, I laid out the historical background to the American teaching on biblical inerrancy and summarized the modern debate on the subject. I noted that the modern debate has essentially divided American evangelicals into two camps. One group holds to the views of Warfield, as articulated by the International Council on Biblical Inerrancy in its Chicago Statement; the other group holds to the views of Rogers and McKim. If offered a straight choice between these two positions, then, given the weaknesses and inadequacies of the Rogers and McKim argument, I would certainly choose the inerrantist position. The argument of this chapter, however, is that we are offered a false dichotomy and do not have to choose between these two views.[1]

I shall argue in this chapter that there is an older and better way to defend a 'high' view of Scripture: the 'infallibilist' view. I shall argue that this is a stronger, more sustainable and, above all, more biblical view of Scripture than

---

1. We must recognize, of course, that some American evangelicals refused to accept this stark choice and developed a range of non-inerrantist positions, not least some of those associated with Fuller Seminary.

the inerrantist view. It will be my contention that many evangelical theologians have historically held to a 'high' view of Scripture without arguing either for inerrant *autographa* (Warfield) or for errors in Scripture (Rogers and McKim).

An evangelical alternative

My argument is that Scripture, having been divinely spirated, is as God intended it to be. Having freely chosen to use human beings, God knew what he was doing. He did not give us an inerrant autographical text, because he did not intend to do so. He gave us a text that reflects the humanity of its authors but that, at the same time, clearly evidences its origin in the divine speaking. Through the instrumentality of the Holy Spirit, God is perfectly able to use these Scriptures to accomplish his purposes.

Lest there be some who suspect that I am really presenting a slightly different version of the Rogers and McKim hypothesis, it is important to clarify the difference between their position and the position advocated in this chapter. As I indicated, the debate in the USA on these matters has essentially forced people into one of two camps, and the impression has been given that you must support one or the other. In reality, the situation is much more nuanced and difficult than this simplistic approach implies. I am arguing that to reduce the options to these two alternatives misses the point. Instead, I am arguing for a high view of Scripture, based on a verbal spiration of the text but one which accepts that God chose to use human authors, with all the implications of that decision. In other words, I am arguing that Scripture is as God intended it to be, in his gracious providential overruling, but reject the implication that thereby the *autographa* must be inerrant.

Rogers and McKim argue that their view is the one held by mainstream Christian theologians through the centuries. Their analysis of the theology of Calvin is particularly striking. They lay heavy stress on his understanding of accommodation, literalism and the nature of 'error' and argue that he was relatively unconcerned with minor discrepancies in the text and certainly did not hold an inerrantist position.[2] John Woodbridge, in his response, produces many references where Calvin appears to have a very high view of Scripture,

---

2. Jack B. Rogers and Donald K. McKim, *The Authority and Interpretation of the Bible: An Historical Approach* (New York: Harper & Row, 1979), pp. 89–116.

even occasionally verging on the dictation theory.[3] On the whole, Woodbridge had the best of the argument, but the problem remains – there are references produced by Rogers and McKim that cannot be accommodated by Woodbridge's hypothesis, and there are references produced by Woodbridge that cannot be accommodated by Rogers and McKim's hypothesis. How are we to explain this difficulty?

The answer lies in recognizing that we are being offered a false choice here. We do not have to choose between Woodbridge's inerrantist text and Rogers and McKim's errantist text. There is a third option, namely that the Scriptures we have are precisely as God intended them to be, but we must take seriously the fact that God used human authors to communicate his Word and did not make them into ciphers in doing so. Calvin and Luther understood this and gave a much higher place to the humanness of the Scriptures than later writers in the Reformed tradition. That is why neither Rogers and McKim nor Woodbridge can get them to 'fit' completely into their theories. These Reformers had a very high view of Scripture as the voice of God speaking by his Spirit through his servants, and they resisted any suggestion that it was unreliable or lacking in authority. On the other hand, however, they were quite dismissive of minor textual discrepancies or varying accounts or whatever. As far as they were concerned, the Scriptures had come from God and could therefore be trusted, but having used human authors one must expect these minor textual difficulties. Certainly, these textual matters should not be regarded as undermining the supreme authority of God's Word.

Thus to speak of the Scriptures as inerrant or errant is to apply an inappropriate classification to them. We must simply accept the Scriptures as they are and trust that what they teach is for our good (and above all for our salvation) because they have come from God. Nineteenth-century rationalist theology led us down a blind alley from which Rogers and McKim did not rescue us, because they too assumed that the issue of errancy or inerrancy was the key question to be answered.

There are many evangelicals from the same Calvinistic tradition as Warfield himself who are not persuaded of the inerrantist position, nor do they affirm errors in Scripture. These scholars have argued consistently for a high view of Scripture and have been among the strongest defenders of Scripture against liberal theology. This tradition of theology has tended to use the word 'infallibility' rather than 'inerrancy', thus referring generally to the nature and

---

3. J. D. Woodbridge, *Biblical Authority: A Critique of the Rogers/McKim Proposal* (Grand Rapids: Zondervan, 1982), pp. 56–67.

purpose of the Scriptures, rather than specifically to *autographa*. This difference can be illustrated by comparing the USA and the UK. Neither the British Inter-Varsity movement nor its constituent organizations use the word 'inerrancy' in their doctrinal basis. The Tyndale Fellowship, for example, speaks of Scripture as 'infallible' and as having 'supreme authority'. In a wider European context, we have the Fellowship of European Evangelical Theologians, led by Professor Henri Blocher. Once again, there is no mention of inerrancy. Rather, the doctrinal statement speaks of 'entire trustworthiness and supreme authority'.

This division between the USA and Europe goes back to the early origins of the word 'inerrancy' and is epitomized by the friendly disagreement on this matter between the Americans B. B. Warfield and A. A. Hodge on the one side and the Europeans James Orr, Abraham Kuyper and subsequently Herman Bavinck on the other side. In order to highlight and expound this European view of Scripture, we shall consider the writings of those who most directly addressed the issue, namely James Orr and Herman Bavinck.

James Orr

James Orr was a Scottish theologian who, as we have seen, contributed to *The Fundamentals*.[4] Orr held a high view of the inspiration and authority of Scripture but did not believe that it was wise, or even possible, to speak of inerrancy. Despite the fact that Orr rejected Warfield's teaching on inerrancy, there was considerable mutual respect between them. For example, in 1897 Orr wrote the introduction to the republication in Scotland of an article of Warfield's, entitled, 'The Right of Systematic Theology'. Even specifically on the matter of Scripture it was clear that their differences over inerrancy did not cause a breach between them, as evidenced by the fact that, as editor of *The International Standard Bible Encyclopaedia*,[5] Orr invited Warfield to contribute the articles on 'Inspiration' and 'Revelation'. Orr spoke at Princeton in 1897, 1903 and 1907.

---

4. I am most grateful to Stephen N. Williams for suggesting that I reread Orr's writings on Scripture. I confess that I had previously rather dismissed Orr, without careful reading, on the basis that he was opposed to the view of B. B. Warfield, which I had taken as the standard by which all other work on the doctrine of Scripture was to be judged!

5. James Orr (ed.), *The International Standard Bible Encyclopaedia* (Chicago: Howard-Severance, 1915).

William Abraham, commenting on the changes in the doctrine of Scripture in recent evangelical theology, says:

> These extremely important changes must not be allowed to blind us from seeing two salient facts. The first is that the doctrine of Scripture associated with much recent Evangelical theology is for the most part that of Fundamentalism. On this there has been little progress. The link at this point is Warfield. It was he who provided Fundamentalism with its theory of inspiration and it is he who stands behind the standard orthodoxy among Evangelicals at present. In this area many Evangelicals are far from progressive; they are extremely conservative in their desire to preserve the beliefs of the late nineteenth century. Indeed if anything they can be more rigid than the original fundamentalists, for the latter happily accepted James Orr as a fellow-traveller, despite the fact that he rejected inerrancy.[6]

Orr spelled out his doctrine of Scripture, including his opposition to the concept of inerrancy, in his book *Revelation and Inspiration*.[7] His own view was that inspiration must be set and understood in the context of revelation, whereas he notes that the older preferred method was to 'prove' inspiration and thereby to establish revelation. He believed that this method was still seen among some inerrantists: 'It is urged, *e.g.*, that unless we can demonstrate what is called the "inerrancy" of the Biblical record, down even to its minutest details, the whole edifice of belief in revealed religion falls to the ground. This, on the face of it, is a most suicidal position for any defender of revelation to take up.'[8]

He was also concerned that some theologians regarded inerrancy as part of the 'essence' of the doctrine of inspiration: 'such "inerrancy" can never be demonstrated with a cogency which entitles it to rank as the foundation of a belief in inspiration. It must remain to those who hold it a doctrine of faith; a deduction from what they deem to be implied in an inspiration established independently of it; not a ground of belief in the inspiration.'[9]

Orr argues that revelation precedes inspiration, nevertheless arguing that they are '*closely and inseparably united*'.[10] Indeed, he says that 'Revelation and inspiration thus go together, and conjointly give to the written word *a quality*

---

6. W. J. Abraham, *The Divine Inspiration of Holy Scripture* (Oxford: Oxford University Press, 1981), p. 115.

7. James Orr, *Revelation and Inspiration* (New York: Charles Scribner's Sons, 1910).

8. James Orr, *Revelation and Inspiration* (London: Duckworth, 1909), pp. 197–198.

9. Ibid., p. 199.

10. Ibid.

which distinguishes it from any product of ordinary human wisdom.'[11] Despite this high view, Orr was very reluctant to use the expression 'verbal inspiration', noting that it 'is one to which so great ambiguity attaches that it is now very commonly avoided by careful writers'.[12] While recognizing the problems caused by this ambiguity, he does recognize the positive value of what is normally being affirmed when the phrase is used:

> It opposes the theory that revelation and inspiration have regard only to thoughts and ideas, while the language in which these ideas are clothed is left to the unaided faculties of the sacred penman. This is a defective view. Thought of necessity takes shape and is expressed in words. If there is inspiration at all, it must penetrate words as well as thought, must mould the expression, and make the language employed the living medium of the idea to be conveyed.[13]

The problem, however, as he goes on to note, is that verbal inspiration

> is often taken to mean much more than this. It is apt to suggest a *mechanical* theory of inspiration, akin to dictation, which all intelligent upholders of inspiration now agree in repudiating. In the result it may be held to imply a *literality* in narratives, quotations, or reports of discourses, which the facts, as we know them, do not warrant.[14]

He gives one example of the kind of fact he has in mind: 'It is well known that in the reports of Christ's words in the Synoptic Gospels there is often a very considerable variation in expression – a difference in phraseology – while yet the *idea* conveyed in all the forms is the same. At most one side or another of the truth is brought out with slightly different emphasis.'[15]

Orr, like Warfield, was writing in the context of post-Enlightenment liberal theology.[16] This school was suspicious of claims to revelation and, based on the current scientific world view, largely rejected the concept of supernatural

---

11. Ibid., p. 200.
12. Ibid., p. 209.
13. Ibid.
14. Ibid., p. 210.
15. Ibid.
16. For a useful comparison of Orr and Warfield see Robert J. Hoefel, 'The Doctrine of Inspiration in the Writings of James Orr and B. B. Warfield: A Study in Contrasting Approaches to Scripture' (PhD diss., Fuller Theological Seminary, 1983).

intervention. Orr was anxious to defend historic Christianity against liberal theology and to maintain a high view of Scripture, albeit one that did not affirm inerrancy.[17] At the beginning of his *Revelation and Inspiration*, Orr outlines the then current views on the matters of revelation and inspiration, with special reference to the way in which the supernatural or miraculous is viewed. He argues that 'the vital question' in his day, into which 'all other questions with regard to revelation and inspiration will be found to resolve themselves', was whether or not a distinction was to be made between natural and supernatural revelation.[18] Given Orr's context, with the predominance of early twentieth-century liberal theology, Kantian philosophy and the Newtonian 'closed causal continuum' world view, which ruled out the possibility of divine intervention, miracles or even certain concepts of the 'supernatural', this is not surprising. Orr notes that the key factor, which he calls the 'large assumption',[19] underlying contemporary theology's rejection of supernatural revelation is the *unbroken continuity* of nature, and consequent impossibility of the miraculous'.[20] One author Orr quotes says that this is a view 'Christianity must incorporate on pain of extinction'.[21] Orr's caustic response is that 'the Christianity which incorporates this "modern" view is, not *threatened* with extinction, but is already extinguished'.[22]

Today, we are in a better position to respond to Orr's opponents because modern science no longer holds to the notion of a Newtonian closed causal universe and therefore liberal theology's accommodation to the prevailing (and temporary) view has left it largely bankrupt.[23] Modern theology is much more able to come to Orr's defence by advocating again the concepts of revelation, the supernatural and the miraculous. T. F. Torrance's work in this area is one of his abiding contributions to theology.[24]

---

17. He defended a high view of Scripture against the higher critics: James Orr, *The Problem of the Old Testament* (New York: Charles Scribner's Sons, 1906); and also against liberal theology: James Orr, *The Ritschlian Theology and the Evangelical Faith* (London: Hodder & Stoughton, 1898).

18. Orr, *Revelation and Inspiration* (1909 ed.), p. 6.

19. Ibid., p. 11.

20. Ibid.

21. Ibid., p. 12.

22. Ibid.

23. Thomas F. Torrance, *Theological Science* (Oxford: Oxford University Press, 1969).

24. See also Thomas F. Torrance, *God and Rationality* (Oxford: Oxford University Press, 1971).

Not all of Orr's opponents rejected the concepts of revelation and the supernatural. Orr writes, 'There is a *believing-critical*, as well as a naturalistic school of thinkers, and their opinions also need to be taken account of.'[25] He goes so far as to argue that certain writers in this school had developed a high view of Scripture as a result of their higher-critical research, not least concerning the religion of Israel and the fact of prophecy. On the whole, however, there was a prevailing anti-supernaturalist view within academia, stemming from German higher-critical scholarship.

Orr throughout stresses the significance and priority of the gospel in his thinking. In responding to many of the critical theories, Orr argues that the 'humblest' can see what critical scholars often fail to see, where these critical scholars neglect the key factor of the gospel itself:

> The one thing criticism can never expunge from this book, the Bible, is what we speak of as the *Gospel* – its continuous, coherent, self-attesting discovery to man of the mind of God regarding man himself, his sin, the guilt and ruin into which sin has plunged him, and over against that the method of a divine salvation, the outcome of a purpose of eternal love, wrought out in ages of progressive revelation, and culminating in the mission, life, death, atoning work, and resurrection of His Son Jesus Christ, and in the gift of His Spirit to the Church and believers. Here also is a fact – the biggest and most solid fact in the universe – a fact patent on the face of Scripture to any one who reads with open eyes, intertwined with ages of Christian experience, with enduring institutions, with efforts and achievements, which furnish a continuous proof of its reality. So long as this fact stands, the Scriptures will also stand. For it is the Scriptures which, in their divers parts and divers manners, embody and convey to us this revelation of God, and by the verifiable presence of this revelation in them, the Scriptures are proved to be, what they claim to be, the living and inspired oracles of God.[26]

Orr goes on to support this argument in a way that highlights his conviction that the gospel comes first and our doctrine of Scripture later. Speaking of the believer, he says this:

> Criticism does not make him anxious, for he knows that excesses of criticism must always be blocked and checked by the presence of this vital evangelical element which runs continuously through Scripture. If he is told, as he will be, that he is beginning at

---

25. Orr, *Revelation and Inspiration* (1909 ed.), p. 12.
26. Ibid., pp. 18–19.

the wrong end, – that he has first to prove that the Bible is God's Word, and only then can go on to speak of its Gospel, – his reply is the simple one, that it is the fact that the Bible has this Gospel in the heart of it which, above all else, proves to him that it *is* God's Word. If that Gospel is in the Bible, he is as sure as he is of his own existence that it was not man who put it there. It is too high for him; he could not attain to it. The Bible reveals man to himself as he could never have known himself without its help. It reveals God to him in lights and aspects of His grace which it could never have entered the wildest dreams of his imagination to conceive. It embodies that grace in a divine plan, working itself out in an extended history, which it is absolutely certain no sinful mind could have invented. A book which contains such a Gospel needs no external attestation to prove that God speaks through it with authority to men.[77]

There are two key points here. First, we do not have to prove the Bible to be God's Word in an a priori fashion before speaking of its content; and second, the Bible needs no 'external attestation'.[28] Interestingly, this emphasis on the gospel as coming before our doctrine of Scripture is a major element in a recent, most helpful book on Scripture written by Peter Jensen.[29]

Orr is not entirely negative about the critical movement. Indeed, he recognizes four positive features that arose out of it:[30]

1. A clearer distinction between Scripture and revelation.
2. Clearer recognition of revelation as something 'historical'.
3. A more dynamic view of inspiration.
4. More accurate discrimination between revelation and inspiration.

Orr also explains that a particular conception of God is vital to the idea of revelation: 'The only idea of God which answers to the idea of revelation is that of a Being who has character and will – power to reveal, and purpose and end in revealing, – who is self-conscious personal, and ethical.'[31] With this view of God, Orr argues that it is possible to reject critical theories on the Old Testament simply by noting the purpose of God (teleology) through it all, 'without insisting on any overstrained theory of "inerrancy"'.[32]

---

27. Ibid., pp. 19–20.
28. This reminds us of Van Til's presuppositionalism as expounded in chapter 2.
29. Peter Jensen, *The Revelation of God* (Leicester: IVP, 2002).
30. Orr, *Revelation and Inspiration* (1909 ed.), pp. 21–25.
31. Ibid., p. 27.
32. Ibid., p. 73.

In expounding his understanding of inspiration, Orr argues that God has given a historical, supernatural revelation and that the Scriptures are the 'record' of this revelation. He notes the importance of there being preserved a permanent record of the revelation and says of the writers, 'that those who produce the record *possess in an eminent degree the Spirit of the revelation,* and are fitted by insight and sympathy to produce the kind of record that is required for the purposes in view'.[33] In this context he also makes a somewhat striking remark: 'The denial of the Holy Spirit in the community of God's people may fitly be described as *the primal heresy* – the heresy of all heresies – in the Christian Church. Scripture assumes as axiomatic a presence and work of the Spirit from its first page to its last.'[34]

He then discusses the relationship between the revelation itself and the record of the revelation. He wants to argue that providence, and not simply inspiration, is important: 'To providence must be entrusted the securing and preserving of such materials as are necessary for a proper presentation of the history . . . Inspiration is seen in the use made of these materials, not in the providing of them.'[35] Despite his distinction between the revelation and its record, he later virtually identifies these:

> We began rightly by distinguishing between revelation and the record of revelation. There is an important truth in that distinction, for it marks the fact that there is an objective revelation in divine acts and words prior to any written record. But we have now found that the line between revelation and its record is becoming very thin, and that, in another true sense, *the record,* in the fulness of its contents, *is itself for us the revelation.*[36]

He concludes the section by affirming the sufficiency of Scripture.

In speaking of Paul's view of the Old Testament, Orr defends a high view of Scripture but also makes an interesting comment about 'degrees' of inspiration:

> Paul, it will be observed, does not give any description of the *nature* or *degree* of the inspiration he attributes to the Old Testament (or other) Scriptures. He does not, e.g., say that it secured verbal inerrancy in ordinary historical, geographical,

---

33. Ibid., p. 156.
34. Ibid.
35. Ibid., p. 157.
36. Ibid., pp. 158–159.

chronological or scientific matters. But (1) it seems at least clearly implied that there was no error which could interfere with or nullify the utility of Scripture for the ends specified; and (2) the qualities which inspiration is said to impart to Scripture, rendering it profitable in so great and rich a degree, make it clear that the inspiration itself was of a high and exceptional kind.[37]

Orr also asserts in this chapter that inspiration pertains to the author, not the text, of Scripture: 'Scripture is spoken of as "God-inspired"; but it is important to notice that inspiration belongs primarily to the *person*, and to the *book* only as it is the product of the inspired person.'[38] He further argues that the existing materials used by the writers of Scripture were not the product of inspiration. Inspiration 'reveals itself in the use it makes of the materials, and in the insight it shows into their meaning'.[39] He says that the writers were dependent on normal historical sources (genealogies, other older documents etc.) for their materials. Further, where there are gaps or errors in these old documents, 'it is not to be supposed that supernatural information is granted to supply the lack'.[40]

Orr also has an important section entitled 'Limits of Biblical Inspiration'. He writes, 'The limitations attaching to inspiration arise from the causes already specified – the *progressiveness* of revelation, the varying *degrees* of inspiration, and the *fragmentariness* or other defects of the materials with which inspiration deals.'[41] He then spells each of these out. First, 'inspiration *cannot transcend the existing stage of revelation*'.[42] Second, another limitation 'arises from the recognition of *degrees in inspiration*'.[43] He compares this with the varying degrees of the operation of the Spirit in history, sometimes acting in revival and sometimes 'operating on a lower plane'.[44] Third, 'account has to be taken also of the character and quality of *the sources of information* inspiration has to work with, and of the fact that, while adequate for the ends of revelation, these sources, judged by a literary standard, may be in various ways

---

37. Ibid., p. 162.
38. Ibid.
39. Ibid., p. 164.
40. Ibid., p. 165.
41. Ibid., p. 175.
42. Ibid.
43. Ibid., p. 177.
44. Ibid., p. 178.

defective.[45] After pointing out a number of the 'defects' to which he is referring he says:

> Is inspiration to take responsibility for these defects? Or is a supernatural
> communication to be assumed, in each case, to supply the missing word, or correct
> the misspelt name or corrupted number? This cannot be reasonably maintained, nor
> does the result in the books show that such correction was made. It did not need to
> be for the ends of inspiration.[46]

He even quotes Matthew Henry in support of this position! In his final chapter he states his purpose:

> It is now time to gather up results, and ask whether a doctrine of Scripture is
> attainable which shall at once be true to the facts of the record and true to the claims
> of Scripture itself on this important subject. In the answer to this question is
> involved the answer to another – Is there for the Church of to-day a tenable doctrine
> of Holy Scripture?[47]

In answering this question, he notes the use made by Calvin and others of the witness of the Holy Spirit to inspiration, so as to avoid the argument that church or tradition determines what is to be called 'inspired'. He wants to affirm this but says the argument cannot be pressed too far: 'How, *e.g.*, can it legitimately be employed, taken by itself, to sustain the canonicity, not to say the inspiration, of books like the Song of Solomon, Esther, or Ecclesiastes, which belong, in the opinion of some, to the lowest grade of inspiration . . .'[48] The interesting point here again is not only the canonical issue but the notion of degrees of inspiration.

Orr denies that inspiration of the biblical writers is simply an example of a wider genre of inspiration that may also be attributed to all great writers. He considers briefly the views of Calvin and Luther. Then he turns to the subject of 'verbal inspiration'. He begins by saying that 'The phrase "verbal inspiration" is one to which so great ambiguity attaches that it is now very commonly avoided by careful writers.'[49] He believes that 'It is apt to

---

45. Ibid., p. 179.
46. Ibid., p. 180.
47. Ibid., p. 197.
48. Ibid., p. 203.
49. Ibid., p. 209.

suggest a *mechanical* theory of inspiration, akin to dictation, which all intelligent upholders of inspiration now agree in repudiating.'[50] He argues instead for the phrase 'plenary inspiration'. He then turns again to the issue of inerrancy:

> Very commonly it is argued by upholders of this doctrine that 'inerrancy'
> in every minute particular is involved *in the very idea* of a book given by
> inspiration of God. This might be held to be true on a theory of verbal
> dictation, but it can scarcely be maintained on a just view of the actual
> historical genesis of the Bible. One may plead, indeed, for 'a supernatural
> providential guidance' which has for its aim to exclude all, even the least, error
> or discrepancy in statement, even such as may inhere in the sources from which
> the information is obtained, or may arise from corruption of anterior documents.
> But this is a violent assumption which there is nothing in the Bible really to
> support.[51]

Interestingly, in the light of the much later International Council on Biblical Inerrancy, he says of inerrancy, 'The theory may be stretched, moreover, by qualifications, admissions, and explanations, till there is *practically* little difference between the opposite views.'[52]

None of this should be taken to mean that Orr does not have a high view of Scripture. Towards the end of the book he can say, 'it remains the fact that the Bible, impartially interpreted and judged, is free from demonstrable error in its statements, and harmonious in its teachings, to a degree that of itself creates an irresistible impression of a supernatural factor in its origin'.[53] Indeed, he believes that in their central concerns the defenders of inerrancy are not far away from his own position:

> The most searching inquiry still leaves them with a Scripture, supernaturally inspired
> to be an infallible guide in the great matters for which it was given – the knowledge of
> the will of God for their salvation in Christ Jesus, instruction in the way of holiness,
> and the 'hope of eternal life, which God, who cannot lie, promised before times
> eternal.'[54]

---

50. Ibid., p. 210.
51. Ibid., pp. 213–214.
52. Ibid., p. 214.
53. Ibid., p. 216.
54. Ibid., p. 217.

In his conclusion Orr has a powerful statement:

> This leads, in closing, to the remark that, in the last resort, the proof of the
> inspiration of the Bible – not, indeed, in every particular, but in its essential
> message – is to be found in the life-giving effects which that message has produced,
> wherever its word of truth has gone. This is the truth in the argument for
> inspiration based on the witness of the Holy Spirit. The Bible has the qualities
> claimed for it as an inspired book. These qualities, on the other hand, nothing but
> inspiration could impart. It leads to God and to Christ; it gives light on the deepest
> problems of life, death, and eternity; it discovers the way of deliverance from sin; it
> makes men new creatures; it furnishes the man of God completely for every good
> work.[55]

As can be seen from this fairly detailed analysis of Orr's position, certain key
elements help us to formulate a balanced doctrine of Scripture, from an evangelical and Reformed perspective, yet without affirming Warfield's notion of
inerrancy. It is, then, genuinely a 'third way' between the 'inerrantists' and the
'errantists'.

My inclination is to support Orr's basic position but, in the light of what I
have argued earlier regarding divine spiration, to disagree with him on two
related matters. First, I would disagree with him on verbal inspiration. It seems
to me that there is no good reason for arguing that the content but not the
form of the Scriptures have come to us from God. Indeed, his own arguments
in favour of verbal inspiration, notwithstanding his concern lest it be misunderstood in some mechanical way, are well taken. Second, I would disagree
with him on the issue of degrees of inspiration.[56] If 'inspiration' is replaced
with 'spiration', thereby placing the emphasis upon the text (in its final canonical form) rather than upon the writers, then the concept of 'degrees of
inspiration' does not make sense.

On the whole, however, I affirm Orr's position that the Scriptures have
been given to us by God, through human instrumentality, and are as God
intended them to be (plenary inspiration). Like Orr, I think it is wrong to pre-
judge the nature of the Scriptures through some deductivist approach, based
on what we believe inspiration must mean, given God's character. That is to
say, it is inappropriate, before we have even considered inductively the nature

---

55. Ibid., pp. 217–218.

56. Interestingly, this notion of 'degrees of inspiration' was also the position of
    Archibald Alexander, for which A. A. Hodge criticized him.

of the Scriptures, to assume that they must be inerrant because God cannot lie. It is important to stress, however, that Orr did not argue that there *were* errors in Scripture, simply that one could not rule this out as an a priori impossibility. This is a vital point. It is possible to say that one does not know of any errors in Scripture, to affirm plenary (even verbal) inspiration and yet to deny the Warfieldian doctrine of inerrancy.

Orr and the Dutchmen

This view of Scripture, ably represented by James Orr, is also to be found in two other significant European Calvinists, Abraham Kuyper and Herman Bavinck. It is perhaps not surprising that they followed Orr, since Kuyper and subsequently Bavinck were also influenced by Orr in other areas of thought and writing. For example, many would regard Abraham Kuyper's Stone Lectures,[57] delivered at Princeton University in 1898, as the classic expression of Calvinism expressed as a world and life view, rather than simply as a particularist soteriology. In the very first footnote of that book, however, he refers appreciatively to Orr's *A Christian View of God and the World*, on the same theme of world and life view.[58] In some ways, that earlier volume by Orr is a more sustained and profound treatment than Kuyper's and clearly influenced the direction of Kuyper's thought.[59]

In thinking about this connection, the natural question arose: 'If Orr and Kuyper were closely agreed on this matter of Christianity as a world and life view, then were they perhaps also agreed on the subject of Scripture?' This proved to be the case. It is also interesting to observe that just as we noted a strong mutual respect between Warfield and Orr, despite their disagreement on inerrancy, so we can see a similar relationship between Warfield and Kuyper. Like Orr, Kuyper disagreed with Warfield's stance on inerrancy. Nevertheless, Warfield in April 1900 wrote the introduction to Kuyper's famous work on *The Holy Spirit*. Their disagreement on inerrancy did not affect their mutual esteem. Each recognized the other's commitment to a high view of Scripture as over against the prevailing liberal theology.

---

57. Abraham Kuyper, *Calvinism: Six Stone Lectures* (Edinburgh: T. & T. Clark, 1989).

58. James Orr, *The Christian View of God and the World* (Vancouver: Regent College Publishing, 2002).

59. This view is supported by Peter Heslam, 'Faith and Reason: Kuyper, Warfield and the Shaping of the Evangelical Mind', *Anvil* 15.4 (1998), pp. 299–313.

There has, however, been some misunderstanding concerning the doctrine of Scripture as espoused by Kuyper and his younger colleague Herman Bavinck that requires clearing up. Rogers and McKim claimed that Kuyper and Bavinck supported their view of Scripture. This was ably and comprehensively challenged by Richard Gaffin.[60] As Gaffin demonstrated, Rogers and McKim held to a form–content distinction between the humanity of Scripture and the divine Word spoken through it. Neither Kuyper nor Bavinck held to this distinction. Unfortunately, many people assumed (because of the closed, two-option dichotomy in the American discussion of the topic) that since Kuyper and Bavinck could not be cited in support of Rogers and McKim, therefore they must have been inerrantists! In fact, this is not the case. As Gaffin himself noted, they did not use the normal Dutch word for inerrancy in their doctrine of Scripture, although they occasionally used similar expressions. Gaffin does show very clearly, however, that they had a high view of Scripture very close to that of Warfield. They certainly did not use the terminology of 'errors' in relation to Scripture. Following James Orr, they rejected the inerrantist position and instead held to an infallibilist position. Others have also recognized this. Donald Bloesch, for example, notes that Bavinck had a high view of Scripture but was not an inerrantist:

> Here again we are confronted with the impenetrable mystery of the dual nature of the Bible. It is both a divine word to a sinful and broken humanity and a human witness to an incomparable divine action in history. There is not only divine splendor but also human weakness and infirmity in the Bible (Herman Bavinck). The Bible contains a fallible element in the sense that it reflects the cultural and historical limitations of the writers. But it is not mistaken in what it purports to teach: God's will and purpose for the world. It bears the imprint of human frailty, but it also carries the truth and power of divine infallibility. We cannot affirm that the propositions in the Bible are a priori infallible, but we can affirm that God's infallible revelation is communicated through these propositions.[61]

---

60. In a two-part article in the *Westminster Theological Journal*. Part 1 dealt with Kuyper: Richard Gaffin, 'Old Amsterdam and Inerrancy', *Westminster Theological Journal* 44 (1982), pp. 250–289; and part 2 dealt with Bavinck: Richard Gaffin, 'Old Amsterdam and Inerrancy', *Westminster Theological Journal* 45 (1983), pp. 219–272.

61. D. G. Bloesch, *Holy Scripture: Revelation, Inspiration and Interpretation* (Downers Grove: IVP, 1994), p. 115.

Given the respect in which Kuyper and Bavinck are held in the Reformed community and given that they clearly had a very high view of Scripture, while rejecting inerrancy, it is natural that Rogers and McKim would readily claim them, but they were wrong to do so, not least because, as we have noted, these Dutch scholars rejected the form–content distinction between the religious-ethical aspects of Scripture and the historical-scientific parts, which is so important in the Rogers and McKim hypothesis. In other words, we can accept Richard Gaffin's argument that it is illegitimate for Rogers and McKim to claim Kuyper and Bavinck for their side of the argument, but still recognize that they were not inerrantists.

Rather than engage in a detailed study of both Kuyper and Bavinck, I shall focus on Bavinck, because he dealt with the doctrine of Scripture in a more sustained and detailed way in his *Dogmatics* than did Kuyper in his writings.

Herman Bavinck

Herman Bavinck (1854–1921) was the second Professor of Systematic Theology at the Free University of Amsterdam, following Abraham Kuyper who was also the founder of the university. Bavinck was followed in the chair by Valentinius Hepp, who in turn was succeeded by G. C. Berkouwer. In order to expound Bavinck's doctrine of Scripture, I shall begin by making three preliminary points.

High view of Scripture

First and most importantly, Bavinck, like James Orr and Abraham Kuyper before him, held to a high view of Scripture. Standing as he did in the Calvinistic tradition of the Protestant Reformation, Bavinck affirms the supreme authority of God, speaking in and through the Scriptures. In response to Rome's argument that dogma rests on pronouncements of the church, Bavinck writes, 'But the Reformation recognises no truth other than that which is given on the authority of God in holy Scripture.'[62] He elaborates on this distinction between the dogmas of the church and the dogmas of God by arguing that the dogmas of the church may function with authority, 'only if and to the degree they are the dogmas of God (δογματα του θεου)'.[63] For

---

62. H. Bavinck, *Reformed Dogmatics*, vol. 1: *Prolegomena* (Grand Rapids: Baker, 2003), vol. 1, p. 30.

63. Ibid., p. 31.

this reason, theology is entirely dependent upon God's self-revelation in the Scriptures. Theology is not a human construct, created entirely in abstraction from the one who is the subject of theology. Rather, theology is human reflection upon the self-revelation of God, who shows himself to be Father, Son and Holy Spirit. As we shall see later, this has implications for Bavinck's theological method.[64] It also means that Scripture is the epistemic standard of truth, since human beings are not themselves the source and standard of religious truth, being sinful and corrupt, including the noetic effects of sin on the mind.[65]

Theologian as believer

Second, Bavinck's whole theology is based on the conviction that the theologian must be a believer. Bavinck was writing at a time when there was a move in theology towards a supposedly objective, unbiased method of 'scientific theology'.[66] This was based on the idea that, as in other sciences, the theological scientist must be detached and independent, weighing up the evidence dispassionately, having no personal engagement with the subject of the investigation. This 'scientific method' (although it is not so scientific) gradually became normative for Christian theology and almost axiomatic within the theological guild. As we shall see in the next chapter, there have even been instances where the academic integrity and quality assurance of faith-based theological colleges have been questioned, on the basis that faculty who are required to affirm a doctrinal basis, cannot possibly be properly 'academic' (interpreted as the freedom to exercise independent judgment, outside the control or guidance of any church, Scripture or creed). In opposition to this developing school of thought, Bavinck insists that 'God has unmistakably revealed himself'[67] and therefore the task of the theologian is to receive and reflect upon the knowledge that comes in this self-revelation of God. This being the case, 'it is absolutely imperative that the dogmatician be active as believer'.[68] After all, if there is a God who has revealed himself and if that self-revelation is to be the basis for Christian

---

64. Bavinck expresses it thus: 'The task of dogmatics is precisely to rationally reproduce the content of revelation that relates to the knowledge of God' (ibid., p. 45).

65. Ibid., p. 80.

66. Ibid., p. 36.

67. Ibid., p. 38.

68. Ibid., p. 42.

theology, then the idea that the theologian can take up the perspective of the objective onlooker who is not personally committed is clearly untenable. The conviction that there is a God who is knowable is that which distinguishes theology from religious studies, the latter discipline being primarily socio- logical and comparative and therefore requiring no personal faith. For Bavinck, then, the dogmatician must be a believer and must base his work on revelation,[69] since no knowledge of God is possible except that which comes from God.[70]

It follows from what I have just said that this revelation must be appro- priated by faith,[71] since only the spiritual person can discern spiritual things.[72] This is an important point because, for Bavinck, faith is a significant element in our doctrine of Scripture. He notes that faith 'is the internal prin- ciple of knowledge (*principium internum cognoscendi*) of revelation and thus of religion and theology'.[73] In opposition to the Enlightenment epistemology and the liberal theology based upon it, he can write, 'Over against those who think that nothing can be considered true that cannot be perceived by the senses or mathematically proven, it is a towering certainty that by far the most and the most important things we know are based, not on proofs, but on immediate certainty.'[74] The relationship between faith and revelation as Bavinck expounds it stands in marked contrast to faith, which in Roman Catholic thought 'is a firm and certain assent to the truths of revelation on the basis of the authority of God in Scripture and the church'.[75] Faith in Reformed theology accepts the truth on the basis of divine authority.[76] This faith 'excludes all doubt. It rests in the Word of God and is satisfied with it.'[77]

Theology as science
Third, Bavinck's conviction about the necessary faith of the theologian should not be taken to mean that he denies the scientific character of theology. In fact,

---

69. Ibid., pp. 78–81.

70. Ibid., p. 212.

71. Ibid., p. 209–210.

72. Ibid., p. 210.

73. Ibid., p. 565.

74. Ibid., p. 567.

75. Ibid., p. 571.

76. Ibid., p. 579.

77. Ibid., p. 603.

he argues strongly that theology is a science.[78] This is evident when he writes, 'The task of dogmatics, however, is always the same. It is and can, from its very nature, be nothing other than a scientific exposition of religious truth, a detailed exposition and interpretation of the Word of God.'[79] Or, as he continues, 'dogmatics is a positive science, gets all its material from revelation, and does not have the right to modify or expand that content by speculation apart from that revelation'.[80] In order to clarify his argument that theology is a science and to respond to those whose understanding of theological science excluded faith and personal commitment, Bavinck makes the point that not all scientific inquiry is carried on in the same manner. He rightly observes that the object of inquiry determines the nature and content of the investigation and so knowledge of God must be acquired 'in a special way that corresponds to the nature of its object'.[81]

As a student, I had a summer job working in a laboratory where we tested the consistency and strength of concrete for the construction industry. We took sample concrete blocks and submitted them to increasing water pressure until the concrete split. We then knew the strength of that batch of concrete. The medical scientist examining a human lung does not approach his object in the same way as we did our concrete blocks, because that method would be inappropriate (and fatal) for the object of investigation. We could note similar differences in the way a botanical scientist might examine a flower or an astronomical scientist might examine a distant planet. Theology is a science, but, like all scientific enterprises, it must develop appropriate methods of investigation based on the nature of the object of study.[82] God is not a concrete block, a mathematical formula or a distant planet. He is a living personal being, in Trinity, who has chosen to make himself known. Our 'scientific' theological method must be appropriate to the nature and forms of this self-revelation. No-one has expounded this better than T. F. Torrance, in a number of his publications, leading to his being awarded the Templeton Prize for his work on the interface between science and theology.

---

78. Ibid., p. 120.

79. Ibid., p. 55.

80. Ibid., p. 44.

81. Ibid., p. 43.

82. As Bavinck notes, 'One cannot see a thing by means of the ear, or weigh them with a yardstick; neither can one test revelation by means of an experiment' (ibid., p. 372).

Bavinck's doctrine of Scripture

In order to draw out Bavinck's doctrine of Scripture in such a way as to show its points of originality, its similarities with the work of James Orr and its dissimilarities with some forms of the inerrantist position, we are going to look at seven key elements of his doctrine of Scripture.

Rejection of natural theology

One significant aspect of Bavinck's theological method, which flows directly from his convictions regarding God's self-revelation, is his rejection of all natural theology. Given that God's self-revelation is the means of obtaining real knowledge of God, no preparatory discipline is required. That is to say, Bavinck rejected the medieval theological method, which insisted that human beings can discover the existence of God and receive some knowledge of him without revelation. Thus philosophy or a form of Christian apologetic was seen as a necessary prerequisite to the study of God's revelation. Crudely, it was argued that the 'proofs' for the existence of God are sufficient to convince us that there is a God but that we must then turn to the Scriptures to discover what this God is like. Bavinck rejects natural theology and all suggestions that philosophy and apologetics come before theology as preparation.[83] As we saw earlier, he was followed in this conviction by two very different twentieth-century theologians in the Reformed tradition, Karl Barth and Cornelius Van Til. The main difference on this issue between these scholars was that, whereas Barth rejected not only natural theology but also the concept of general revelation, Van Til followed Bavinck in affirming general revelation. In other words, Bavinck rejected the idea that it is possible to know God without revelation but recognized that there are different forms or types of revelation. Bavinck was also openly critical of Calvin and certain Protestant rationalists, whom he regarded as having moved towards natural theology.[84] This should not be misinterpreted as a complete rejection of philosophy. Just as Bavinck does not deny the value of a scientific method, so also he does not question the importance of philosophy. He is clear, however, that science, philosophy and theology must respect each other, especially the limits of each other's competence and the methodology used by each discipline.[85] What Bavinck cannot accept is that philosophy lays the foundation for dogmatics. Rather,

---

83. Ibid., p. 55.
84. Ibid., pp. 512–513.
85. Ibid., p. 371.

dogmatics must have its own *principia*, drawn from God's revelation.[86] As he puts it, God's self-revelation is the only *principium cognoscendi* of our knowledge of God.[87]

Theological method

Having rejected natural theology, Bavinck could not use the same theological method as many of those who had gone before him, because the prevailing method, in both Catholic and Protestant theology, had been based on a dual source of the knowledge of God, part natural and part revealed. Bavinck sums up very succinctly the reasons why he rejected the scholastic method of beginning with 'natural knowledge of God', saying that it is rationalistic, abandons the viewpoint of faith and subsumes dogmatics to philosophy.[88] Instead, as we saw earlier, dogmatics must be carried out from a standpoint of faith: 'The recognition of revelation, of Scripture as the Word of God, is an act of faith as well as its fruit. Dogmatics is from start to finish the work of a believer who is confessing and giving an account of the ground and content of his faith.'[89]

In advocating a theological method in which theology is viewed as a science concerned with the study of God's self-revelation, Bavinck was perfectly in line with the Reformed theology of his day, not least the theology of Princeton Seminary, with which he and Abraham Kuyper had a close relationship.[90] At one critical juncture, however, he rejected a key aspect of the theological method of Charles Hodge of Princeton. Hodge had adopted a theological method he believed to be scientific but that Bavinck thought to be somewhat rationalistic or 'mechanical'. Bavinck believed that Scripture must be viewed as a living organism: 'Scripture is not a legal document, the articles of which only need to be looked up for a person to find out what its view is in a given case. It is composed of many books written by various authors, dating back to different times and divergent in content. It is a living whole, not abstract but organic.'[91] In adopting an organic rather than a mechanical view of Scripture (see below), Bavinck understands Scripture to be the foundation (*principium*) of theology, rather than its source (*fons*). In elaborating this distinction he writes:

---

86. Ibid., p. 209.

87. Ibid., p. 213.

88. Ibid., p. 108.

89. Ibid., p. 109.

90. E.g. Kuyper and Bavinck each gave the Stone Lectures at Princeton.

91. Bavinck, *Reformed Dogmatics*, vol. 1, p. 83.

The term *principium* is, in fact, to be preferred over that of *fons*. The latter describes the relation between Scripture and theology as a mechanical one, as though dogmas could be drawn from Holy Scripture like water from a well. But 'first principle' suggests an organic connection. In a formal sense there are no dogmas in Scripture but the material for them all is to be found in it. Hence dogmatics can be defined as the truth of Scripture, absorbed and re-produced by the thinking consciousness of the Christian theologian.[92]

We noted earlier that Vanhoozer expressed problems with Charles Hodge's theological method. Bavinck had similar issues. As the editor of his *Dogmatics* quite rightly points out:

> Bavinck's theological method distances itself at this point from the Princeton tradition represented by Charles Hodge, who advocates an empirical-inductive method that sees the Bible as a 'storehouse of facts'. The task of the theologian is then 'to ascertain, collect, and combine all the facts in an orderly system, guided by the same rules as the man of Science'.[93]

Bavinck calls Charles Hodge's theological method 'the empirical or experimental method' (also the method of R. Edgar of Dublin) and shows that it is based on Bacon's experimental method. First, the facts are collected; second, a hypothesis is framed to explain the facts; and third, the hypothesis is tested. Bavinck rejects this method:

> When examined, this method fails to stand up. In divine revelation, word and fact are always connected; it does not merely convey facts that we have to explain, but itself clearly illumines those facts. Scripture does not show us some facts that we then summarize under the rubric of sin, but it tells us itself what the essence of sin is. It not only tells us what Jesus has done but also who he was. Without this explanation we would not understand the facts at all and would give them a totally wrong interpretation. Accordingly, the term *hypothesis* is completely inappropriate here. In the first place, the doctrine of the origin and essence of sin, to cite an example, or the doctrine of the deity of Christ, is not a hypothesis we have conceived but part of the witness of Holy Scripture. Furthermore, that doctrine, based as it is on this witness, is not a human hypothesis but a word of God that as such demands faith. Hodge, accordingly, speaks of truth alongside of facts, and

---

92. Ibid., p. 89.
93. Ibid., n. 49.

Edgar substitutes the term *doctrine* for that of *hypothesis*. With that the entire theory collapses. Finally, if God has spoken in his Word, there is no longer any room for 'experiment.' Subsequent to the witness of Scripture, verification is in the nature of the case impossible in this area.[94]

Bavinck opts instead for a 'synthetic-genetic method'. This method

receives from revelation both fact and word, word and fact, and the two in conjunction with each other. The fact, for that matter, is made known to us in Scripture precisely by means of the word and is for that very reason inseparable from it. Of the person of Christ, for example, we have no knowledge other than what we gain from the witness of the apostles. As the history of Gnosticism and of recent idealism has made very clear, one who rejects this witness no longer has the facts of revelation either. The synthetic-genetic method also gives the dogmatician the advantage that he can show the unity and organic interconnectedness of dogmatics. The different dogmas are not isolated propositions but constitute a unity. Actually there is only one dogma, one that is rooted in Scripture and that has branched out and divided in a wide range of particular dogmas. Consequently, the method of the dogmatician cannot and may not be other than systematic. Finally, he is also called, in this genetic and systematic unfolding of the dogmas, to point out possible deviations, to fill possible gaps, and so to work at the development of dogmas in the future. That is the critical task to which the dogmatician is called but which is already and automatically implied in the systematic nature of the work he does on the dogmatic material. In that way he attempts in dogmatics to furnish an exposition of the treasures of wisdom and knowledge that are hidden in Christ and exhibited in Scripture.[95]

I have quoted these passages at length because this difference between Bavinck and Hodge takes us into the most crucial area for an understanding of Bavinck's doctrine of Scripture. It is precisely Bavinck's rejection of Hodge's 'empirical' view and his own adoption of an 'organic' view that enables him to offer a real Reformed alternative to the 'inerrantist' views that came out of Old Princeton, particularly (as we saw in an earlier chapter) in the writings of B. B. Warfield and of Charles Hodge's son, A. A. Hodge. As we shall see, however, this view of Bavinck also stands over against the 'central church tradition' of Rogers and McKim. It thus offers a 'high' view of Scripture but is not the inerrantist view.

---

94. Ibid., p. 94.
95. Ibid., pp. 94–95.

Dual authorship of Scripture

The full richness and strength of Bavinck's position comes out when he discusses the authorship of Scripture. It is interesting to note here that Bavinck affirms the Vatican I statement that the Scriptures are to be recognized because they have God as their author and not because they contain revelation without error.[96] Were an inerrantist to be asked the same question, he or she might well argue that the Scriptures are to be recognized because, being inspired, they are inerrant. Bavinck's primary concern is with authorship and not inerrancy. For him, the key point is that the Scriptures have come into existence because God is their primary author. This point is well made when Bavinck responds to those who argue that inspiration means simply the arousing of religious affections:

> All of revelation in Scripture is one continuous proof, however, that God not only speaks to human beings metaphorically, by nature and history, facts and events, but also repeatedly comes down to them to convey his thoughts in human words and language. Divine inspiration is above all God speaking to us by the mouth of prophets and apostles, so that their word is the word of God.[97]

There could hardly be a stronger statement than this, of the nature of Scripture as God's Word.

In making this affirmation, Bavinck is aware of the problem from the other side, namely developing a doctrine of Scripture that advocates 'a *mechanical* inspiration, thereby failing to do justice to the activity of the secondary authors'.[98] He argues, however, that it is precisely at this point that the organic view of the doctrine of Scripture is most helpful. He writes:

> This organic view, far from weakening the doctrine of Scripture at this point, enables it more fully to come into its own. It is Scripture itself that requires us to conceive inspiration – like prophecy – organically, not mechanically. Even what it teaches us in general about the relationship between God and his creature prompts us to suspect that also the leading of God's Spirit in divine inspiration will confirm and strengthen, not destroy, the self-activity of human beings. For in creation God confers on the world a being of its own, which, though not independent, is distinct from his. In the preservation and government of all things, God maintains this distinct existence of

---

96. Ibid., p. 429.
97. Ibid.
98. Ibid., p. 430.

his creatures, causes all of them to function in accordance with their own nature, and guarantees to human beings their own personality, rationality, and freedom. God never coerces anyone. He treats human beings, not as blocks of wood, but as intelligent and moral beings.[99]

This enables Bavinck faithfully and clearly to emphasize both sides of any orthodox doctrine of Scripture, namely that God is the author but yet human beings are the authors. This concursive understanding of authorship is the key to understanding his position. How is this dual authorship possible? It is possible because of the work of the Holy Spirit: 'The Spirit of the Lord entered into the prophets and apostles themselves and so employed and led them that they themselves examined and reflected, spoke and wrote as they did. It is God who speaks through them; at the same time it is they themselves who speak and write.'[100] These writers 'also retain their own character, language, and style'.[101] In taking this position, Bavinck can emphasize and maintain the genuine humanity of the authors of Scripture. This stands in marked contrast to many inerrantist writers who pay lip service to the humanity of the authors but often descend almost into a 'dictation theory', so anxious are they to safeguard God's authorship of Scripture. One gets the impression that some of these writers are almost embarrassed by the humanity of the writers of Scripture and want to play it down as much as possible. On the other hand, we must note that Bavinck's view is not that of Rogers and McKim and their supporters, who, in affirming the humanity of Scripture, so stress the mistakes and inadequacies of the human authors that one is sometimes left wondering about the nature and extent of God's involvement in the process.

Bavinck's position, then, like that of James Orr before him, stands directly between the inerrantists on the one side and Rogers and McKim on the other side, offering a solidly evangelical position in identifying the Scriptures as the Word of God, breathed out by God, but yet recognizing that God took and used human authors with all their humanity intact. The human authors did not become dictating machines or ciphers: they remained themselves. And when they wrote the Scriptures, they did so using all the normal skills, tools and practices of anyone writing a book, including 'research, reflection and deliberation', and exercised freedom of the will as they worked. As Bavinck

---

99. Ibid., pp. 431–432.
100. Ibid., p. 432.
101. Ibid., p. 434.

concludes, 'So far from being spurned or excluded by divine inspiration, these means are incorporated into it and made to serve the goal that God has in mind.'[102]

Bavinck is thus able to affirm that the human authors of Scripture were genuinely involved in the writing process. Their minds did not go blank while God told them what to write. Nevertheless, in the mysterious providence of God, he so overruled providentially in their nature, character, upbringing, education and so on that what they wrote was what God wanted them to say. Bavinck sums up the paradox thus:

> Just as every human thought and action is the fruit of the action of God in whom we live and have our being, and is at the same time the fruit of the activity of human beings, so also Scripture is totally the product of the Spirit of God, who speaks through the prophets and apostles, and at the same time totally the product of the activity of the authors.[103]

One consequence of the nature of Scripture's dual authorship is that the theologian must be confident that God has spoken and therefore Scripture is infallible, not in the sense of inerrant *autographa* but in the sense that God has given us the Scriptures and they will infallibly achieve God's purpose in giving them. Among other things, this means that if we find passages that are in apparent contradiction, we must not try to force them into some artificial agreement. Rather, where there occurs the dilemma of apparent contradiction in the revelation, the dogmatician must let the truths stand side by side rather than failing to do justice to one truth or the other. As Bavinck says, 'God's thoughts cannot be opposed to one another and thus necessarily from [*sic*] an organic unity.'[104] Bavinck is not suggesting for one moment that theologians must not struggle to understand the relationship between different passages of Scripture. Like all orthodox Reformed theologians, he advocates the method called the 'analogy of faith', which affirms the fundamental unity and agreement of the Scriptures as the Word of God and seeks to understand difficult and obscure passages in the light of clear and easily understood passages. Indeed, he believes that 'The imperative task of the dogmatician is to think God's thoughts after him and to trace their unity.'[105] What he wants to avoid is forced harmonization and the

---

102. Ibid., p. 433.
103. Ibid., p. 435.
104. Ibid., p. 44.
105. Ibid.

determination to get passages to 'fit' our neat theological systems when we ought rather to admit that we do not understand how two passages relate to one another. Honest admission of failure and prayerful study towards the resolution of the difficulty are the appropriate method in such cases.

Testimony of the Holy Spirit

One of the major keys to opening up Bavinck's understanding of the doctrine of Scripture is the use he makes of the internal testimony of the Holy Spirit. As we saw in chapter 2, so convinced is he of the self-authenticating nature of Scripture, through the work of the Holy Spirit in enabling the believer to recognize God's Word for what it is, that he can write (as quoted earlier):

> Holy Scripture is self-attested (αυτοπιστος) and therefore the final ground of faith. No deeper ground can be advanced. To the question 'Why do you believe Scripture?' the only answer is: 'Because it is the word of God.' But if the next question is 'Why do you believe that Holy Scripture is the word of God?' a Christian cannot answer.[106]

This is very similar to what Calvin argued in his *Institutes* when, in answer to the apologetic question as to how we can be sure that Scripture has come from God (if we do not accept it on the authority of the church), Calvin replies, 'it is as if someone asked: Whence will we learn to distinguish light from darkness, white from black, sweet from bitter? Indeed, Scripture exhibits fully as clear evidence of its own truth as white and black things do of their color, or sweet and bitter things do of their taste.'[107] Calvin sets this conviction in the context of the internal testimony of the Holy Spirit:

> Since for unbelieving men religion seems to stand by opinion alone, they, in order not to believe anything foolishly or lightly, both wish and demand rational proof that Moses and the prophets spoke divinely. But I reply: the testimony of the Spirit is more excellent than all reason. For as God alone is a fit witness of himself in his Word, so also the Word will not find acceptance in men's hearts before it is sealed by the inward testimony of the Holy Spirit. The same Spirit, therefore, who has spoken through the mouths of the prophets must penetrate into our hearts to persuade us that they faithfully proclaimed what had been divinely commanded.[108]

---

106. Ibid., p. 589.
107. J. Calvin, *Institutes of the Christian Religion* (Philadelphia: Westminster, 1977), 1.7.2.
108. Ibid. 1.7.4.

Bavinck even uses dispensational language at this point in his argument, speaking of how the 'dispensation of the Son' gives way to the 'dispensation of the Spirit'.[109] He means by this that the objective revelation in Scripture becomes subjective or personal as it is appropriated by individuals through the work of the Holy Spirit. He is not arguing, however, that this work of the Spirit that enables the believer to accept and understand Scripture is somehow a special revelation.[110] Like Calvin before him, he views this internal testimony of the Spirit as an aspect of Scripture's self-authenticating character, as that whereby believers are enabled to recognize Scripture as God's Word: 'The testimony of the Holy Spirit is not a source of new revelations but establishes believers in relation to the truth of God, which is completely contained in Scripture.'[111] He likens this to an organ of the body: 'Just as the eye answers to light, the ear to sound, the logos (reason) within us to the logos (rationality) outside of us, so there has to be in human beings a subjective organ that answers to the objective revelation of God.'[112] Bavinck is also very careful to distinguish his view of the internal testimony of the Spirit from later developments within Reformed theology towards an 'evidentialist' apologetic. He notes that

> gradually the doctrine of the internal testimony began to lose its place of honor even in Reformed theology. Already in Turretin, Amyrald, Molina, et al., it was weakened and identified with the so-called illumination of the Holy Spirit by which the intellect is enabled to note the marks and criteria of the divinity of Holy Scripture. Faith no longer connects directly and immediately with Scripture but is the product of insight into the marks of truth and divinity it bears. Inserted between Scripture and faith, then, are the marks of the truth of Scripture. This occurred first in the sense that the recognition of those criteria was attributed to an illumination of the intellect by the Holy Spirit. But rationalism soon also considered this illumination unnecessary, assigned the study of the truth of revelation to reason, and based the authority of Scripture on historical proofs.[113]

Bavinck is very careful to avoid any misunderstanding here. He is quite clear that the internal testimony of the Holy Spirit must not be viewed as some kind

---

109. Bavinck, *Reformed Dogmatics*, vol. 1, p. 383.

110. Ibid., p. 384.

111. Ibid., p. 584.

112. Ibid., p. 505.

113. Ibid., p. 584.

of special revelation or event or vision, as Calvin and the Reformers were in danger of doing. Rather, it must be seen as part of the overall work of the Spirit in the life of the believer.[114] He writes, 'The testimony of the Holy Spirit is first of all the assurance that we are children of God. That is the central truth, the core and focus of this witness.'[115] This means that the internal testimony does not provide access to new truths or reveal anything to which we previously had no access. Instead, 'It only gives us a spiritual understanding of these same things, one that is different and deeper.'[116] He is also careful to point out that 'We believe Scripture, not because of, but by means of the testimony of the Holy Spirit.'[117] Indeed, he can speak in exalted terms about the witness of the Spirit: 'Take away the testimony of the Holy Spirit, not only in relation to Scripture, but to all the truths of redemption, and there is no more church.'[118]

Despite the strength of these statements, Bavinck is also pastorally sensitive in this area, conscious that many Christians experience difficulties with issues of assurance, and so he notes the importance of spiritual life and health in our perceptions, such that our convictions about Scripture are stronger or weaker depending upon our spiritual condition at any given time.[119]

Revelation and inspiration

It is important to note that, in Bavinck's theology, Scripture is situated in the context of revelation. Indeed, he argues that there is no religion without God and no religion without revelation.[120] Bavinck defines revelation as 'systematic disclosure of the words and deeds of God; it encompasses a world of thoughts and has its center in the incarnation of the Logos'.[121] As to the purpose of revelation, Bavinck believes that it is to transform and not simply to inform.[122] This revelation was not made necessary by the fall, since God revealed himself prior to the fall. The only difference the fall made was in

---

114. Ibid., p. 593.
115. Ibid., p. 594.
116. Ibid.
117. Ibid., p. 598.
118. Ibid., p. 599.
119. Ibid., p. 598.
120. Ibid., pp. 276–277.
121. Ibid., p. 605.
122. Ibid., p. 346.

terms of the content of the revelation, namely 'special grace, the revelation of God in Christ, the incarnation of God'.[123] When this revelation comes to human beings from God, we are able to receive it because of the way in which God has graciously created us: 'Corresponding to the objective revelation of God, therefore, there is in human beings a certain faculty or natural aptitude for perceiving the divine. God does not do half a job. He creates not only the light but also the eye to see it.'[124]

Bavinck gives an important place in his theology to general revelation.[125] He regards it as the foundation for special revelation. Indeed, without general revelation, special revelation 'loses its connectedness with the whole cosmic existence and life'.[126] The first occurrence of revelation is the creation itself and God's work of maintaining and sustaining the creation is the continuing aspect of that initial revelation.[127] Following Calvin,[128] he affirms that general revelation cannot lead to regeneration but notes that it does convey certain truths and information.[129] Reformed theologians developed their understanding of common grace around this concept of general revelation and Bavinck too follows this trend.[130] He presses this point to the extent that he views general revelation as the 'point of contact' with the natural man: 'In that general revelation, moreover, Christians have a firm foundation on which they can meet all non-Christians. They have a common basis with non-Christians.'[131] Again following Calvin,[132] Bavinck argues that it is only in the light of special revelation that general revelation comes fully into its own. Only when we see through the 'spectacles' of Scripture, do we see the creation for what it is and understand all things as a revelation of God's eternal power and divine nature.[133]

Ultimately, however, it is in special revelation that God makes himself known to believers, and this special revelation centres in Christ. 'The person

123. Ibid., p. 359.

124. Ibid., pp. 278–279.

125. Ibid., p. 322.

126. Ibid.

127. Ibid., p. 307.

128. Calvin, *Institutes* 1.3.1.

129. Bavinck, *Reformed Dogmatics*, vol. 1, p. 313.

130. Ibid., p. 319.

131. Ibid., p. 321.

132. Calvin, *Institutes* 1.6.1.

133. Bavinck, *Reformed Dogmatics*, vol. 1, p. 321.

and work of Christ is the central revelation of God; all other revelation is grouped around this center.'[134] He repeatedly emphasizes this point: 'The Incarnation of God is the central fact in special revelation, the fact that sheds light upon its whole domain.'[135] Jesus Christ 'constitutes the central content of the whole of special revelation'.[136] And again, 'The whole of revelation, summed up in Scripture, is a special revelation that comes to us in Christ. Christ is the centre and content of that whole special revelation, which starts in Paradise and is completed in the Apocalypse.'[137] This special revelation is not a completed act in history but rather requires the ongoing work of the Holy Spirit.[138]

Bavinck is careful to distinguish between revelation and Scripture, since these cannot simply be identified.[139] One of the problems in modern evangelical theology is that, in response to neo-orthodoxy, which was perceived as separating revelation from Scripture in order to put more focus on revelation in Christ, evangelicals have insisted on a precise identification between revelation and Scripture. Bavinck was able to see that this is neither helpful nor theologically necessary. As he carefully distinguishes between Scripture and revelation, he notes a number of mistaken attempts to relate the two,[140] and then summarizes his own position thus: 'The right view is one in which Scripture is neither equated with revelation nor detached from it and placed outside of it.'[141] He says this not least because some Scripture involved no revelation at all (the historical books).[142] In explaining his position, Bavinck says that 'inscripturation keeps pace with revelation . . . Inasmuch as in his person and work Christ fully revealed the Father to us, that revelation is fully described for us in Scripture.'[143] Notice the words 'fully described for us'. This confirms that Bavinck does not directly identify Scripture with revelation but sees it as a recording or description of revelation. Nevertheless, although for Bavinck the spoken word of revelation has priority over the 'inscripturation'

---

134. Ibid., p. 339.
135. Ibid., p. 344.
136. Ibid.
137. Ibid., p. 321.
138. Ibid., p. 347.
139. Ibid., p. 288.
140. Ibid., p. 381.
141. Ibid., p. 382.
142. Ibid., p. 381.
143. Ibid., p. 383.

of that word, Scripture remains vital: 'Thought is richer than speech, and speech is richer than writing. Still the written word is of immense value and importance . . . The written word is the incarnation of the [spoken] word.'[144] In our own situation, however, although revelation has priority over Scripture, revelation is only known to us through Scripture.[145] Thus he can say, 'For us, for the church of all the ages, revelation exists only in the form of Holy Scripture.'[146]

When he comes to speak of the nature of inspiration, Bavinck openly admits that 'Holy Scripture nowhere offers a clearly formulated dogma on inspiration but confronts us with the witness of its God-breathed character and in addition furnishes us all the components needed for the construction of the dogma.'[147] In seeking to draw out this dogma from Scripture, Bavinck builds upon what he has already said about the relationship between revelation and Scripture. Just as he made the distinction between revelation and Scripture, so too he wants us to distinguish carefully between revelation and inspiration. Noting that the Son is the agent of revelation whereas the Spirit is the agent of inspiration, Bavinck points out that revelation often (but not always) comes before inspiration. He concludes, 'Hence for the church of all ages, Scripture is *the* revelation, i.e., the only instrument by which the revelation of God in Christ can be known. Accordingly, in inspiration the revelation is concluded, gets its permanent form, and reaches its end point.'[148]

In discussing inspiration, Bavinck makes the very important point that Scripture does not just connect us to the past but rather connects us to the living God and thus is an ongoing reality. Hence he can write, 'Divine inspiration, accordingly, is a permanent attribute of Holy Scripture. It was not only "God-breathed" at the time it was written; it *is* "God-breathing."'[149] He spells this out later: 'The Holy Spirit does not, after the act of inspiration, withdraw from Holy Scripture and abandon it to its fate but sustains and animates it and in many ways brings its content to humanity, to its heart and conscience.'[150] Although expressed differently, this was one of the key points Karl Barth was

---

144. Ibid., p. 378.
145. Ibid., p. 382.
146. Ibid.
147. Ibid., pp. 422–423.
148. Ibid., p. 427.
149. Ibid., p. 385.
150. Ibid., pp. 439–440.

trying to make in his doctrine of Scripture, as we saw earlier, namely that Scripture is not simply something God the Holy Spirit brought into being in the past, such that we now own and control these texts but rather the Holy Spirit continues to be active in speaking to his church today in and through the Scriptures. Barth's argument that Scripture 'becomes' the Word of God in the experience of the believer was highly criticized by evangelicals, who argued that this cast aspersions on the objective nature of Scripture as the Word of God. It did also seem to confuse inspiration and illumination, a mistake Bavinck urges us to avoid.[151] Looked at in its most positive light, however, we might suggest that Barth was making the same point Bavinck is making when he notes the difference between what he calls 'objective and subjective revelation'.[152] This identification is strengthened when Bavinck notes that the latter of these should be called 'illumination'.[153] Whether or not we are persuaded by Barth's overall treatment of the doctrine of Scripture we must surely recognize the importance of this issue: Scripture is not an end product, owned and controlled by the church, but rather an instrument of God, who first brought it to completion and continues to use it as part of his self-revelation.

Bavinck stands firmly against any interpretation of inspiration that appears to follow a fundamentalist 'dictation theory'. Noting that the Holy Spirit is the true witness and not the apostles, who are his instruments, Bavinck says:

> He will take the disciples into his service *with* their personalities and gifts, their memory and judgment (etc.). He will not add to the revelation anything that is materially new, that was not already present in Christ's person, word, and work, for he takes everything from Christ and only to that extent brings everything to the apostles' remembrance, thus guiding them into all truth (John 14:26; 16:13, 14).[154]

In this regard, for example, he argues that 'The Synoptic Gospels show so much kinship between them that the one must have been known either totally or in part to the others.'[155]

His understanding of inspiration naturally impacts on his view of canonicity. On this subject, Bavinck is careful to recognize the actions of the

---

151. Ibid., p. 345.
152. Ibid., p. 348.
153. Ibid., p. 350.
154. Ibid., pp. 398–399.
155. Ibid., p. 400.

church, while at the same time denying any final authority to the church in respect of the decisions made regarding what was and was not canonical. He holds that the eventual conciliar decisions in respect of the canon were merely formalizing what had been the case in the church for many years.[156] He is thus able to write, 'The canonicity of the Bible books is rooted in their existence. They have authority of themselves, by their own right, because they exist. It is the Spirit of the Lord who guided the authors in writing them and the church in acknowledging them.'[157] He goes even further by arguing that

> If the church had raised to the rank of an inspired book any writing that was in fact not inspired, it would have been guilty of deception. Therefore, it is impossible even for God himself, by a simple declaration at a later date, to put a document that had been written without the special leading of the Holy Spirit in a group of writings that had originated with such leading.[158]

The books that make up the canon can rightly be called the 'Word of God'. Bavinck recognizes that this term is used in Scripture in a range of ways[159] and mostly in relation to the spoken rather than the written communication from God by his servants. Nevertheless, Scripture may be called the Word of God 'both on account of its origin and on account of its content'.[160] In any case, the Scriptures have been recognized by the church from the beginning as the Word of God.[161]

Organic view

As we noted earlier, Bavinck, in developing his view of inspiration, takes an 'organic view'. This view did not originate with him but rather can be traced back to the medieval church, notably to Agobard of Lyon.[162] This view, he says, 'offers a better explanation of the Bible's language, style, grammatical irregularities, etc.'[163] He believes that a somewhat 'mechanical' view

---

156. Ibid.
157. Ibid., p. 401.
158. Ibid., p. 429.
159. Ibid., pp. 401–402.
160. Ibid., p. 404.
161. Ibid., p. 402.
162. Ibid., p. 407.
163. Ibid., pp. 407–408.

had been dominant and is bold enough to say of Reformation views on Scripture that 'Occasionally one can discern a feeble attempt at developing a more organic view of Scripture'!¹⁶⁴ In what, then, does this organic view consist? 'It implies the idea that the Holy Spirit, in the inscripturation of the word of God, did not spurn anything human to serve as an organ of the divine.'¹⁶⁵ Above all, the organic view takes seriously the work of the human authors of Scripture in a way that inerrantists often fail to do. Aspects of Scripture that the inerrantists 'explain away' pose no problem for Bavinck. He goes so far as to say that 'the guidance of the Holy Spirit promised to the church does not exclude the possibility of human error'.¹⁶⁶ Such a claim could never be made by an inerrantist. One good example of what this organic view implies concerns the so-called 'Synoptic Problem'. Bavinck dismisses this problem, quoting approvingly from Abraham Kuyper:

> Inspiration was evidently not a matter of drawing up material with notarial precision. 'If indeed in the four gospels words are put in Jesus' mouth with reference to the same occasion but *dis*similar in the form of their expression, Jesus naturally could not have used four different forms; but the Holy Spirit only aimed to bring about for the church an impression which completely corresponds to what came forth from Jesus.'¹⁶⁷

In his organic view, Bavinck focuses not on the text of Scripture as such but upon its meaning and purpose. By so doing, he is able to avoid complex arguments as to whether or not the authors of Scripture knew that the world was round or whether they were supernaturally enabled to make statements that went beyond the scientific knowledge of their day. Instead, we must understand that 'Scripture does not satisfy the demand for exact knowledge in the way we demand it in mathematics, astronomy, chemistry, etc. This is a standard that may not be applied to it.'¹⁶⁸ In a most striking passage immediately following this comment, Bavinck even argues that the loss of the *autographa* and the existence in our day only of corrupted versions and translations was part of God's plan:

---

164. Ibid., p. 415.
165. Ibid., p. 442.
166. Ibid., p. 32.
167. Ibid., p. 444.
168. Ibid.

For that reason, moreover, the autographa were lost; for that reason the text – to whatever small degree this is the case – is corrupt; for that reason the church, and truly not just the layman, has the Bible only in defective and fallible translations. These are undeniable facts. And these facts teach us that Scripture has a criterion of its own, requires an interpretation of its own, and has a purpose and intention of its own. That intention is no other than that it should make us 'wise unto salvation.'[169]

H. M. Vroom notes that Kuyper also held to this 'organic' view of Scripture. He also makes the most interesting point that this emphasis enables us to say much more about Scripture than is possible for those who focus on *autographa*.[170] He writes, 'Inspiration by the Spirit obtains not only for prophets, writers of history, and apostles but also for collectors of sources and redactors. The entire process of the wording of the Bible was under God's guidance.'[171]

Form–content distinction
Bavinck dealt with this issue in connection with some theologians who, already in the nineteenth century, continued to use the word 'inspiration' in respect of the Scriptures but who limited the action of the Holy Spirit to doctrinal or ethical matters:

> The split between 'that which is needed for salvation' and 'the incidentally historical' is impossible, since in Scripture doctrine and history are completely intertwined. The distinction fails to do justice to the consciousness of the authors, who certainly did not limit their authority to the religious-ethical dimension but extended it to the whole content of their writings. It is at variance with the way Jesus, the apostles, and the whole Christian church used Scripture.[172]

He later rejects any kind of distinction between 'word and fact, the religious and the historical dimensions, that which was spoken by God and that which was spoken by human beings', arguing that these two aspects are 'so tightly interwoven and intertwined that separation is impossible. The

---

169. Ibid.
170. H. M. Vroom, 'Scripture Read and Interpreted: The Development of the Doctrine of Scripture and Hermeneutics in Gereformeerde Theology in the Netherlands', *Calvin Theological Journal* 28N (1993), pp. 352–371.
171. Ibid., p. 355.
172. Bavinck, *Reformed Dogmatics*, vol. 1, p. 417.

historical parts in Scripture are also a revelation of God.'[173] In refusing to distinguish between different parts of Scripture in respect of truth and authority, Bavinck helpfully links his 'world and life view' (following Kuyper) to his doctrine of Scripture:

> Precisely as the book of the knowledge of God, Scripture has much to say also to the other sciences. It is a light on our path and a lamp for our feet, also with respect to science and art. It claims authority in all areas of life. Christ has [been given] all power in heaven and on earth. Objectively, the restriction of inspiration to the religious-ethical part of Scripture is untenable; subjectively the separation between the religious life and the rest of human life cannot be maintained. Inspiration extends to all parts of Scripture, and religion is a matter of the whole person.[174]

He traces the beginnings of this distinction between the religious-ethical and the rest of Scripture to the school of liberal theology that began with Schleiermacher but found its impetus in those who followed. He is aware, of course, that liberal theology was not a monolithic movement but that there was a range of opinions on Scripture among liberal scholars, ranging from the earlier writers for whom the word 'inspiration' can be used only in a 'metaphorical sense' through to 'the radicals who have completely finished with Scripture, shed all feelings of reverence toward it, and frequently have nothing left but mockery and contempt for it'.[175] This should not be taken to mean, however, that Bavinck simply dismissed this whole theological movement and learned nothing from it. He was well aware of the difficulties presented by modern scholarship concerning the nature of Scripture and the dilemma thus posed to theologians.[176]

As we have seen, one of the key aspects of Bavinck's doctrine of Scripture is his emphasis on the importance of the self-testimony of Scripture. In this context, he wants to distance himself from those who argued that the actual nature of Scripture as we possess it must be set against any claims that Scripture makes for itself. This is an argument used widely in the modern debate on Scripture. Bavinck is firm in his response: 'The so-called phenomena of Scripture cannot undo this self-testimony of Scripture.'[177] The

---

173. Ibid., p. 438.
174. Ibid., p. 445.
175. Ibid., p. 420.
176. Ibid., pp. 419 and 439.
177. Ibid., p. 424.

proper way to deal with the problems of Scripture as identified by the liberal scholars is to develop an 'organic' approach and, above all, by 'putting the primary author and the secondary authors in the right relationship to each other'.[178] Following James Orr, he also stresses the importance of distinguishing between parts of Scripture. He says that 'There is therefore a vast amount of difference in the character of personal inspiration and hence also between the different parts of Scripture: not all the books of the Bible are of equal value.'[179]

G. C. Berkouwer

As we reach the end of this chapter it is appropriate to say a word about G. C. Berkouwer. Much of what I have pointed out concerning Bavinck's doctrine of Scripture is also to be found in G. C. Berkouwer. Indeed, Berkouwer quotes Bavinck approvingly more than any other author and is as close to Bavinck as almost anyone. Berkouwer also rejected the notion of inerrancy, and advocated a more organic view. In many ways he continued Bavinck's emphasis on the need to take seriously the humanity of the writers of Scripture, arguing that 'Amidst many dangers, the conviction has gradually become stronger that the human character of Scripture is not an accidental or peripheral condition of the Word of God but something that legitimately deserves our full attention.'[180]

If there is a difference between Berkouwer and Bavinck it concerns the emphasis upon the human authorship of Scripture. This is a much needed emphasis, and I am indebted to the Dutch Reformed theologians for their work in this area. Indeed, more work is now being done in this area that acknowledges this contribution.[181] It can be argued, however, that Berkouwer so emphasized the human authorship that he lost the balance to be found in Bavinck, thus opening the way for Rogers and McKim to go even further and to make the fatal distinction between those areas in which the Scriptures could be trusted (religious, doctrinal, ethical) and those where Scripture could not

---

178. Ibid., p. 428.
179. Ibid., p. 437.
180. Berkouwer, *Holy Scripture*, p. 19.
181. See the article by Paul Wells, 'The Doctrine of Scripture: Only a Human Problem', in Ron Gleason and Gary L. W. Johnson (eds.), *Post Conservative Evangelicals: A Critique* (Wheaton: Crossway, forthcoming).

necessarily be trusted (historical, geographical, scientific). Some evangelicals have argued that Berkouwer represents a departure from orthodoxy, a move normally blamed on the influence upon him of Karl Barth. It may well prove to be true that this was the 'hole in the dyke' of Dutch theology that allowed a departure from Bavinck's high view of Scripture, although my own view is that Berkouwer's theology is closer to Bavinck than to Rogers and McKim and deserves further careful study. Much of the criticism of Berkouwer has come because his position has been compared to the inerrantist position. When compared to Orr, Kuyper and Bavinck (his own European tradition), it is possible to come to a more generous assessment of his position.

Summary

Herman Bavinck, then, is a theologian from whom we can learn a great deal. On the doctrine of Scripture in particular, he has much to teach us and offers us a perspective that is Reformed but that does not become rationalist or mechanical. In short, he offers a high doctrine of Scripture that is different from the inerrantist model, although no less evangelical in its affirmations. Let me spell out the strengths of his position.

First, Bavinck's stress on the infallibility rather than the inerrancy of Scripture enables us to affirm a strong view of Scripture, without making any particular claims concerning hypothetical *autographa* that we do not possess and have not seen. In Europe, the word 'infallibility' has generally been used by evangelicals rather than the word 'inerrancy'. It has the sense of purpose, meaning that God will infallibly achieve what he has determined to achieve in and through his Word. It avoids sterile textual arguments that, by their very nature, can never be proved. It also avoids the somewhat arrogant position of telling God what means he must use to guarantee the reliability of Scripture. As we saw in the last chapter, inerrancy is not a biblical doctrine but an implication that some theologians have drawn from the doctrine of inspiration. The argument is that, given the character of God, he could not possibly have given us Scriptures that were errant in the *autographa*. Bavinck rejects this implication, arguing that God chose to use human beings as the secondary authors, with all their human frailty and tendency to error. For Bavinck the authority of Scripture rests on the fact that its primary author is God and not upon supposed inerrant *autographa*.

Second, Bavinck's view also makes more sense of Calvin and the other early Reformed theologians by offering a way of interpreting them that takes a middle line between Rogers and McKim on the one hand and John Woodbridge on the other. In examining the arguments of Rogers and McKim and of Woodbridge and observing the polarization, one can see the force of Richard Muller's comment that 'Altogether too much of the discussion of the Reformation and Protestant orthodox doctrines of Scripture has approached the subject from theologically biased perspectives and with the specific intention of justifying one or another twentieth-century view of Scripture.'[182] In Bavinck we find someone who shared Calvin's high view of Scripture but who, because of his similar understanding of the nature of the human authorship of Scripture, has no problems with the apparent discrepancies, contradictions and other difficulties that so trouble inerrantists. In short, Bavinck presents a high doctrine of Scripture that can be traced back to Calvin (and beyond) and that offers a middle way between the errantists and inerrantists.

Third, Bavinck's doctrine of Scripture enables us to avoid a rationalistic theological method and a mechanical understanding of inspiration. His critique of Charles Hodge's theological method is profound, despite his great respect for Hodge in so many other areas of theology. It is no coincidence that the Princeton school of theology, following Hodge's theological method, devised an inerrantist (or mechanical) view of the Scriptures. In an age when liberal theology was fast becoming the dominant academic position in the theological institutions and when scientific truth was regarded as the ultimate test of everything, the Princetonians became somewhat rationalistic in their approach, including in their defence of the doctrine of Scripture. Their reaction to the prevailing academic climate led them to rest the authority of Scripture on original manuscripts, a view that could not be successfully challenged – because they no longer existed.

Fourth, Bavinck's 'organic' view of Scripture helps us to understand the relationship between revelation and Scripture, confirms the importance of viewing the testimony of the Holy Spirit as a 'permanent quality' attaching to Scripture and enables us to identify with Bavinck's refusal to distinguish between the 'religious-ethical' content of Scripture and the 'historical-scientific' content, thus resisting the move towards a 'Bible inside the Bible' with all the accompanying difficulties of deciding what is reliable and what is unreliable.

Fifth, and more generally, we can also learn a great deal from Bavinck's way of engaging in theological debate. Bavinck opposed the developing liberal theology and challenged the Enlightenment epistemology on which it was based, not least Kant's view that God could not be known and that real knowledge must come from sense experience or from the use of reason by

---

182. Richard A. Muller, *Post-Reformation Reformed Dogmatics*, vol. 2: *Holy Scripture: The Cognitive Foundation of Theology* (Grand Rapids: Baker, 1993), p. 4.

autonomous human beings.[183] He consistently affirmed the authority of
Scripture and defended orthodox Christianity against the onslaughts of its
opponents. In all of this, however, he wrote and spoke graciously, yet firmly,
always seeking to find the best in each writer, even those with whose core theological position he was in disagreement. He was also a model of careful and
thorough scholarship, showing a determination to understand the views of
other theologians properly. Having done this, he sought always to describe
their views in a way that demonstrated studied familiarity with their writings,
which were read in the most generous and sympathetic light. In all of this he
was and remains a model for Reformed theology.

Conclusion

My argument in this chapter is that Orr and Bavinck have shown us a way of
understanding the nature and authority of Scripture that is quite different from
both the inerrantist and the errantist positions. It is my argument that the
recovery of this position will liberate us from some very sterile arguments
about *autographa* and yet enable us to maintain a high view of Scripture.

In terms of the vocabulary of the doctrine, the proposal is that we use the
word 'infallibility' instead of the word 'inerrancy'. We might also usefully
employ the word 'authenticity', which focuses much more on the work of the
Holy Spirit, who authenticates it to our hearts by his internal testimony. In 1
Corinthians 2:13, Paul says that God communicates to us 'in words not taught
by human wisdom but taught by the Spirit, interpreting spiritual truths to those
who are spiritual'. Instead of trying to safeguard the Scriptures by arguing that
the *autographa* are verbally inerrant, it will be more productive to emphasize that
the Scriptures are the authentic Word of God, given to us by the Holy Spirit.

Having come to the conviction that this infallibilist view of Scripture, as
spelled out by Bavinck and other Reformed theologians, is the best way to
present and defend a high view of Scripture, it is my hope and prayer that just
as Warfield, Orr and Kuyper retained a high respect for one another despite
their differences on inerrancy, this book might promote a constructive dialogue
between theologians who share a common high view of Scripture as God's
Word.

---

183. Bavinck, *Reformed Dogmatics*, vol. 1, p. 55.

6. SCRIPTURE AND CONFESSION

Introduction

Up to this point I have been arguing for a reconstruction of the doctrine of Scripture. In particular, I have argued that the *locus*, the vocabulary and aspects of the theology itself need to be revisited. I now move on, in the next two chapters, to deal with the use of Scripture in the life of the church. In this chapter I shall argue that evangelical theologians must give some thought to a thorny ecclesiastical issue, namely the relationship between Scripture and our confessional statements.[1] This is not an easy subject. As Herman Bavinck noted, 'Now one of the greatest difficulties inherent in the dogmatician's task lies in determining the relation between divine truth and the church's confession.'[2]

The primary question to be addressed is this: 'Given the many different ways in which Scripture has been approached and interpreted and given that these approaches and interpretations have often been encapsulated in confessional

---

1. An earlier version of this chapter was presented as the 2006 Tyndale Doctrine Lecture.
2. H. Bavinck, *Reformed Dogmatics*, vol. 1: *Prolegomena* (Grand Rapids: Baker, 2003), vol. 1, p. 31.

statements, what authority do such statements have and how do they relate to the authority of the voice of God speaking in and through the Scriptures?'

In this chapter, I shall do three things. First, I shall address various proposals regarding the relationship between Scripture and confession that I hold to be problematic. Second, I shall say something about the relationship between Scripture and tradition, dealing with the way in which councils, creeds and confessions have functioned in the history of the church. Then third, I shall offer a way forward in defining the relationship between Scripture and confession.

Scripture and confession

Four proposals in respect of the relationship between Scripture and confession are problematic. First, some people reject the use of confessions, believing that our only authority is Scripture and that to place a confession alongside Scripture is to undermine the authority of Scripture. Second, some people explicitly, or in practice, reject the use of confessions because it restricts them in their desire to abandon past beliefs and create a new theology. Third, some people believe it is simply impossible for Christians in general and theologians in particular to be bound by a confession, since this restricts 'academic freedom'. Fourth, some people place so much emphasis on their confession that, in practice if not in theory, it is given a higher place than Scripture itself in theological discussion. Let us examine these problematic views.

Scripture alone

Some do not believe that confessions should have any formal place within the church and believe they are free to establish all things from an open Bible. Anyone who holds a high view of the authority of God speaking in the Scriptures must have a certain sympathy with this view, but it is not as 'evangelical' as it sounds. It is also the case that many of those who take this 'only Scripture' position, in practice are very firmly ensconced within a particular theological and exegetical tradition. For example, some of those who eschew confessional statements are very happy to allow the Scofield Reference Bible to determine their theological position. This is a confessional statement in practice if not in name. Having said this, we must recognize that some take the 'only Scripture' position and do indeed have a high regard for those have gone before them, even if they are unwilling formally to identify with a confessional statement. Some evangelicals have reached a point in their thinking where they are unwilling to make any doctrinal affirmation beyond the authority of Scripture itself, while not ignoring the wisdom of earlier centuries.

Many of those who hold to the 'only Scripture' position are in the charismatic and Pentecostal traditions. Interestingly, many of these are becoming disillusioned and are now seeking some deeper connection with the church through the ages. One example of this is the number of evangelical Protestants who have recently become Eastern Orthodox.[3] Some fascinating books have been written by these converts, where they describe their move.[4] These books make it clear that one of the main reasons for their decisions to join Orthodoxy was the desire for a more profound spirituality and a more rooted worship practice. Clearly, the authors felt spiritually fed, uplifted and fulfilled through their involvement in the life and worship of the Orthodox Church. They were clearly dissatisfied with what they had experienced before. The argument was that the 'me and Jesus' type of Christianity, fostered by a daily quiet time and Sunday worship services, had left them empty and looking for something deeper and more satisfying. On this point, it is interesting that a number of them came from a charismatic background, not least Michael Harper, and some of them had previously worked with Campus Crusade. The constant pressure for that which was new and innovative in worship ultimately gave way to a desire for a tradition of worship with roots far back in history. The issues of spirituality and worship, however, were merely symptomatic of the underlying issue that was the need for a sense of history, a sense of continuity with the past. For many of them, the slogan 'only Scripture' had left them rootless and open to the wind of every new idea that swept through their churches.

Nevertheless, many still hold to the 'only Scripture' position. Those who do, would argue that creeds and confessions have often supplanted the authority of Scripture in the church. Some who come from a congregationalist tradition would also argue that no church body has the right to impose on other Christians a particular theological viewpoint. The problem is that those who take this approach often act as if they were the first Christians and see no need to give any consideration to what has been said by earlier Christians, except perhaps one

---

3. I use this generic term because, due to the divided jurisdiction, there are (at least) Greek, Russian, Serbian and Antiochene Orthodox churches.

4. P. E. Gillquist, *Becoming Orthodox* (Ben Lomond, Calif.: Conciliar, 1992); P. E. Gillquist, *Coming Home: Why Protestant Clergy Are Becoming Orthodox* (Ben Lomond, Calif.: Conciliar, 1992); M. Charles Bell, *Discovering the Rich Heritage of Orthodoxy* (Minneapolis: Light & Life, 1994); Frank Schaeffer, *Dancing Alone: The Quest for the Orthodox Faith in the Age of False Religions* (Brookline, Mass.: Holy Cross, 1994); and Michael Harper, *The True Light* (London: Hodder & Stoughton, 1997).

or two noted leaders in their own circles. This often leads to a sectarian attitude highly critical of other Christians. Where such a view is held consistently, it almost inevitably leads to error and heresy because there are no checks and balances, such as are provided in other traditions by creeds and confessions.

Semper reformanda

In most mainline Presbyterian denominations, ministers and elders take vows that include an affirmation of Scripture as the Word of God and an affirmation of the Westminster Confession of Faith as the church's 'Principal Subordinate Standard'. In practice, however, the relationship between Scripture and confession is often ill-defined and complicated by the addition of a Declaratory Article. For example, in the Church of Scotland, one of the ordination vows taken by ministers and elders requires commitment to the doctrines contained in the Westminster Confession of Faith. The Declaratory Article, however, conditions this commitment by adding the words 'except in those matters which do not pertain to the substance of the faith'. The problem is that the 'substance of the faith' has never been defined, thus allowing some ministers and elders to deny the incarnation or the resurrection without any kind of church discipline. The 'substance of the faith' sometimes appears to mean whatever anyone wants it to mean, although when the phrase was first used in the Scottish church it had a narrow and fairly specific compass.

Such a situation suits those who wish to remain part of a historic Reformed denomination but who no longer accept many of the core beliefs of Reformed theology. Those who are in this position often use traditional language to defend their position. In particular, they invoke two principles: first, the Reformed principle of *semper reformanda* (always reforming); and second, the confessional notion of 'liberty of conscience'. Unfortunately, these important Reformed principles are often used to mask a wholesale abandonment of Reformed theology!

We can illustrate the use (or abuse) of these two principles by reference to a recent debate within the Church of Scotland. The Church's Legal Questions Committee, at the beginning of 2006, intimated that it would bring to the General Assembly in May an Act that would permit ministers to conduct a service marking a same-sex civil partnership. In the course of the debate that followed, a group called 'One Kirk' produced a booklet presenting the case for a recognition of homosexuality as a valid alternative lifestyle and arguing against a proposed counter-motion prepared by an evangelical group:

> This is precisely why we would urge wariness of the Counter Proposal 'debarring
> ministers and deacons from conducting services to mark civil partnerships.' Contrary

to the stated aim of this counter-proposal, however well-meant, the effect will be to shut down all debate. We will have enshrined in Church Law a statement of a particular understanding of Scripture. This in itself is a significant departure from the practice and procedure of the Church of Scotland, which has for centuries been at the forefront of theological thinking and developments. Allowing ministers and deacons to follow their conscience, whether for or against conducting such services, while guaranteeing an ongoing theological discussion is much more in keeping with our tradition.[5]

It is clear that those who advocate this position see it as *semper reformanda*. We must not be bound in any way by the past, not even by Scripture itself, if modern thinking and modern social consensus favours change.

When this issue was debated at the General Assembly of the Kirk in Edinburgh in May 2006, the other argument was also used, concerning 'liberty of conscience'. In the course of the debate, it was argued that the Church of Scotland should not bind the consciences of its ministers and that the right of private judgment, based on individual conscience, must be permitted. One minister gave an emotional speech, citing the occasion when he found himself at the bedside of a dying woman who wanted him to conduct a service of blessing on her and her lesbian partner. He did so and insisted that his right of private judgment, based on his own conscience, should be recognized. He also indicated that, in similar circumstances, he would do the same again, whatever the Church might say.

Both of these arguments are based on traditional Reformed language (*semper reformanda* and liberty of conscience), but in fact the arguments presented actually represent an abuse of these important principles. I have argued elsewhere that *semper reformanda* must be interpreted carefully within certain biblical and theological parameters,[6] so let me now address the issue of liberty of conscience, with particular reference to this debate within the Kirk.

It has, of course, never been the case that a private right of judgment, based on individual conscience, supersedes church law or precludes discipline. Indeed, it is contrary to all previous theology and practice within the Church and such an argument would not be allowed on other matters. Ministers who have had problems with women's ordination, for example, were accorded no

---

5. See <http://www.onekirk.org/resources/stepping-forward/pdf> (p. 10), accessed 28 June 2006.

6. A. T. B. McGowan (ed.), *Always Reforming: Explorations in Systematic Theology* (Leicester: IVP, 2006), pp. 13–18.

right of conscience. Those who oppose an evangelical position justify their
views by constantly affirming that the Church of Scotland is a broad church,
but this is not true. The Church of Scotland is a confessional church in the
Reformed tradition. In such a church, Scripture and confession are the decision-making factors in any matter of faith or practice. We must strongly resist
the emotive cries for freedom of conscience, when ultimately what is asked for
is freedom to disobey the authority of God speaking in the Scriptures.

It is true that the Westminster Confession of Faith speaks of 'liberty of
conscience', but it is very carefully worded. It does not propose complete
freedom to believe or to do anything. Rather, it says that 'God alone is Lord of
the conscience, and has left it free from the doctrines and commandments
of men, which are, in any thing, contrary to His Word; or beside it, if matters
of faith, or worship.'[7] It is also very specific in restricting liberty of conscience,
lest anyone use it as an excuse for sin.

The deeper issue, of course, concerns the way in which a denomination is
related to the world church. Wolfhart Pannenberg, dealing with this same issue
of homosexuality, puts it like this:

> Here lies the boundary of a Christian church that knows itself to be bound by the
> authority of scripture. Those who urge the Church to change the norm of its
> teaching on this matter must know that they are promoting schism. If a church
> were to let itself be pushed to the point where it ceased to treat homosexual activity
> as a departure from the biblical norm, and recognised homosexual unions as a
> personal partnership of love equivalent to marriage, such a church would no longer
> stand on biblical ground but against the unequivocal witness of scripture . . . A
> church which took such a step would thereby have ceased to be one, holy, catholic
> and apostolic.[8]

That is to say, there comes a point when those who deny any doctrinal or
confessional commitment effectively exclude themselves from Christianity.
When James Orr wrote his book *The Problem of the Old Testament*, a devastating
analysis of German liberal biblical criticism, he argued that liberal theology
was not Christianity. As we have seen, J. G. Machen later echoed this view in
his book *Christianity and Liberalism*. This principle can perhaps be illustrated
using the example of a game of chess. If someone develops a new variation

---

7. J. W. Ross (ed.), *The Westminster Confession of Faith* (Glasgow: Free Presbyterian,
    1986), ch. 20, sect. 2.

8. Wolfhart Pannenberg, 'Amor Vincit Omnia – or Does it?', *Church Times*, June 1996.

of, say, the Scotch defence, then although it may never have been seen or played before, it is still a legitimate option. If, however, a player moves his bishop horizontally instead of diagonally, moves his king two squares at a time instead of one and allows his pawns to move backwards as well as forwards, then he is no longer playing chess. It might become an exciting new board game but it is not chess.

We may reasonably conclude, then, that much of what is called for under the spurious use of *semper reformanda* and the call for a right of private judgment based on individual conscience is akin to developing a new religion. Scripture and confession together must define the boundaries of exploration and private judgment.

Academic freedom

The third approach to this question of the relationship between Scripture and confession involves a complete rejection of confessions. This approach is the one often used within the academy in relation to evangelical theology. As mentioned earlier, it is normally expressed thus: 'How can you combine academic rigour with confessional subscription?' The argument is that complete academic freedom and detachment are necessary in order to be able to engage in serious study. Any kind of prior faith or commitment makes it virtually impossible to be truly 'academic'.

This position was not held during the first 1,800 years of the church's history. Virtually all the early universities were founded as theological colleges. Indeed, only members of the Church of England could register as students at the Universities of Oxford and Cambridge until relatively recently. Many writers, of course, have responded to this argument that one can have true academic freedom only if one has no presuppositions. For example, Cardinal John Henry Newman faced it head on in the lectures he gave providing the rationale for a Christian university being established in Dublin. Later published as *The Idea of a University*, his argument is powerful and has hardly been surpassed.[9] Newman was quite clear that theology, based as it is in revelation from God, is real knowledge and so deserves its place within the university. He argued at length concerning the importance of this knowledge and for the useful effect of Christianity on all other disciplines. I could, however, press his argument still further and argue, as I did in chapter 2, that not only is it legitimate to have presuppositions but in fact without the presupposition of the existence of the Triune God nothing in the world makes any kind of sense.

---

9. John Henry Newman, *The Idea of a University* (London: Longmans, 1931).

Interestingly, Bavinck chose to go to a university rather than to a seminary because he argued that the knowledge of God is real knowledge and that it is to succumb to the Enlightenment if we concede that there is no place for theology in the university. Not every evangelical seems to accept this, however. D. A. Carson, in reviewing John Webster's book on Holy Scripture includes the following as part of his 'critique': 'Would it be churlish of me to wonder why a scholar as helpfully committed to reforming theological education as he is, distancing it from the prevailing mindset of university faculties, isn't teaching at a church-based theological college instead of in a university department?'[10] Webster is right to remain in the university. To do otherwise would be to admit what Richard Dawkins and others have argued for years, namely that there is no place in the university for theology because it has no real knowledge.

The origins of the argument concerning the incompatibility of academic freedom and confessional subscription (or indeed of any deep faith commitment) can, of course, be traced to the Enlightenment. The logical conclusion of having accepted Kantian dualism is that religion becomes a private matter, separated from the real world of sensory experience and hence unable to make definitive truth claims. In this context, one cannot speak confidently about God, since his existence or otherwise is not provable by reason, which, based upon the presupposition of human autonomy, is the only acceptable basis for decision-making. The result is that one can speak only about religion and religious people. Thus theology becomes religious studies and God-talk is replaced by sociology. In a postmodern society where the very concept of truth is denied, this position is reinforced. As theology transmogrifies into religious studies and is taken out of the sphere of faith and the church, to be absorbed into the academy, all authentic truth claims are lost.

A paradigm shift now rarely challenged has taken place in Western society since the Enlightenment. No-one has exposed this more clearly than Allan Bloom in his brilliant book *The Closing of the American Mind*.[11] He opens his argument thus:

> There is one thing a professor can be absolutely certain of: almost every student
> entering the university believes, or says he believes, that truth is relative. If this
> belief is put to the test, one can count on the students' reaction: they will be

---

10. D. A. Carson, 'Three More Books on the Bible: A Critical Review', *Trinity Journal* 27.1 (2006), p. 18.

11. Allan Bloom, *The Closing of the American Mind* (New York: Simon & Schuster, 1987).

uncomprehending. That anyone should regard the proposition as not self-evident astonishes them, as though he were calling into question $2+2=4$. These are things you don't think about. The students' backgrounds are as various as America can provide. Some are religious, some atheists; some are to the Left, some to the Right; some intend to be scientists, some humanists or professionals or businessmen; some are poor, some rich. They are unified only in their relativism and in their allegiance to equality. And the two are related in a moral intention. The relativity of truth is not a theoretical insight but a moral postulate, the condition of a free society, or so they see it. They have all been equipped with this framework early on, and it is the modern replacement for the inalienable natural rights that used to be the traditional American grounds for a free society. That it is a moral issue for students is revealed by the character of their response when challenged – a combination of disbelief and indignation: 'Are you an absolutist?' the only alternative they know, uttered in the same tone as 'Are you a monarchist?' or 'Do you really believe in witches?' This latter leads into the indignation, for someone who believes in witches might well be a witch-hunter or a Salem judge. The danger they have been taught to fear from absolutism is not error but intolerance. Relativism is necessary to openness; and this is the virtue, the only virtue, which all primary education for more than fifty years has dedicated itself to inculcating. Openness – and the relativism that makes it the only plausible stance in the face of various claims to truth and various ways of life and kinds of human beings – is the great insight of our times. The true believer is the real danger. The study of history and of culture teaches that all the world was mad in the past; men always thought they were right, and that led to wars, persecutions, slavery, xenophobia, racism, and chauvinism. The point is not to correct the mistakes and really be right; rather it is not to think you are right at all.[12]

Bloom's analysis is surely correct and widely applicable. The number of departments of Christian theology in universities that have become, since the 1970s, departments of religious studies, is itself testimony to the problem. It may be that the right to think from a Christian perspective and to have that thinking recognized as legitimate is the greatest challenge facing Christian theologians in the present day.

Strong confessionalism
Most of those who advocate what I regard as inappropriate relationships between Scripture and confession seek to undermine the effective teaching of

---

12. Ibid., pp. 25–26.

the confessions. There are, however, those on the other side. Some churches and individuals affirm that Scripture is the final authority but, in practice, act as if their confession were the final authority. Those who take this position would normally affirm the priority of Scripture, but their confession would condition their exegesis, becoming a prism through which Scripture is read, thus undermining the free translation and exegesis of Scripture.

The way in which a confession is treated and the status it is accorded depends to some extent on the form of subscription.[13] When church office bearers are required to affirm a particular confessional statement, it usually has some rubric or declaratory article attached. For example, in some Presbyterian denominations, ministers and elders are expected to say that in affirming the Westminster Confession of Faith, they do so *simpliciter* and without any liberty of opinion, whereas, in other denominations, as noted earlier, the ordination vow is less strict. The Presbyterian Church in America, which has the Westminster Confession of Faith as its subordinate standard, has had an ongoing dispute over the nature of subscription to the confession. On the one hand, some affirm 'good-faith subscription', and, on the other hand, some affirm 'strict subscriptionism'.

The good-faith subscriptionists argue that a certain liberty of opinion must be permitted and that individual Presbyteries should judge whether or not a particular 'exception' to the confession should preclude ordination or induction. The strict subscriptionists argue that if someone cannot accept the confession in its entirety, then they should not be ordained into the denomination. Their position would be that if any member of the denomination believes that the confession needs to be amended, then they ought to argue for this change through the courts of the church. Amending a historical document may seem somewhat odd on this side of the Atlantic, but, in fact, the American Presbyterians already use an amended version of the confession, having made changes to chapters 20, 22, 23, 24, 25, 26 and 31. The good-faith subscriptionists believe that the strict subscriptionists are narrow and legalistic, whereas the strict subscriptionists believe that the good-faith subscriptionists are becoming liberal. Both sides fear for the future of the denomination if the other side triumphs.

A strong confessionalism can easily lead to a situation where, although Scripture is affirmed as the final authority, in practice the confession becomes the controlling authority. One example of this relates to recent debates in

---

13. For examples of various practices in regard to subscription see David W. Hall (ed.), *The Practice of Confessional Subscription* (London: University Press of America, 1995).

some Presbyterian denominations in the USA on the days of creation, particularly on the issue as to whether the 'days' of creation were literal twenty-four-hour days or longer periods. Some participants in some denominations were so strongly confessional in their approach to the problem that they did not focus on exegetical matters, nor was the matter argued on the basis of the teaching of Scripture. The issue became one of subscription to the confession, with some arguing that we must establish what the authors of the confession had in mind when they spoke about the days of creation. If they meant normal twenty-four-hour days, then ministers and elders who took a different view would have to take an 'exception' to the confession (which some Presbyteries would not permit). Thus, instead of a serious biblical debate, with different sides bringing forward exegetical arguments, the debate often focused on subscription and ordination. In that case at least, the clear priority of Scripture over confession was in danger of being lost.

This is not a problem confined to America. An English Presbyterian minister, who was serving in a Scottish denomination, once wrote in his denominational magazine that the Westminster Confession of Faith must be permanently accepted in its entirety and that those who disagreed with even a small part of it should be stripped of office in the church. It almost seemed as if the confession was being put on a par with Scripture as an untouchable final authority. There was no suggestion that God the Holy Spirit could yet shed new light on Scripture. Nor was there any recognition that the issues and heresies of today are different from the seventeenth-century battles against medieval Roman Catholicism and that we might need a new confession to deal with such matters.

Having identified four problematic suggestions as to the proper relationship between Scripture and our confessional statements, let us turn to look at the issue of tradition, to see if it might provide a helpful structure in enabling us to approach confessional statements without these problems.

Scripture and tradition

Given that the Scriptures have been subject to many different and indeed contradictory interpretations, the church has consistently issued statements as to what Christians ought to believe. In some cases, these statements have become part of the tradition of the church and affirmation of them has become a test of faith. This is particularly true of the church's creedal statements. From the earliest days of the church, councils have been called to deal with particular issues. Some of the conciliar statements issued at the end of these deliberations ultimately became creedal, for example the *Nicene Creed*, following discussions at the Council of Nicaea (AD 325) and the Council of Constantinople (AD 381). Others, for example the Chalcedonian Definition, produced after the Council of Chalcedon (AD 451), have virtually the same authority as the creeds themselves.

As we noted in chapter 2, three creeds, with some variations,[14] are almost universally accepted and, indeed, are often referred to as the 'Three Ecumenical Symbols', namely the Apostles' Creed, the Nicene Creed and the Athanasian Creed. The doctrinal statements in these creeds are regarded as being definitive of Christianity itself. A discussion between representatives of the Orthodox, Catholic, Anglican, Lutheran, Presbyterian, Baptist, Methodist and Pentecostal churches will soon demonstrate that there is substantial unity on these creeds and also with the main conciliar decisions of the first four centuries. Those who reject key elements of these creeds and conciliar decisions are normally regarded as being outside the boundaries of orthodox Christianity, even where they ostensibly give affirmation to the authority of Scripture. For example, the Mormons and Jehovah's Witnesses, who deny the co-equal divinity of Christ with the Father and the Holy Spirit.

Within the camp of those who affirm the creeds, however, there are major divisions concerning the proper interpretation of Scripture. A common commitment to the authority of Scripture does not mean that Christians agree on the nature of faith, the atonement, the sacraments, ecclesiastical structures and much more besides. These divisions have come about through different interpretations of the Scriptures and these different interpretations have become entrenched through their adoption as part of an ecclesiastical tradition or statement of faith. Different traditions within Christianity have sought to define their interpretations of Scripture and subsequent doctrinal affirmations by various means. The Orthodox churches of the East would say that they affirm the teaching of all seven of the Ecumenical Councils of the early church and can neither depart from nor add to the teaching of these councils. The Roman Catholic Church affirms a similar conciliar position but recognizes later councils, up to and including the Council of Trent (1545–63), the First Vatican Council (1870) and the Second Vatican Council (1962–5). The Orthodox churches do not regard these (and other councils) as Ecumenical Councils of the whole church but merely local councils of the Roman Catholic Church. The Roman Catholic Church, in addition to its conciliar position, also allows the magisterium the right to interpret (or reinterpret) these decisions and even to introduce new teaching.

---

14. E.g. the argument between the Eastern and Western church over the inclusion of the *filioque* clause in the Nicene Creed.

The teaching of the councils is identified in both Orthodoxy and Roman Catholicism as 'tradition' and this word is vital to a proper understanding of the theological position held by both Orthodoxy and Roman Catholicism. There is, however, a significant difference in the way that tradition is understood in these two communions. In the Roman Catholic Church, tradition is regarded as a parallel source of authority alongside Scripture. It is taught that the gospel was passed on in two ways, orally and in writing. The written handing on is Scripture but the oral handing on refers to tradition, whereby the apostles handed on the gospel to bishops, who in turn by apostolic succession passed it on to their successors until the present day. As the *Catechism of the Catholic Church* says, 'This living transmission, accomplished in the Holy Spirit, is called Tradition, since it is distinct from Holy Scripture, though closely connected to it.'[15] The position of the Roman Catholic Church is that 'Sacred Tradition and Sacred Scripture' are 'bound closely together'. Indeed, quoting from *verbum Dei*, The *Catechism of the Catholic Church* says that 'the Church . . . "does not derive her certainty about all revealed truths from the holy Scriptures alone. Both Scripture and Tradition must be accepted and honoured with equal sentiments of devotion and reverence." '[16]

In Orthodoxy, however, tradition is not a parallel authority alongside Scripture. Rather, it includes Scripture. As Timothy Ware, Bishop Kallistos of Diocleia, writes:

> A tradition is commonly understood to signify an opinion, belief or custom handed down from ancestors to posterity. Christian Tradition, in that case, is the faith and practice which Jesus Christ imparted to the Apostles, and which since the Apostles' time has been handed down from generation to generation in the Church. But to an Orthodox Christian, Tradition means something more concrete and specific than this. It means the books of the Bible; it means the Creed; it means the decrees of the Ecumenical Councils and the writings of the Fathers; it means the Canons, the Service Books, the Holy Icons – in fact, the whole system of doctrine, Church government, worship, spirituality and art which Orthodoxy has articulated over the ages. Orthodox Christians of today see themselves as heirs and guardians to a rich inheritance received from the past, and they believe that it is their duty to transmit this inheritance unimpaired to the future.[17]

---

15. *Catechism of the Catholic Church* (Dublin: Veritas, 1994), p. 24.

16. Ibid., p. 25.

17. Timothy Ware, *The Orthodox Church* (London: Penguin, 1993), p. 196.

Although mainstream Protestant churches would accept most of the decisions of the seven Ecumenical Councils, with the main exception being on the matter of icons, these churches do not normally accord the creeds and councils the same authority as do the Orthodox and Roman Catholic churches. That is to say, they value these creeds and councils but do not regard them as having undisputed authority. They take this position in order to maintain the principle of *sola scriptura*. Despite this concern, most of these churches will use the creeds in worship. Some Protestant churches take a different view, however, and refuse to give any place in their worship to a conciliar or creedal statement. Within the Reformed tradition particularly, this is part of a more general refusal to have any set forms of prayers or rubrics and has come about because of a certain confusion between sixteenth- and seventeenth-century Reformed views on worship.

Whatever place they might give or not give to the creeds, however, it is certainly true that Protestants have tended to define their distinctive doctrinal beliefs by means of confessions and catechisms, mostly produced during the Reformation and post-Reformation periods. In general, a creed is a statement of the Christian faith universally accepted by all the major branches of the church, whereas a confession or a catechism is normally an expression of the particular beliefs of a denomination or a distinctive grouping within the church. For example, the Lutherans produced the Augsburg Confession (1530) and the Calvinists produced the Genevan Confession (1536) and Calvin's Catechism (1537 revised 1541).

Different countries or regions also produced statements of faith. From the French came the Gallic Confession (1559), known also as the Confession de la Rochelle. From the Scots came the Scots Confession (1560), presented to Parliament as part of the Reformation settlement. The Dutch, to this day, affirm the 'Three Forms of Unity', being the Belgic Confession (1561), the Heidelberg Catechism (1563) and the Canons of Dort (1619). The Swiss gave us the Second Helvetic Confession (1566), which was widely accepted as a Reformed confession across Europe. The Church of England, after various earlier versions, settled on the Thirty-Nine Articles (1571).

In addition to these national (or regional) confessional statements, there were those adopted by particular ecclesiastical traditions. The Presbyterians in the Church of Scotland adopted the Westminster Confession of Faith in 1647, the Congregationalists (or Independents) produced their own slightly revised version, called the Savoy Declaration (1658) and the Baptists followed with another revision, called the Baptist Confession of Faith (written in 1677 and reissued in 1689). This Baptist confession is also known as the Old

London Confession and (in America) as the Philadelphia Confession of Faith (1744).

All of these confessions, often with associated catechisms, were intended to define precisely how Scripture was to be interpreted, particularly on points that had been in theological dispute. We are left, however, with the same problem in relation to confessional statements I identified in relation to the creeds, namely precisely what authority is to be accorded to them and on what basis?

The Orthodox and Roman Catholic Churches have solved this problem to their satisfaction by a theology of tradition. Can Protestants also have a theology of tradition? Certainly, within the ecumenical movement, Catholics have strongly urged Protestants to give serious consideration to this matter. No-one pressed this point more than Yves M.-J. Congar, whose main concern in his writing was the ecumenical purpose of seeking reconciliation on this matter of the place of tradition between Protestants and Catholics.[18] His position was that the Spirit enables the church to understand Scripture and thus tradition develops. In other words, it is the Spirit who brings tradition into being, just as he brought the Scriptures into being.

Defining the relationship

How should we define the relationship that ought to exist between Scripture and our confessional statements? In answering the question, I shall do two things. First, I shall argue that we need to reconstruct our doctrine of the church and within that reconstruction to develop an evangelical understanding of the place of tradition. Second, I shall make certain comments about the nature of confessional statements.

The doctrine of the church

My argument here is that evangelicals, in practice, have a much higher view of tradition than our theology implies and therefore we need to formalize this by developing an evangelical theology of tradition within a reconstructed doctrine of the church.

In the early church it was recognized that no one individual or even one fellowship had the right to determine conclusively the will of God. This was a

---

18. See Yves M.-J. Congar, *The Meaning of Tradition* (New York: Hawthorn, 1964); and Yves M.-J. Congar, *Tradition and Traditions: An Historical and a Theological Essay* (London: Burns & Oates, 1966).

matter for the church and particularly for the church gathered in assembly, as in Acts 15. Some good work has been done recently on this theme, not least by D. H. Williams, in helping evangelicals to 'reconnect' to the ancient catholic tradition of the church and not to see this as in any way a departure from the authority of Scripture.[19]

The importance of tradition to Christians cannot be denied, whether in the Orthodox sense of tradition as representing the whole life of the church including Scripture, or the Roman Catholic sense of tradition as a parallel source of authority alongside Scripture, or in the sense of the 'Reformed tradition', meaning a school of thought that shares a common history, based on an agreed interpretation of the Scriptures. Christians share a conviction that our beliefs are firmly rooted in the Scriptures but also that we can trace some continuity back through history, indicating that we stand alongside those who have gone before us in the faith. To give just one example, those in the Scottish Reformed tradition believe that they stand in line with the early Fathers, especially Augustine, with Calvin, Zwingli and Knox. Then, depending on your view of these things, the tradition either goes on through Robert Rollock, Samuel Rutherford, Thomas Boston, William Cunningham and on to John Murray; or alternatively, through Robert Bruce, Robert Leighton, John Macleod Campbell and Karl Barth to Tom Torrance! We even occasionally (although not nearly often enough) also give a nod to the Dutch. The significance of this appeal to history and tradition is most noticeable when the line of succession is challenged, as it was during the Calvin versus Calvinism debate. At such times people feel very threatened because their tradition is very important to them.

It is also true to say that those evangelicals who belong to different 'traditions' also have a deep sense of need for belonging, to be part of an identifiable community that can trace its origins. This is what we saw earlier in the case of those who had become Orthodox. Their search for deep spiritual roots led them to reconstruct their ecclesiology. That is to say, ultimately they became Orthodox because they had come to a different understanding of the church. In Protestant churches, if the question is asked, 'What is the church?', there would probably be several strands to the answer. It would be noted that the church has certain marks as identified by the early Fathers (unity, sanctity,

---

19. See D. H. Williams, *Retrieving the Tradition and Renewing Evangelicalism: A Primer for Suspicious Protestants* (Grand Rapids: Eerdmans, 1999); and D. H. Williams, *Evangelicals and Tradition: The Formative Influences of the Early Church* (Milton Keynes: Paternoster, 2005).

catholicity and apostolicity) and other marks identified by the Reformers (the Word rightly preached and the Sacraments rightly administered – with the later addition of discipline rightly maintained). A more contemporary strand would certainly emphasize the need for mission and evangelism and the importance of being concerned for issues of poverty and justice. Additionally, it would be pointed out that there are many biblical motifs that can aid our understanding (the body of Christ, the bride of Christ, the kingdom of God etc.). Some emphasis would also clearly be placed on the meaning and significance of the Greek word *ekklēsia*.

Unfortunately, all of this taken together does not enable us to answer a number of key questions that are hugely difficult, if not impossible, for Protestants, but that provide no problem at all for the Orthodox. For example, can any group of Christians who choose to do so begin to meet and call themselves a church, without any reference to other Christians? Would it make any difference if some of those who met had previously been set apart as elders? If they left their former congregation to escape charges of heresy or immorality, what is the status of their new congregation? Are Christians entitled to leave a congregation of believers and begin a new congregation just because they prefer a different worship style? Where a schism, disruption or secession takes place, can each of the new bodies arising out of these crisis events call themselves the church? Given that there are over 25,000 Protestant denominations, how can we tell what is a true church, or is it arrogant even to consider such a designation?

The Othodox answer, of course, is that the only true church is the one that has unbroken continuity with the apostles themselves. They recognize that there are Christians who are not part of that true church but believe that these Christians ought to 'come home'. They would have little difficulty answering my list of difficult Protestant questions! Similarly, the Roman Catholic Church would have no difficulty in answering these questions and the ability of that church to give a clear and unambiguous answer to questions about the nature of the church and its authority has been very attractive to Protestants. In his biography of Cardinal Basil Hume, Anthony Howard devotes a chapter to the decision of the Anglican Church to ordain women and the response of the Catholic Church to this decision. The context is that many High Anglicans believed that the church would effectively become a sect if it cut itself off from the tradition of the church and ordained women. In the course of this analysis, Howard quotes the infamous article by John Wilkins, editor of *The Tablet*, who, in speaking about Anglicans coming over to Rome, used the expression 'the conversion of England', which naturally caused enormous furore. If, however, we pass over that remark and the row that followed, there is another interesting comment in the article. Wilkins says that '[the cardinal] finds a certain irony in that just at the moment when Catholics seem to be irked by the teaching authority, High Church Anglicans are finding a need of it'.[20] This is surely the same need I identified in those who have become Orthodox.

In all of this discussion, the problem arises when we try to ask what we mean by 'tradition'. Protestants tend to accuse Catholics of placing tradition alongside Scripture as a parallel authority, proudly insisting that we hold to the Bible alone. As we have seen, however, our Protestant confessions of faith, while not being accorded the place that tradition has in the Roman Catholic and Orthodox churches, can nevertheless become a hermeneutical prism through which we read the Scriptures and therefore a controlling factor in our exegesis. In any case, we have to admit that some teaching was passed on to the early Christians by word of mouth and was binding upon them (2 Thess. 2:15; 3:6). The argument of the Orthodox and of the Catholics is that this constitutes part of the sacred tradition that has been passed down through the centuries to the church. This, however, has never been a satisfying or persuasive theological interpretation for Protestants. The issue is clear: 'How can we develop an evangelical theology of tradition that rightly gives priority to Scripture but that recognizes our historical development and the importance to us of our creeds and confessional statements?'

Some evangelical theologians have sought to develop an evangelical understanding of tradition.[21] This is evidenced by what has come to be known as the Wesleyan Quadrilateral, where Scripture, tradition, experience and reason are seen as the sources or norms for theology. Perhaps the most significant recent attempt to identify an evangelical theology of tradition has been the work of Stan Grenz.[22] Grenz, in the course of his argument against the notion that Scripture is primarily to be understood as propositional revelation, proposes that theology has three sources of authority: Scripture, tradition and culture.[23] This argument brought considerable counter-reaction from other evangelicals, notably Don Carson, who goes so far as to say that he 'cannot see

---

20. Anthony Howard, *Basil Hume: The Monk Cardinal* (London: Headline, 2005), p. 222.

21. See Williams, *Retrieving the Tradition* and *Evangelicals and Tradition*.

22. Stanley J. Grenz, *Revisioning Evangelical Theology: A Fresh Agenda for the 21st Century* (Downers Grove: IVP, 1993); Stanley J. Grenz, *Theology for the Community of God* (Nashville: Broadman & Holman, 1994).

23. Grenz, *Theology for the Community*, pp. 21–26.

how Grenz's approach to Scripture can be called "evangelical" in any useful sense'.[24]

Whatever we may think of Grenz's attempts, however, evangelicals need to take seriously the place tradition has in our theology, not least so that we can give a clear answer to questions concerning the place of creeds and confessions in the church. Our inability to give clear answers to the 'difficult Protestant questions' mentioned earlier highlights the need for a clearer theology of the church. It might well be argued that at the Reformation we recovered the doctrine of justification by faith but lost our doctrine of the church.

More recently, some evangelicals have argued that we need to recover the importance of the church's tradition, as an authority alongside Scripture. William Abraham, for example, has argued that we need a canon of tradition as well as a canon of Scripture. In fact, he holds that there are two types of canons: ecclesial (creed, Scripture, liturgy, iconography, the Fathers and sacraments) and epistemic (reason, experience, memory, intuition and inference).[25] He avers that over the years ecclesial canons were transformed into epistemological categories and that this 'warped their original use and purpose', since an ecclesial canon is not an epistemic category but a means of grace.[26] He stresses the key place of the Christian community in these matters: 'In a real sense canonical material is actually constituted by the community. The two ideas, canon and community, are logically and reciprocally related. A community constitutes its canonical heritage, and in doing so, that community is itself constituted along certain lines.'[27] In the early Christian community there developed 'a network of canonical practices' that included Scriptures, a creed, a liturgy and so on, which together represented the tradition of the church.[28]

In some post-conservative evangelical theology, an attempt has been made to give much more place to the interpretative community, both in relation to the doctrine of Scripture and in relation to tradition. Stanley Grenz and John Franke, in seeking to develop a postmodern evangelical theology, consider various 'norms'. They expound Scripture as the 'norming norm'[29] and then go

---

24. D. A. Carson, *The Gagging of God* (Leicester: Apollos, 1996), p. 481.

25. William J. Abraham, *Canon and Criterion in Christian Theology: From the Fathers to Feminism* (Oxford: Clarendon, 1998), p. 1.

26. Ibid., p. 2.

27. Ibid., p. 30.

28. Ibid., p. 467.

29. Stanley J. Grenz and John Franke, *Beyond Foundationalism: Shaping Theology in a Postmodern Context* (Louisville: Westminster John Knox, 2001), pp. 57–92.

on to discuss tradition. They note that 'Christianity is also a tradition; its beliefs and practices are rooted in its historical contexts as well as in its corporate reflection on Scripture.'[30] How precisely does this tradition relate to Scripture? They write:

> We come to the texts as participants in the story of faith who seek to understand the whole of Scripture as the instrumentality of the Spirit's speaking to us. Yet we realise that the Spirit has been speaking to the church through Scripture over the course of history. Therefore, we do well to take account of the reception of the Spirit's voice mediated to us and passed on by the faith community through the ages.[31]

In the remainder of the chapter they note the demise of tradition in Protestant theology in general and in evangelical theology in particular, as part of a conscious determination towards *sola scriptura*. They conclude that 'the biblical narratives function as the norming norm for Christian faith and life. Nevertheless, the tradition of the community provides a crucial and indispensable hermeneutical context and trajectory in the construction of faithfully Christian theology.'[32]

Kevin Vanhoozer follows Congar in arguing that the Holy Spirit is the ultimate author of good tradition and devotes four chapters to the subject in his *Drama of Doctrine*.[33] He resists the post-conservative approach, however, arguing that the interpretative community (church) does not create its own tradition by its receiving and interpreting of Scripture. Rather, he is careful to insist that normativity belongs with the authors of Scripture and not the interpretative community. When the community reads Scripture, it does not create meaning but helps understanding.

As we have seen, Bavinck was quite clear that the Reformers did not completely dispense with tradition but only with 'bad' tradition.[34] Philip Schaff echoes this as he explains the way in which the Reformers distanced themselves from Roman Catholicism while still asserting their continuity with historic Christianity. He notes that 'Tradition is not set aside altogether, but is

---

30. Ibid., p. 94.
31. Ibid.
32. Ibid., p. 129.
33. Kevin J. Vanhoozer, *The Drama of Doctrine: A Canonical Linguistic Approach to Christian Theology* (Louisville: Westminster John Knox, 2005), pp. 115–241.
34. E.g. in bk. 4 of the *Institutes*, Calvin insists that his view is in line with the Fathers, rather than with medieval theology.

subordinated, and its value made to depend upon the measure of its agreement with the Word of God.'[35]

What shape, then, should an evangelical doctrine of tradition take? We might usefully identify four principles. First, tradition is vital and must be recognized as an integral part of being the church. We are not the first Christians and we cannot pretend that with an open Bible we can ignore all those who have gone ahead of us in the faith. Second, tradition must never stand alongside Scripture as a parallel source of authority, nor as an inclusive concept that includes Scripture. The voice of God the Holy Spirit speaking in and through the Scriptures must be our final authority. Third, tradition in the evangelical sense must always mean a recognition of the biblical, theological and ecclesiastical decisions made by those who have gone before us in the faith and the importance of these decisions for our self-understanding. Fourth, tradition must always be subject to review and reformation, in the light of God continuing to speak to us by his Spirit through his Word. In short, our evangelical theology of tradition must guard the authority of the voice of God speaking in Scripture and yet at the same time take seriously the concept of tradition as the collective voice of the church through the ages.

The nature of confessional statements

Having indicated that any confessional statements must be set in the context of an understanding of tradition within a reconstructed ecclesiology, I want to finish by making a few comments about the nature of any confessional statements we do develop.

Perhaps the first thing to be said is obvious, namely that confessional statements are important and useful. Philip Schaff makes this point well in his classic work on the creeds. He writes, 'Confessions, in due subordination to the Bible, are of great value and use. They are summaries of the doctrines of the Bible, aids to its sound understanding, bonds of union among their professors, public standards and guards against false doctrine and practice.'[36]

When we affirm a confession, we are saying that, in the light of our own understanding and that of those who have gone before us, this is the best summary we can give of what we believe the Scriptures mean and teach. Scripture (or rather, the voice of God speaking in and through Scripture) has authority and priority over any confession and indeed is that which determines

---

35. Philip Schaff, *The Creeds of Christendom*, vol. 1: *The History of the Creeds* (New York: Harper & Brothers, 1877), p. 206.

36. Ibid., p. 8.

the shape and content of any confession. Any attempt to give a confession priority over Scripture, or to assume that a confession's interpretation of Scripture is somehow permanently privileged, must be resisted. At the same time, any attempt to use the *semper reformanda* principle to develop confessional statements that clearly depart from Scripture and enshrine in the church's theology doctrines and practices contrary to Scripture is equally to be rejected. Schaff underlines this when he writes:

> In the Protestant system, the authority of symbols, as of all human compositions, is relative and limited. It is not co-ordinate with, but always subordinate to, the Bible, as the only infallible rule of the Christian faith and practice. The value of creeds depends upon the measure of their agreement with Scripture. In the best case a human creed is only an approximate and relatively correct exposition of revealed truth, and may be improved by the progressive knowledge of the Church, while the Bible remains perfect and infallible. The Bible is of God; the Confession is man's answer to God's word. The Bible is the *norma normans*; the Confession the *norma normata*. The Bible is the rule of *faith* (*regula fidei*); the Confession the rule of doctrine (*regula doctrinae*). The Bible has, therefore, a divine and absolute, the Confession only an ecclesiastical and relative authority.[37]

We must also note that confessional statements ought to be constantly subjected to scrutiny by careful exegetical work and should always be recognized as transient documents. Confessions should be written regularly so that the church always has a doctrinal statement that deals with the issues and concerns of the day. The fact that most of the confessions in use in Protestant churches were written in Western Europe in the seventeenth century is a strange phenomenon. Is it not remarkable that none of us has confessions that deal with the principal difficulties that have assailed and are assailing the church, namely liberalism, pluralism, relativism, postmodernism and so on?[38]

Finally, we must be open to the possibility that both the structure and the content of our confessions need to be revised. Like the writers of the Scots Confession, we must be willing to change anything in our confessions if it can be shown from Scripture that we have made a mistake in exegesis or

---

37. Ibid., p. 7.

38. One attempt is being made to rectify this. The Theological Commission of the World Reformed Fellowship, made up of scholars in the Reformed tradition from many different countries, is writing a new statement of faith for the twenty-first century.

interpretation. That is to say, we must be prepared to admit that we are fallen human beings, whose thinking is often faulty and hence approach our theology with a profound sense of humility. As evangelicals we are not good at holding up our hands and admitting our mistakes. Let me give one example. As a Presbyterian whose church affirms the Westminster Confession of Faith I have been deeply challenged by the recent publication in English of Karl Barth's lectures on the Reformed confessions.[39] In particular, I was challenged by his argument that the Westminster Confession of Faith heralds a departure from earlier creedal and confessional statements in that its main preoccupation is not with God but with personal salvation and the doctrine of assurance. Barth goes so far as to suggest that it represents an attempt 'to make Reformed theology into anthropology'.[40] Whether or not one agrees with his whole argument, it clearly deserves serious consideration.

Conclusion

In conclusion, then, I would argue that the need to define properly the relationship between Scripture and our confessional statements is both vital and urgent. It is also important that we carry out this work in an attitude of humble willingness to learn from our brothers and sisters in the faith.

---

39. Karl Barth, *The Theology of the Reformed Confessions*, ed. Darrell L. Guder and Judith J. Guder (Louisville: Westminster John Knox, 2002).
40. Ibid., pp. 150–151.

7. PREACHING SCRIPTURE

Introduction

Having considered a number of significant theological issues in relation to Scripture, it is important now to conclude with the matter of how Scripture is to be used. If we were to continue the development of new pneumatological vocabulary for our doctrine of Scripture, then the word here would be 'fruition'.[1] God the Holy Spirit brings forth fruit in the lives of believers as they are exposed to the teaching of Scripture.

Scripture was given to us by God and is continually interpreted for us and applied to us by God, for our life and salvation. The academic arguments over the nature and authority of Scripture are important but are ultimately pointless if Scripture does not play its vital role in the lives of individual Christians and the life of the church. In this chapter, I shall consider the use of Scripture in the preaching of the church, noting particularly the lessons that can be learned from one of the greatest expositors of Scripture, John Calvin.[2]

---

1. I am grateful to my friend Dominic Smart for this suggestion.
2. This chapter, in an earlier form, was given as a paper at the Leicester Ministers' Conference in 2004.

Scripture and the believer

To carry out this study of the church's preaching, we must first ask ourselves what the church is seeking to achieve in the lives of believers by its preaching of Scripture. Or, to put it another way, in order to ensure that the preaching of Scripture is appropriate to God's purpose, we must begin by asking why God has given us the Scriptures. There are at least three places in the New Testament where we are given specific answers to this question.

First, we have the purpose of Scripture as explained by the apostle John. In John 20:31 the apostle gives his reason for writing the gospel. He says, 'these are written so that you may believe that Jesus is the Christ, the Son of God, and that by believing you may have life in his name'. The Scriptures were not given to satisfy our curiosity, nor to provide information for theologians; they were written that we might believe and have life. That is to say, they were written in order that we might know God and, in knowing God, find salvation.

Second, Paul writes in Romans 15:4 that 'whatever was written in former days was written for our instruction, that through endurance and through the encouragement of the Scriptures we might have hope'.

Third, Paul in 2 Timothy 3:16–17 gives a number of reasons why Scripture is useful: 'All Scripture is breathed out by God and profitable for teaching, for reproof, for correction, and for training in righteousness, that the man of God may be competent, equipped for every good work.'

In the earlier chapters we looked at the 'God-breathed' or divinely spirated nature of Scripture, but here we see why God breathed it out. It was given that men, women and children might come to faith in Jesus Christ and so receive the gift of eternal life. It was given for our instruction and for our encouragement. It was given that we might be fully equipped for every good work. On this last point, it is useful to note in some detail Paul's statement in 2 Timothy 3 concerning the purpose of Scripture.

Paul tells us that God has given us the Scriptures, first, for *teaching*. Everything that is necessary for life and salvation is to be found in the Scriptures. There we are taught about the nature and character of God and his law, about the human condition and about our need of salvation. In short, we are taught everything we need to know in order to live the life of faith. This teaching must not be neglected but rather must be studied in the context of private reading, in the context of the family and in the context of the church. It should be part of our daily pattern of living to read and learn from Scripture and to pass this teaching on to our children. One of the astonishing features of Scripture is that we can read it every day for the rest of our lives and never plumb the depths of the teaching we find there.

God has given the Scriptures, second, for *reproof*. All human beings are fallen creatures and as we read the Scriptures God confronts us with our sin and need for forgiveness. When David sinned with Bathsheba, God sent the prophet Nathan to reprove David and call him to repentance. In one sense, that happens each day as we open God's Word. We must, however, be willing to accept this judgment upon our sin and be open to the work of God's Spirit as he confronts us with our fallenness. There is in the heart of every human being a determination to assert our own autonomy and to try to justify ourselves. That is precisely what we saw earlier in Genesis 3. We must overcome this and welcome God's reproof, knowing that it stems from his love and is intended to make us more like Christ.

God has given the Scriptures, third, for *correction*. This notion of 'correction' has the sense of being 'straightened out' and comes from the same Greek root as the word 'orthopaedic'. The sense is that God, through the Scriptures, gradually reshapes our twisted and fallen humanity and enables us to become what he intends us to be. By nature we are twisted and damaged creatures, much in need of this straightening. One of the glories of the Christian gospel is to see those who have made shipwreck of their lives being gradually enabled to rebuild and become new creatures in Christ. Often new Christians are almost unrecognizable after Christ has begun to do his work.

God has given the Scriptures, fourth, for *training in righteousness*. This has the sense of being schooled in goodness and holiness. One of the marks of Christian discipleship is that believers are to live good lives, showing forth the fruit of the Spirit. Believers should be markedly different from unbelievers, because the Holy Spirit is remaking us in the image of Christ who is perfectly holy and righteous. God does this by his Spirit through his Word, as we read the Scriptures and meditate on their meaning and significance.

The result of this is 'that the man of God may be competent, equipped for every good work'. It is one of the sad results of a declining Christian situation in the West that so many believers are so ill-equipped for the life of faith. This is often because they have neglected the Scriptures and so have failed to benefit from all that God intended the Scriptures to accomplish in their lives. On the other hand, those Christians who are best equipped to serve God in the world are usually those who have given themselves to the Scriptures and to prayer, not as a retreat from the world but precisely in order to be able to engage with the world.

The preaching of Scripture

As we saw in chapter 2, orthodox Christian theologians teach that God has revealed himself in a number of ways but that these different ways can be brought together under two headings, namely general revelation and special revelation. We also noted that there are several forms of special revelation and these are usually expressed in terms of the 'Threefold Word of God': *Jesus Christ*, the incarnate Word; *Scripture*, the written Word; and *preaching*, the Spoken Word.

It is this third form of the Word of God, preaching, with which we are concerned here. In one sense we might say that this is the most controversial of the three. Most people can accept that Jesus Christ is the Word of God and that Scripture is the Word of God, but in what sense can preaching be described as the Word of God? Professor Klaas Runia put it succinctly when he said this: 'Both Luther and Calvin were convinced that, when the message of the gospel of Jesus Christ is being proclaimed, God himself is heard by the listeners.'[3]

The Second Helvetic Confession (1566), written by Heinrich Bullinger, gave classic expression to this theme. In chapter 1 of that confession it is affirmed quite unambiguously that 'the preaching of the word of God is the word of God'.[4] This was Calvin's view also. As the Calvin scholar T. H. L. Parker puts it:

> According to Calvin . . . preaching so to say 'borrows' its status of 'Word of God' from Scripture. It is the Word of God inasmuch as it delivers the Biblical message, which is God's message or Word. But 'God's Word' means, for Calvin, that which is spoken by God; not simply in its first giving but in its every repetition. It does not somehow become weakened by repetition so as to become less and less God's Word.[5]

We must be careful, however, to hedge this statement round with an important qualification. Runia puts it like this: 'The indispensable condition for true preaching is the faithful proclamation of the message of Scripture.'[6] Notice, not *all* preaching is to be accorded the designation 'Word of God' but only that preaching which properly expounds the Scriptures.

---

3. Klaas Runia, 'Preaching', in Sinclair B. Ferguson and David F. Wright (eds.), *New Dictionary of Theology* (Leicester: IVP, 1988), pp. 527–528.

4. Arthur C. Cochrane (ed. and comp.), *Reformed Confessions of the Sixteenth Century* (Louisville: Westminster John Knox, 2003), p. 225.

5. T. H. L. Parker, *Calvin's Preaching* (Edinburgh: T. & T. Clark, 1992), pp. 23–24.

6. Runia, 'Preaching', p. 528.

In order to open up this theme of preaching from the Scriptures, we are going to consider the place Calvin gave to preaching. This subject should not simply be of historical interest to us but should represent a challenge to our own understanding and practice of preaching. It is certainly the case that if we were to recover some of the key elements in the preaching of Calvin, the church as a whole would be rescued from the shallowness that so often pervades worship today.

Reformed preaching

The magisterial Reformers were among the truly great preachers and the legacy they left us in the Reformed church is a valuable one indeed. Calvin himself was undoubtedly a giant among preachers, even in such company. As T. F. Torrance has said:

> If it fell to the lot of Martin Luther to transform the theological scene and to introduce or reintroduce into the understanding of the Christian faith elements of far-reaching importance which have not ceased to have their impact upon Christian thought, it was certainly the destiny of John Calvin to be the father both of modern theology and of modern biblical exposition. It was he who in his *Institutes of the Christian Religion* laid the foundations for biblical and dogmatic theology as they are now pursued, and he who in his many *Commentaries* upon the books of the Old and New Testaments paved the way for the systematic interpretation of the Holy Scriptures in which so many scholars have engaged ever since.[7]

In order to spell out Calvin's legacy, I shall highlight five elements or characteristics of his preaching, many of which he shared with the other Reformers:

1. Calvin's preaching was founded upon the authority of Scripture.
2. Calvin's preaching was expository.
3. Calvin's preaching was systematic.
4. Calvin's preaching was doctrinal.
5. Calvin's preaching reflected his views on ministry and worship.

Let us consider each of these in turn.

---

7. Thomas F. Torrance, *The Hermeneutics of John Calvin* (Edinburgh: Scottish Academic Press, 1988), p. 61.

Calvin's preaching was founded upon the authority of Scripture

Prior to the Reformation, the Bible had not been available in the languages of everyday speech but only in Latin, and it was generally believed that, without a priest to interpret, ordinary people should not have access to the Bible. The Reformers overturned this and insisted on the need for vernacular translations of the Bible. Convinced as they were of the perspicuity of Scripture, they believed that by the use of a right method (comparing Scripture with Scripture) people could and should read and understand the Scriptures.

Calvin had a very high view of Scripture, believing it to have been given by God. For example, in his commentary on the word *theopneustos* in 2 Timothy 3:16, he says, 'This is the principle that distinguishes our religion from all others, that we know that God has spoken to us and are fully convinced that the prophets did not speak of themselves, but as organs of the Holy Spirit uttered only that which they had been commissioned from heaven to declare.'[8] This attitude was reflected in the amount of time and energy he gave to preaching, teaching and writing, often preaching five times a week in addition to lecturing and writing. As T. H. L. Parker puts it, it 'is clear that this single-minded concentration on the Holy Scriptures could come only from a particular view of the Bible. No-one would spend so much time on a book to which he did not attach an extraordinary importance.'[9]

This view of Scripture naturally came out in his theology and practice of preaching. He was steeped in Scripture and everything he wrote was based upon Scripture. Quite apart from specific statements in which he affirms a high view of Scripture (such as the one just quoted), his very method of study and writing demonstrates a commitment to its authority. One of the implications of this high view of Scripture was that Calvin expounded Scripture 'without exception'. Parker sums up Calvin's attitude: 'The preacher, then, is to receive "without exception everything contained in Holy Scripture", even what his reason tells him to reject. Reason, that necessary guide in things earthly, is out of its depths in the realm of revelation and must submit to the infinite superiority of God's wisdom.'[10]

Calvin himself, in a sermon on Ephesians 6:1–4, puts it like this:

---

8. David W. Torrance and Thomas F. Torrance (eds.), *The Second Epistle of Paul the Apostle to the Corinthians and the Epistles to Timothy, Titus and Philemon*, Calvin's Commentaries (London: Oliver & Boyd, 1964), p. 330.

9. Parker, *Calvin's Preaching*, p. 1.

10. Ibid., p. 38.

Here again I must remind you of something that I spoke of before, namely, that when God's will is once known to us, we must restrain ourselves and not take leave to reply against God and ask why God is pleased with this, or displeased with that, but admit his will as the sovereign righteousness and equity. And where shall we find that will of his? In his Word! For when St Paul wishes to ratify God's will to us, he does not soar in the air above the clouds, but brings forward and alleges the things that are contained in the law. So then, to rule our lives aright, let us apply our whole minds to seek out the things that are pleasing and acceptable to God, as he shows them to us in his law, in the prophets, and in the gospel. This is all our wisdom. And let us beware of that boldness which I said was devilish, which consists in being wise in our own conceits, and saying, How this? And Why that? But let us simply obey our God.[11]

This high view of the authority of the Bible was most clearly expressed in chapters 6 and 7 of Book 1 of his *Institutes of the Christian Religion*. For example, he writes of Scripture, 'This, therefore, is a special gift, where God, to instruct the church, not merely uses mute teachers but also opens his own most hallowed lips.'[12] God having done this, the Word he has spoken must be accepted. As he writes, 'When that which is set forth is acknowledged to be the Word of God, there is no one so deplorably insolent – unless devoid also both of common sense and of humanity itself – as to dare impugn the credibility of Him who speaks.'[13]

He also makes the point that 'daily oracles are not sent from heaven, for it pleased the Lord to hallow his truth to everlasting remembrance in the Scriptures alone [cf. John 5:39]. Hence the Scriptures obtain full authority among believers only when men regard them as having sprung from heaven, as if there the living words of God were heard.'[14] In this way he acknowledges the innate authority of Scripture. He then goes on to acknowledge the place of the church in relation to Scripture, while rejecting the notion that the Scriptures derive their authority from the church or that we accept them on the basis of the church's authority: 'Thus, while the church receives and gives its seal of approval to the Scriptures, it does not thereby render authentic what

---

11. J. Calvin, *Sermons on the Epistle to the Ephesians* (Edinburgh: Banner of Truth, 1973), p. 624.

12. J. Calvin, *Institutes of the Christian Religion* (Philadelphia: Westminster, 1977), 1.6.1.

13. Ibid. 1.7.1. See also ibid., p. 74, n. 2; and cf. ibid. 4.8.1ff.

14. Ibid. 1.7.1.

is otherwise doubtful or controversial. But because the church recognises Scripture to be the truth of its own God, as a pious duty it unhesitatingly venerates Scripture.'[15]

In answer to the apologetic question as to how we can be sure that Scripture has come from God (if we do not accept it on the authority of the church), Calvin, as we saw in chapter 5, insists that its authority is self-evident. He even goes so far as to say, 'it is clear that the teaching of Scripture is from heaven'.[16]

As we noted in chapter 2, Calvin speaks of the 'inward testimony of the Spirit' as the means whereby we are enabled to recognize the Scriptures as the Word of God:

> For as God alone is a fit witness of himself in his Word, so also the Word will not find acceptance in men's hearts before it is sealed by the inward testimony of the Holy Spirit. The same Spirit, therefore, who has spoken through the mouths of the prophets must penetrate into our hearts to persuade us that they faithfully proclaimed what had been divinely commanded.[17]

Calvin can say of the Scripture that 'we affirm with utter certainty . . . that it has flowed to us from the very mouth of God by the ministry of men. We seek no proofs, no marks of genuineness upon which our judgement may lean; but we subject our judgement and wit to it as to a thing far beyond any guesswork!'[18] Thus Calvin is 'fully conscious that we hold the unassailable truth!' and can affirm that 'the undoubted power of his divine majesty lives and breathes there'.[19]

There can be little doubt, surely, that Calvin held to a high view of Scripture and that this affected deeply his understanding of the task of preaching.

Calvin's preaching was expository

Expository preaching is preaching that begins with the text of Scripture and seeks to interpret, explain and apply that text. Calvin's preaching was exegetical in style, the exegesis being based on the text in its original languages. Scholars have studied Calvin's sermons to try to establish the text he used in

---

15. Ibid. 1.7.2.
16. Ibid. 1.7.4.
17. Ibid.
18. Ibid. 1.7.5.
19. Ibid.

the pulpit, whether French or Latin or whatever. By a diligent comparison of the texts available to him, it is clear that if he went into the pulpit to preach on the Old Testament, then what he had in front of them was his Hebrew text, making his own translation as he went along. This explains why sometimes when the passage is given at the beginning of the sermon, it differs slightly from the text as repeated during the exposition. The evidence for the New Testament sermons is not quite so clear cut, but the general view is that his method was the same; hence when he preached from the New Testament, he used a Greek text and translated as he went along.

We now take it for granted that the study of Greek and Hebrew is a sound basis from which to progress to exegesis, but that was by no means the case in the sixteenth century. It was the Reformers themselves who introduced this practice. In order to understand this, we have to go back behind the Reformation to the humanist movement.

There were different forms of humanism arising out of the pre-Reformation Renaissance, but the type that affected Christian theology came out of northern Europe. Humanism was a multifaceted endeavour, but at its heart it involved a recovery of interest in the classical languages. Humanism sent people back to the original texts in their original languages. Initially, this meant a rediscovery of the great Latin and Greek classical texts, but ultimately the lessons learned in this type of scholarship were applied to the Christian faith and the Christian Scriptures.

It has been said that humanism had a significant effect on John Calvin. Alister McGrath puts it like this:

> The origins of Calvin's methods as perhaps the greatest biblical commentator
> and preacher of his age may be argued to lie in his study of law in the advanced
> atmosphere of Orléans and Bourges. There is every indication that Calvin learned
> from Budé the need to be a competent philologist, to approach a foundational
> text directly, to interpret it within the linguistic and historical parameters of its
> context, and apply it to the needs of his own day. It is precisely this attitude
> which undergirds Calvin's exposition of Scripture, especially in his sermons, in
> which he aims to fuse the horizons of Scripture and the context of his audience.
> French humanism gave Calvin both the incentive and the tools to enable the
> documents of yesteryear to interact with the situation of the city of Geneva in
> the 1550s.[20]

---

20. Alister E. McGrath, *Christian Theology: An Introduction*, 2nd ed. (Oxford: Blackwell, 1997), p. 42.

When scholars began to engage in this discipline, it had considerable significance for Christian theology. In particular, it had the effect of bringing to light many of the mistakes in the Latin Vulgate text of the Scriptures, which was used in the church. Not only so, but a number of doctrines and church practices were based on these mistranslations of the original, so that careful, scholarly study of the original texts led to doctrinal reform.

The humanist slogan was *ad fontes* (to the sources). As McGrath points out, 'Applied to the Christian church, the slogan *ad fontes* meant a direct return to the title-deeds of Christianity – to the patristic writers, and supremely to the Bible, studied in its original languages.'[21] Here we have the beginning of the modern understanding of biblical scholarship. As McGrath suggests, the first texts the humanists studied were the ancient Latin and Greek texts, but gradually they became interested in ancient Christian writings (especially the New Testament and the writings of the early church Fathers) and began to study them. Many of these scholars began to see that what they were reading had implications for the church and that there was great need for reform.

One of the first to apply this humanist exegetical method to the Scriptures was a young man from England called John Colet. He was the 'son of a wealthy London merchant who had been several times Lord Mayor'.[22] Colet began to study the Bible in earnest after hearing the humanist scholar Savonarola preach. When he returned to England, he lectured at Oxford University on Paul's epistles. T. M. Lindsay writes, 'His method of exposition, familiar enough after Calvin had introduced it into the Reformed Church, was then absolutely new, and proves that he was an original and independent thinker.'[23]

Colet abandoned the scholastic method of using texts to prove church teaching and also rejected allegorical methods of interpretation. He wanted to let the Bible speak for itself, believing it to be personal revelation from God. Many of his views were distinctly Protestant. The Lollards in England delighted in Colet's preaching, but he did not join them or even obviously identify himself with them. We can perhaps underline his influence by mentioning two points. First, one of his pupils was William Tyndale; and second, he was the one who persuaded Erasmus to give up purely classical studies in favour of work on the New Testament and the church Fathers. In mentioning

---

21. Ibid., p. 52.

22. Thomas M. Lindsay, *A History of the Reformation*, vol. 1, 2nd ed. (Edinburgh: T. & T. Clark, 1907), pp. 163–164.

23. Ibid., p. 164.

Erasmus, it is worth taking a moment or two to consider his contribution to this new scholarly approach to Scripture.

Desiderius Erasmus (c. 1469–1536) was undoubtedly one of the greatest scholars of his day, if not the greatest and certainly the most significant scholar of the Renaissance. He was one of the humanists who was determined to hold on to Christianity while at the same time being critical of the church. He prepared a critical edition of the Greek New Testament and also prepared editions of the early church Fathers. He was convinced (partly because of the influence of Colet) that if he could get people to return to the original text of the New Testament and to a simplified Christianity, then reform would take place and the peace of the church would be maintained.

It has been argued that he had a considerable influence on Calvin, who began his life as a classical scholar and humanist. It is certainly true to say that the Reformer's great emphasis upon an educated ministry and upon the necessity of such ministers studying the Scriptures in the original languages comes from his background in Christian humanism.

And so the Reformers developed this method of expository preaching, based on the lessons they had learnt from the humanists. Commentaries began to appear and collections of sermons, both of which were exegetical and expository. For the first time in centuries men and women were exposed to the Bible in a new and living way, as a book by which God was speaking rather than as a collection of documents to support the teaching of the church.

Calvin put it like this:

> When we read the epistles which St Paul wrote to a variety of places, we should always consider that God meant that they should serve not only for one time alone, or for certain people only, but for ever, and in general for the whole church. And truly if a man considers well the doctrine that is contained in them, it will be easy to discern that God's intention was to be heard in the things that are spoken there, even to the world's end; and also that he has such a care for us that he has not passed over or forgotten anything that might further our salvation . . . We see then that the doctrine which is contained in this epistle is directed and dedicated to us at this present day, and that God has by his wonderful providence so disposed things beforehand that we not only have had the foundations of the gospel upon which to ground ourselves, but also the means by which our faith may from day to day grow and increase, so that we may still go forward until we reach perfection.[24]

---

24. John Calvin, *Sermons on the Epistle to the Ephesians* (Edinburgh: Banner of Truth, 1973), pp. 7–8.

Being expository also meant, of course, that their preaching was less liable to distortion on the basis of a 'system'. Some evangelicals have occasionally done their arguments more harm than good by trying to squeeze passages into a preconceived mould to get them to 'fit' their theological system. Calvin never did that and, indeed, has sometimes been misquoted and misunderstood precisely because of this. When Calvin was expounding a passage that speaks of individual responsibility, he expounded it in that way. If he was dealing with a passage that deals with the sovereignty of God, he expounded it in that way. Which is why it is so important to read his *Institutes*, because, as he said himself, the commentaries are to be read in the light of the *Institutes*. This point is well made by Ian Hamilton.[25] In other words, Calvin allowed the Bible to speak for itself. Instead of seeking to press it into a mould, he developed his theological system on the basis of his exegesis.

Calvin's preaching was systematic

The third mark of Calvin's preaching is that it was systematic. Indeed, it can probably be argued that his involvement in the recovery of this method was one of his most significant contributions to the method of Christian preaching. I say 'recovered' because this was already a well-established pattern in the fourth and fifth centuries of the church, as we see in preachers such as Chrysostom and Augustine; and although it was largely absent from the preaching of the four or five hundred years before the Reformation, some systematic exposition of Scripture did take place in the medieval theological schools.[26]

Calvin took books of the Bible and either preached or lectured through them, chapter by chapter, verse by verse, although he was not the first to do so. In the earliest period of the Reformation, perhaps the most notable of those who followed this method was Zwingli. Zwingli had studied in Basle, where his involvement with the humanists brought him into personal contact with Erasmus. Like many of the Christian humanists he learned Greek so that he could read the New Testament in its original language, and gave himself seriously to the study of Scripture. In the course of his academic life (partly because of his interest in Greek, the Fathers and the classics) he became an enthusiastic Erasmian. From 1506 until 1516 he was parish priest in Glarus, and it was during this time that he began to study Greek and began to be more

---

25. Ian Hamilton, *Calvin's Doctrine of Scripture: A Contribution to Debate*, Rutherford Monographs (Edinburgh: Rutherford House, 1984), p. 4.

26. Parker, *Calvin's Preaching*, p. 80.

deeply involved in study along Christian humanist lines. He became people's priest in the Great Minster in Zurich in 1518.

After 1520, however, Zwingli's views underwent a major change. He was no longer an Erasmian. Nor was he, like Bucer, one of those who changed from being Erasmian to being Lutheran. Instead, he created for himself a new theological position. There is no agreement as to the factors that brought about this change, although two things may be said. First, he was committed to what might be called the Scripture principle. That is to say, he was convinced that all decision-making must be done on the basis of what the Bible says. Second, he had given himself seriously to the study of Augustine. It is no coincidence that the influence of Augustine is seen in the Calvinist side of the Reformation much more than in the Lutheran. Zwingli, Bucer and Calvin were all influenced by the great Father of the church and it showed in their theological writings.

Above all, however, his preaching was systematic, going through books of the Bible. Indeed, as Hughes Oliphant Old points out, when Zwingli went as preacher to the Great Minster in Zurich, 'He started out by taking the Gospel of Matthew and preaching through it verse by verse, day after day for a whole year.'[27] Zwingli was certainly not alone in following this method. Martin Bucer did the same in Strasburg. As Old says, 'he did a long series of sermons on the Gospel of Matthew, the Gospel of John, the first epistle of Peter and the book of Psalms'.[28] Old is careful to point out that these Reformers did not rediscover preaching. There had always been preachers, even some very good preachers. Rather, 'It was far more that their reform of preaching consisted in establishing regular and systematic expository preaching. It was this approach to preaching which Calvin introduced to Geneva and which the Marian exiles took with them when they returned to England and Scotland.'[29]

In commenting on Calvin's method of preaching, Old writes:

> Calvin preached through most of the books of the Bible and he preached slowly through each book. Normally, he took three to six verses at a time. This system produced, for example, 123 sermons on Genesis, 200 sermons on Deuteronomy, 159 sermons on Job, 176 sermons on 1 and 2 Corinthians, and 43 sermons on Galatians.

27. Hughes Oliphant Old, *Worship*, Guides to the Reformed Tradition (Atlanta: John Knox, 1984), pp. 68–69.

28. Ibid., p. 71.

29. Ibid., p. 73.

In more than twenty years as preacher at Geneva, Calvin must have preached through almost the entire Bible.[30]

As early as 1538 there is evidence to indicate that Calvin had already adopted a systematic pattern of preaching through books of the Bible.[31] Prior to 1549 the records are not too reliable, but from 1549 until his death in 1564 the records of his preaching are very dependable. We can be almost certain that we know the text of every sermon he preached in this period, even where the sermons themselves are no longer extant. One striking feature of these records is that Calvin was rigorous in maintaining his systematic exposition through books of the Bible, with one exception: he always interrupted a series on the great Christian festivals.[32] On the Sunday before Christmas he would preach a sermon on the nativity from Luke, on Easter Sunday he would preach on the passion narratives and on Whitsun he would preach from Acts 2.[33] On these occasions he would also administer the Lord's Supper.

Interestingly, systematic preaching through books of the Bible gradually began to wane, even in the Reformed church, and preaching began to be exposition of a single text or theme or doctrine. In many ways we see this happening during the period of the Puritans, where the preaching was certainly powerful and effective but tended to be based on a text rather than an extended systematic exposition of a chapter or a book.[34] James Philip of Edinburgh traced this gradual loss of the Reformers' emphasis on systematic ministry and noted that it was only in the twentieth century that this pattern was re-established on a large scale.[35] The recovery of this method in the middle of the century in the UK was effected largely through the influence of William Still in Scotland and Martyn Lloyd-Jones in England.

---

30. Ibid., p. 75.

31. Parker, *Calvin's Preaching*, p. 60.

32. Ibid., p. 63.

33. Parker helpfully provides a 'List of Sermons on Church Festivals' (ibid., pp. 160–162).

34. There were exceptions to this, however, and some consecutive expository ministry did undoubtedly take place, as demonstrated by David Jussely, 'The Puritan Use of the Lectio Continua in Sermon Invention (1640–1700)' (PhD diss., University of Southern Mississippi, 1997).

35. James Philip, 'Expository Preaching: An Historical Survey', in N. M. de S. Cameron and S. Ferguson (eds.), *Pulpit and People* (Edinburgh: Rutherford House, 1986), pp. 5–16.

Calvin's preaching was doctrinal

Calvin's preaching was doctrinal in the sense that it involved *teaching* the Christian faith. His preaching did not consist in some homily on a theme or in some reflection on personal experience but rather his preaching was teaching.[36] This is not to suggest that his sermons were lectures by another name, since there was always exhortation and application.[37] Nor did he avoid contemporary issues. If there was an important matter that concerned his congregation, Calvin would often deal with that issue in his preaching. For example, on Sunday 27 January 1555, in anticipation of the elections to the Genevan City Councils that were about to take place, Calvin addressed the subject in his sermon.[38]

His preaching was self-consciously doctrinal. He was concerned to expound the great doctrines of the faith in a way that would be comprehensible to the men and women in the pews. His sermons were not overburdened with detailed academic matters or full of theological language; rather, the reverse is the case. He preached in a simple, conversational style, used familiar vocabulary and spoke in short sentences.[39] He often used rhetorical questions[40] and dialogue[41] and, although he did not tell humorous anecdotes, there was often humour in his satire as he debated with imaginary opponents.[42]

He also wore his scholarship lightly. It is clear that he was always aware of complex exegetical issues underlying a passage but he did not trouble his congregation with these finer points. Having decided the matter for himself, he was content to pass on his conclusions without always feeling the need to explain how he arrived at a particular interpretation. This is one of the marked differences between his sermons, on the one hand, and his lectures and commentaries, on the other hand.

It is good to stress the fact that Calvin preached doctrinally lest the impression be given, by the earlier references to humanism, that he was merely a language scholar or an exegete, opening up the Bible as an interesting ancient text. He expounded Scripture in order that men and women might be

---

36. Parker, *Calvin's Preaching*, p. 35.
37. Ibid., pp. 114ff.
38. Ibid., pp. 122ff.
39. Ibid., pp. 140, 142–143.
40. Ibid., p. 144.
41. Ibid., p. 145.
42. Ibid., p. 148.

changed by the power of God and naturally he paid particular attention to those doctrines that, taken together, describe the work of God in the life of the believer. That is to say, he focused on God's work of salvation and sanctification. As Calvin expounded these doctrines, doctrinal truth was laid out before sinners.

He did not avoid even the most difficult doctrinal matters in his preaching. For example, in one sermon on election he writes this:

> In short, we have to note here that we shall never know where our salvation comes from till we have lifted up our minds to God's eternal council by which he has chosen whom he pleased and left the remainder in their confusion and ruin. Now then it is no marvel that some men think this doctrine to be strange and hard, for it does not fit in at all with man's natural understanding. If a man asks of the philosophers, they will always tell him that God loves such as are worthy of it, and that since virtue pleases him, he also marks out such as are given that way to claim them for his people. You see then that, after our own imagination, we shall judge that God puts no other difference between men, in loving some and in hating others, than each man's own worthiness and deserving. But, at the same time, let us also remember that in our own understanding there is nothing but vanity and that we must not measure God by our own yardstick, and that it is too excessive a presumption to impose law upon God such that it would not be lawful for him to do anything but that which we could conceive and which might seem just in our eyes.[43]

Calvin was not afraid to open up the whole counsel of God but did it clearly and simply.

Calvin's preaching reflected his views on ministry and worship

Calvin was committed to preaching and teaching as his primary tasks because he recognized that this was the function of the Protestant minister. In the Reformed church it was understood that ministers were 'teaching elders' and that this is the key to a proper understanding of ministry in the Reformed church. There was, nevertheless, still a lingering sense of the 'ordained clergy' even in Reformed Protestantism. That legacy remains today when we still speak of a clergy–laity divide and have a doctrine of ordination that could do with some serious examination.

If we were to carry out the full implications of Calvin's teaching on the minister as a teaching elder, it would have astonishing ramifications. Whatever the

---

43. Calvin, *Ephesians*, pp. 23–24.

limitations of the way in which the Reformers worked out this key principle, one thing is clear. Since preaching was to be at the centre of worship, this determined the nature of Christian ministry, not least because it required an educated ministry. To create such a ministry was a huge task given the situation in pre-Reformation Europe, as we can see if we use the situation in Scotland as an example of the problems involved.

Provision had to be made for the ministry and oversight of the people. John Knox and his associates were concerned that there should be an educated ministry, well trained in the Word of God, so as to avoid the ignorance and neglect of earlier days. They recognized, however, that in these earliest days they would never find enough suitably qualified ministers to cover the whole country. The result was that they spoke of three permanent orders of ministry and oversight (minister, elder and deacon) but also of two temporary offices (superintendent and reader). Of the permanent offices, the minister and elder were largely understood in the same way as they would be today. In addition to them, the deacon was responsible for financial and property matters, not least the collection of church rents and tithes and the care of the poor. Readers were also responsible for the teaching of the young. Elders and deacons were to be chosen annually.

The superintendent was responsible for the oversight of and provision of ministry to a large area of the country. He was not like a diocesan bishop because he was under the authority and supervision of the ministers and elders in his area of responsibility. This office was regarded as essential only until ministers could be placed in every parish. The reader was someone who was not sufficiently capable to be a minister but who could read distinctly and clearly. He would read the prayers and the Scriptures and perhaps a sermon. Later the office of reader was itself divided into two categories: those who could only read and those who could 'exhort'. This latter category were to be encouraged to develop their gifts so that they might eventually become ministers.

The shortage of properly educated and trained preachers is highlighted by the numbers attending the General Assembly of the Church of Scotland that was established right at the beginning of the Scottish Reformation in 1560 and continued to meet twice each year. The very first Assembly met in Edinburgh on 20 December 1560 and there were 42 members, of whom only 6 were ministers! Hay Fleming tells us that as late as 1596 there were still 'four hundred parishes, not reckoning Argyle and the Isles, which still lacked ministers'.[44] It

---

44. D. Hay Fleming, *The Scottish Reformation* (Edinburgh: Hope Trust, 1960), p. 106.

was a long time before the necessary education and training were fully in place to produce in numbers the type and quality of men required for this pulpit ministry. It was a task to which they were committed, however, and the high academic standards demanded of Reformed ministers was testimony to that commitment. They were determined never to go back to the pre-Reformation situation, where many of the clergy were ignorant and lazy and where some of them could hardly read, far less expound the Scriptures.

Calvin's view of preaching as the central act of the teaching elder also had implications for worship. Whereas in the Middle Ages worship had centred on the sacraments (which were held to communicate the grace they signified), Calvin and the other Reformers put preaching at the heart of their worship. When they met, the preaching of the Word of God was central. This commitment was even incorporated into the design and architecture of Reformed church buildings, with a pulpit at the centre as opposed to an altar.

These views on the centrality of preaching to ministry and worship also implied a certain understanding of the person and work of the Holy Spirit. Calvin believed that the Holy Spirit, who brought the Scriptures into being, was also the one who applied them to the life of the individual believer. He understood that without the work of the Holy Spirit, even the best preaching would be ineffective.

Application

We have a great deal to learn, then, from Calvin, the preacher. We must not make the mistake, of course, of believing that we can simply take Calvin's sermons and preach them today. That would be entirely contrary to his own concern for proper engagement with the congregation in their real-life situation and to his concern for appropriate and relevant language and application. Yet there are lessons to be learned. T. H. L. Parker said that 'clarity, force and persuasiveness are the three necessary ingredients in preaching like Calvin's'.[45] Leroy Nixon, in his book on Calvin's preaching summed up in this way:

> The Application of this study to preaching today can be stated very briefly. There are four points to be noted. (a) Be a real student of the Bible. Stress content. (b) Preach often. (c) Appeal to the deepest spiritual needs of the congregation. (d) Speak

---

45. Parker, *Calvin's Preaching*, p. 131.

plainly. Let the subject bear the weight of the interest. Be conversational, not oratorical.[46]

We might sum up the argument in this way. First, preaching should be founded on a commitment to the authority of Scripture. Without this we have no foundation upon which to say anything. Scripture alone is the authority and foundation for our preaching. Second, our preaching should be expository. The task is to open up the Scriptures, to explain and apply them, not to force anything upon them. We are to bring out what is there and not to use the Scriptures as a 'peg' upon which to hang our prejudices and distinctives. Third, preaching should be systematic. The Scriptures come to us in the form of books, and the best way to expound them is to open up those books. The historical sections of Scripture, the Gospels, the New Testament letters and so on have form, structure and development. Only as we see them in a connected way and show the progression through ideas and arguments can we truly preach the whole counsel of God. Fourth, preaching should be doctrinal but without imposing upon the Scriptures a system that does not arise naturally from them. In other words, we should expound the great doctrines of the Christian faith, emphasizing the grace, mercy and love of God to lost sinners as they turn to him in faith and repentance. Fifth, preaching, like that of Calvin's, should be at the centre of what it means to be a minister. We must emphasize the need for teaching elders, not Protestant priests or door-to-door social workers. Ministers are not the chief executives of congregations (as in so much of American practice) but rather teaching elders. The task is to expound Scripture and this should have a central place in worship. It should also be accompanied by much prayer, in recognition of our dependence upon the work of the Holy Spirit.

---

46. Leroy Nixon, *John Calvin, Expository Preacher* (Grand Rapids: Eerdmans, 1950), p. 129.

8. CONCLUSION

In the introduction, I indicated that the purpose of this book is to contribute to discussions about the nature and function of Scripture in evangelical Christianity. The words 'contribute' and 'discussions' should not be passed over too quickly or too lightly. This is genuinely a contribution to debate, rather than any vain attempt at a final word on the subject. To that end, I shall now draw together the threads of this contribution by doing three things. First, I shall sum up the main points I have been trying to make and that I offer for discussion. Second, I shall respond to some anticipated objections to the thesis presented. Third, I shall offer a constructive suggestion for taking the work forward to another stage.

Summary of chapters 2–7

Scripture and the Holy Spirit
In chapter 2, I argued that, as evangelicals, we ought to reconstruct our doctrine of Scripture in three ways. First, our doctrine of Scripture must be set within the context of the doctrine of God. More specifically, we must develop a pneumatological doctrine of Scripture, emphasizing that the origins, interpretation and use of Scripture must be viewed as part of the work of the Holy Spirit. Second, our doctrine of Scripture must be relocated within the theological

corpus, thus identifying Scripture clearly as an aspect of God's self-revelation. God and not Scripture must be given priority in our theology, and so the chapter on Scripture should not be the first chapter in our confessional statements but ought to come after our doctrine of God, as one aspect of his self-revelation. Third, the vocabulary of our doctrine of Scripture must be adapted, in order to clarify the pneumatological position being advocated, speaking of 'divine spiration' (which can refer to the final canonical form and not just to *autographa*), 'recognition', 'comprehension' and 'fruition'.

Scripture and liberal theology

In chapter 3, I described in summary form the rise and development of liberal theology out of its roots in the Enlightenment. We saw that this led to an entirely new doctrine of Scripture, different from anything that had gone before, in which the Scriptures became human reflections on religious experience, rather than documents created by a divine speaking. The writers of Scriptures were viewed as men reflecting on their religious experience rather than men speaking from God as they were carried along by the Holy Spirit. This new doctrine saw the Scriptures as an interesting collection of what Jewish and Christian believers have thought through the centuries, from which we can learn a great deal but that have no real authority over our own thinking. Liberal theology thus, with every good intention, tried to accommodate Christianity to human beings who had rejected the supernatural. Unfortunately, it ended up creating a Christianity with virtually nothing to say about incarnation, resurrection, salvation and eternal life, focusing instead on the ethical or sociopolitical sphere. I then identified two of the main responses to liberal theology: neo-orthodoxy and conservative evangelicalism. I highlighted the doctrine of Scripture as presented by each of these movements and prepared the way for an analysis of their disagreement over inerrancy.

Scripture and fundamentalism

In chapter 4, I charted the rise and development of fundamentalism and its opposition to liberal theology and to the higher-critical methods that were a part of it. I outlined the creation of the new terminology of 'inerrancy' and then noted the battles over this word in the USA, mainly between conservative evangelicals, on the one hand, and those influenced by neo-orthodoxy, on the other hand. I then highlighted some of the problems in using the word 'inerrancy'. First, I noted that the term is often used with so many qualifications that it is emptied of real meaning, or defined in such a way that no evidence is ever allowed to count against it. Second, I asked why, if textual inerrancy is so vital to the doctrine of Scripture, God did not preserve the *autographa*, since this surely undermines the doctrine of God's providence that underlies the inerrantist proposal. In other words, what was the point of God acting supernaturally to provide an inerrant text providentially if it ceased to be inerrant as soon as the first or second copy was made? Third, I looked at issues of textual disagreements (such as the Synoptic Problem), noting that if God is able to use the extant Scriptures in order to do his work, why invest so much theological capital in hypothetical originals we do not possess? Most importantly, I made the point that inerrancy is not a biblical doctrine but rather an implication of 'inspiration', based on an unsubstantiated (and somewhat presumptuous) view of what God could and could not do.

Scripture and infallibility

In chapter 5, I offered an alternative evangelical understanding of the doctrine of Scripture, focusing on the word 'infallibility' and describing the work of James Orr and Herman Bavinck. We saw that it was possible to develop a high view of Scripture, without taking an inerrantist view of the *autographa*. Indeed, as we saw, this is a much stronger position. After all, if one name in one genealogy in 2 Chronicles is demonstrably mistaken, the entire inerrantist doctrine of Scripture collapses, despite protests to the contrary, skilful footwork and unpersuasive arguments! The notion of infallibility, on the other hand, argues that Scripture is as God intended it to be but that he chose to use human authors with all the implications of that decision. In other words, to argue that the only kind of Bible God was able to give us was one with inerrant *autographa* is untenable. Rather, we must take seriously the Bible that God did, in fact, give us and allow the empirical data rather than theological assertion to determine our doctrine of Scripture. Above all, we saw that, in affirming infallibility, we are not weakening an evangelical doctrine of Scripture but rather strengthening it. God infallibly achieves his purposes in giving us the Scriptures and is not in any way hampered by the lack of *autographa*.

Scripture and confession

In chapter 6, I explored the relationship between Scripture and the creeds and confessions of the church. I recognized that there were several inappropriate ways to understand the relationship between Scripture and confession, ranging from those, on the one hand, who had no place at all for confessions in their thinking to those, on the other hand, who gave their confessional statement such a high place that it eclipsed Scripture, or at least curtailed the exegesis of Scripture. In seeking a way forward on these matters, I recognized the importance of our traditions but also the need for these traditions to be brought to the bar of Scripture constantly for review. I argued that there is a need for an evangelical doctrine of tradition. As evangelicals, we do give creeds and confessions an important place in our theology and in our churches but often without any carefully worked out theology of tradition to justify and regulate this.

Scripture and preaching

In chapter 7, I noted that Scripture must be preached, since it belongs to the church and not primarily to theologians. I made the point that, whatever our disagreements about its nature, God gave us Scripture for various purposes, perhaps the most important of which is that men, women and children might believe and have life. Nevertheless, a great deal of what goes under the name of 'preaching' does not properly open up the Scriptures and apply them in a way that achieves these purposes, and so I identified what I believe to be a better way. Using Calvin as a fine model, I advocated preaching founded upon the authority of Scripture, that is expository, systematic and doctrinal and reflects a solidly biblical understanding of ministry and worship.

Anticipating the critique

Clearly, some of the argument presented in this book is controversial, particularly the proposition that evangelicals should no longer use the term 'inerrancy'. One of the friends who read this book in manuscript form said that it was like putting 'a stick in a hornet's nest'. He later talked about the dangers of being 'on thin ice'. In anticipation of some of the criticisms that might be levelled against my argument, what follows is a pre-emptive strike! The following three questions might reasonably be asked by inerrantists.

The first question is this: 'If the Bible is not inerrant, how can we believe what it says?' The key point made in this book is that this question is inappropriate. In other words, I am arguing that recent evangelical debate on Scripture has led to a division of evangelicals into inerrantists and errantists and that this is a false dichotomy. This situation arose because of a genuine desire to demonstrate that the Scriptures can be shown to be scientifically accurate. This desire, quite natural in its time, led theologians to make assertions about the nature of Scripture that the Scriptures do not claim for themselves. That is to say, these theologians imposed an inappropriate standard of accuracy. Nevertheless, my rejection of the use of the term 'inerrancy' does not mean that I am arguing for 'errancy'. I am simply saying that to speak of inerrant *autographa* is not the way to present and defend a 'high' view of Scripture. We can believe what the Bible says because God gave us the Scriptures and he does not deceive. What we must not do is rest its reliability on inerrant autographic text. The Bible infallibly achieves the purposes for which God gave it and we can depend upon the voice of God speaking by his Spirit through the Scriptures, which are his Word.

The second question is this: 'Surely there are continuities between Warfield and Bavinck, since Warfield himself did not downplay the humanity of the authors of Scripture?' There is undoubtedly some truth in this assertion. Indeed, one of the reasons why Warfield was on such good terms with Orr, Kuyper and Bavinck, despite their formal differences on the doctrine of Scripture, was because he himself had a strong view of the humanity of Scripture (much more so than modern inerrantists). For example, in the famous essay *Inspiration* with A. A. Hodge, we are told that neither the Scriptures nor their authors are omniscient and that the Scriptures are in the limited forms of human thought. Further, the Scriptures were not intended to teach philosophy, science or human history, not even a system of speculative theology! Most striking, however, are these words:

> They are written in human languages, whose words, inflections, constructions and
> idioms bear everywhere indelible traces of human error. The record itself furnishes
> evidence that the writers were in large measure dependent for their knowledge upon
> sources and methods in themselves fallible, and that their personal knowledge and
> judgments were in many matters hesitating and defective, or even wrong.[1]

Given this statement, it is difficult to see why Warfield preferred to speak of 'inerrancy', rather than follow his European colleagues in speaking of 'infallibility'. It is also difficult to imagine many modern inerrantists using language like this. I cannot but agree, however, that there are strong similarities and continuities between the inerrantists and infallibilists. There remains, however, this major difference: the inerrantists insist that God was able to give us only one kind of Bible (inerrant *autographa*), whereas the infallibilists regard that as presumptuous and believe that it does not take account of the empirical evidence and seriously underplays the role of the human authors.

The third question is this: 'In the final analysis, is not what Warfield says about inerrancy in practice the same as what Bavinck says about infallibility?' That is to say, is it only a verbal and not a real difference? Or, to put it another

---

1. A. A. Hodge and B. B. Warfield, *Inspiration*, ed. Roger R. Nicole (Grand Rapids: Baker, 1979), pp. 27–28.

way, is the difference between Bavinck and Warfield really a question of theology, rather than simply a question of accent? Could we not argue that Bavinck rests his argument more on the method and mode of inspiration (which is mysterious), whereas Warfield tends to accent the product or result of inspiration (the text), but the two positions are complementary, not contradictory?

As I have noted above, there is a fundamental contradiction between them in terms of their doctrine of Scripture and I would not want to minimize this. Nevertheless, there is no doubt that the differences between inerrantists and infallibilists are far less significant than that which unites them. Their common opposition to liberal theology, to neo-orthodoxy and even to the form–content distinction of Rogers and McKim unites them. Even if we focus on Warfield and Bavinck, we would want to affirm that they were in agreement on most of the fundamentals of Reformed theology and that their respective doctrines of Scripture did not make this difficult.

We might sum up these points by saying that members of the Evangelical Theological Society in the USA who affirm 'inerrancy' and members of the Fellowship of European Evangelical Theologians who affirm 'infallibility' may disagree strongly on the doctrine of Scripture but yet retain a fundamental unity as evangelicals. This is a family disagreement, rather than a cause for division and mutual condemnation and recriminations.

Charting the way forward

My argument, then, is that Herman Bavinck (even more so than James Orr) offers the finest model for an evangelical doctrine of Scripture, with all his emphasis both on the divine speaking and on the humanity of the authors of Scripture. His defence of the infallibility of Scripture can hardly be stronger. The Scriptures are God's Word and God does not mislead us.

Nevertheless, this does leave evangelicals somewhat polarized. Is there no way forward beyond this inerrantist–infallibilist impasse? As noted in the chapters above, if I were to have to choose between the inerrantist position and the views of Rogers and McKim, I would unhesitatingly choose inerrancy. If I reject that dichotomy and am offered the choice between inerrancy and infallibility, I unhesitatingly choose infallibility. If, however, I were to have the opportunity to begin with a blank sheet of paper, avoiding all of the theological arguments that have been fought out over several centuries, I would offer for discussion the word 'authenticity'. I mentioned earlier, in passing, my interest in using this word to describe the nature of Scripture. As I come to the close of this work, I leave this as a possible way forward for evangelicals, although to develop it properly will require more sustained thought over a longer period. It might, nevertheless, be helpful at this point to outline briefly the usefulness of the term.

First, the word 'authenticity' is useful because of its fundamental meaning and connotations. Essentially, to ask if something is 'authentic' is to ask if it is a genuine product of the one who is claimed to be its creator or author. This is the way the word is used in the world of art. Is a painting, sculpture, book or poem an authentic work of the author whose name is attached to it? This is a matter of great importance. A debate has been taking place in Scotland recently over a famous painting whose provenance is now being questioned. It has been argued by a prominent art historian that it may well be the work of a different (and less famous) painter than the one to whom it had formerly been attributed. Essentially, the argument is over its authenticity. In other words, are the claims that have been made for this painting over many years true and persuasive? Is it authentic? Similarly, the primary claim I make about the Scriptures is that they have their origin in the divine speaking and are the authentic product of God's action in communicating with us by his Spirit through certain human authors. Are the Scriptures authentic? Do they bear the undeniable marks of the Creator's handiwork?

Second, the word 'authenticity' is useful because it is capable of being used in reference to the various genres of Scripture, whereas 'inerrancy' only really makes sense in relation to propositional statements. To ask if a psalm or some wisdom literature or an ethical statement or a parable is *inerrant* is to ask a somewhat strange question, but to ask if it is *authentic*, if it truly has its origin in God and thus bears the identifiable marks of his creative operation, makes perfect sense.

Third, the word 'authenticity' is useful because it can refer not only to autographic manuscripts but to the manuscripts, translations and editions we possess today. No-one claims that our current Bibles are inerrant, yet God is able to use them to do his work. Why is this? It is because they are truly his Word, despite the contradictory manuscripts and disputed texts. They can be recognized as 'authentic', even in their present condition.

Fourth, the word 'authenticity' is useful because it takes further the reconstruction of the doctrine of Scripture under the work of the Holy Spirit. We might put it like this: God himself authenticates the Scriptures to our hearts and minds by the work of his Holy Spirit.

So, then, if it were properly developed, the word 'authenticity' might avoid not only the division between inerrantists and errantists but also the divide between inerrantists and infallibilists. It might therefore become a word around which evangelicals could unite.

Conclusion

Finally, may I make a plea for some serious transatlantic scholarship. Without unnecessarily polarizing the matter (since there are inerrantists in Europe and infallibilists in the USA), it is my hope that evangelicals might take time to learn more from the European Reformed tradition of infallibility and thus moderate the dominance of the American inerrantist tradition. Indeed, I might press this point further and say that, even beyond the immediate confines of the doctrine of Scripture, there is a great deal that can be learned from the rich tradition of Scottish and Dutch Reformed theology, these being in many ways quite different from the English Puritan and American Princetonian traditions. May God help us towards a deeper understanding of his Word, through the work of his Holy Spirit in his church.

BIBLIOGRAPHY

ABRAHAM, W. J., *Canon and Criterion in Christian Theology: From the Fathers to Feminism* (Oxford: Clarendon, 1998).

—, *The Divine Inspiration of Holy Scripture* (Oxford: Oxford University Press, 1981).

ALAND, K., and ALAND, B., *The Text of the New Testament: An Introduction to the Critical Editions and to the Theory and Practice of Modern Textual Criticism* (Grand Rapids: Eerdmans, 1989).

AMMERMAN, N. T., *Bible Believers: Fundamentalists in the Modern World* (New Brunswick: Rutgers University Press, 1987).

BAHNSEN, G. L., *Van Til's Apologetic: Readings and Analysis* (Phillipsburg, N. J.: Presbyterian & Reformed, 1998).

BALMER, R. H., 'The Princetonians and Scripture: A Reconsideration', *Westminster Theological Journal* 44 (1982), pp. 352–365.

BARTH, K., *Church Dogmatics*, vol. 1/2: *The Doctrine of The Word of God* (Edinburgh: T. & T. Clark, 1956).

—, *The Epistle to the Romans* (Oxford: Oxford University Press, 1975).

—, *The Theology of the Reformed Confessions*, ed. D. L. Guder and J. J. Guder (Louisville: Westminster John Knox, 2002).

BARTON, J., *People of the Book? The Authority of the Bible in Christianity* (London: SPCK, 1988).

BARTSCH, H.-W., *Kerygma and Myth: A Theological Debate* (London: SPCK, 1972).

BAVINCK, H., *Reformed Dogmatics*, vol. 1: *Prolegomena* (Grand Rapids: Baker, 2003).

BELL, M. C., *Discovering the Rich Heritage of Orthodoxy* (Minneapolis: Light & Life, 1994).

BERKHOF, L., *Systematic Theology: New Combined Edition* (Grand Rapids: Eerdmans, 1996).

BERKOUWER, G., *General Revelation* (Grand Rapids: Eerdmans, 1955).

—, *Holy Scripture* (Grand Rapids: Eerdmans, 1975).

BLOESCH, D. G., *Holy Scripture: Revelation, Inspiration and Interpretation* (Downers Grove: IVP, 1994).

—, *The Holy Spirit: Works and Gifts* (Downers Grove: IVP, 2000).

BLOOM, A. *The Closing of the American Mind* (New York: Simon & Schuster, 1987).

BOSTON, T., 'The Nature of Regeneration', in R. A. Torrey (ed.), *The Fundamentals*, vol. 3 (Grand Rapids: Baker, 1970), pp. 128–132.

BRAATEN, C. E., and JENSON, R. W. (eds.), *Reclaiming the Bible for the Church* (Grand Rapids: Eerdmans, 1995).

BRAY, G., *Biblical Interpretation, Past and Present* (Leicester: IVP, 1996).

BROMILEY, G. W., *Introduction to the Theology of Karl Barth* (Edinburgh: T. & T. Clark, 1979).

BRUCE, F. F., *The Canon of Scripture* (Downers Grove: IVP, 1988).

BRUCE, S., *The Rise and Fall of the New Christian Right: Conservative Protestant Politics in America 1978–1988* (Oxford: Clarendon, 1988).

BRUEGGEMANN, W., *The Book That Breathes New Life: Scriptural Authority and Biblical Theology* (Minneapolis: Fortress, 2005).

BURGON, J. W., *The Revision Revised* (London: John Murray, 1883).

CALVIN, J., *Institutes of the Christian Religion*, ed. F. L. Battles (Philadelphia: Westminster, 1977).

—, *Sermons on the Epistle to the Ephesians* (Edinburgh: Banner of Truth, 1973).

CARSON, D. A., *The Gagging of God* (Leicester: Apollos, 1996).

—, *The King James Version Debate: A Plea for Realism* (Grand Rapids: Baker, 1979).

—, 'Three More Books on the Bible: A Critical Review', *Trinity Journal* 27.1 (2006), pp. 1–62.

Catechism of the Catholic Church (Dublin: Veritas, 1994).

CHRISOPE, T. A., *Toward a Sure Faith: J. Gresham Machen and the Dilemma of Biblical Criticism, 1881–1915* (Fearn: Christian Focus, 2000).

CLARK, T., *The Theory of Inspiration: Composition as a Crisis of Subjectivity in Romantic and Post-Romantic Writing* (Manchester: Manchester University Press, 1997).

COCHRANE, A. C. (ed. and comp.), *Reformed Confessions of the Sixteenth Century* (Louisville: Westminster John Knox, 2003).

COLE, S. G., *The History of Fundamentalism* (Westport, Conn.: Greenwood, 1931).

CONGAR, Y. M.-J., *The Meaning of Tradition* (New York: Hawthorn, 1964).

—, *Tradition and Traditions: An Historical and a Theological Essay* (London: Burns & Oates, 1966).

DAVIS, D. C., 'Princeton and Inerrancy: The Nineteenth Century Philosophical Background of Contemporary Concerns', in J. D. Hannah (ed.), *Inerrancy and the Church* (Chicago: Moody, 1984), pp. 359–378.

DIXON, A. C., MEYER, L., and TORREY, R. A. (eds.), *The Fundamentals: A Testimony to the Truth*, 12 vols. (Chicago: privately printed and distributed, 1910–15).

DOLLAR, G. W., *A History of Fundamentalism in America* (Greenville, S. C.: Bob Jones University Press, 1973).

DUNCAN III, J. L., 'Common Sense and American Presbyterianism: An Evaluation of the Impact of Scottish Realism on Princeton and the South' (MA thesis, Covenant Theological Seminary, 1987).

EHRMAN, B. D., and HOLMES, M. W. (eds.), *The Text of the New Testament in Contemporary Research: Essays on the Status Quaestionis* (Grand Rapids: Eerdmans, 1995).

ELLINGSEN, M., *The Evangelical Movement: Growth, Impact, Controversy, Dialog* (Minneapolis: Augsburg, 1988).

ENNS, P., *Inspiration and Incarnation* (Grand Rapids: Baker, 2005).

ERDMAN, C. R., 'The Holy Spirit and the Sons of God', in R. A. Torrey (ed.), *The Fundamentals*, vol. 2 (Grand Rapids: Baker, 1970), pp. 338–352.

—, 'The Church and Socialism', in R. A. Torrey (ed.), *The Fundamentals*, vol. 4 (Grand Rapids: Baker, 1970), pp. 97–108.

—, 'The Coming of Christ', in R. A. Torrey (ed.), *The Fundamentals*, vol. 4 (Grand Rapids: Baker, 1970), pp. 301–313.

FERGUSON, S. B., *The Holy Spirit* (Leicester: IVP, 1996).

FLEMING, D. H., *The Scottish Reformation* (Edinburgh: Hope Trust, 1960).

FOWL, S. E., *Engaging Scripture: A Model for Theological Interpretation* (Oxford: Blackwell, 1998).

FRAENKEL, P. (ed.), *Natural Theology: Comprising 'Nature and Grace' by Professor Dr Emil Brunner and the Reply 'No!' by Dr Karl Barth* (London: Geoffrey Bles; Centenary, 1946).

FRAME, J. M., *Apologetics to the Glory of God* (Phillipsburg, N. J.: Presbyterian & Reformed, 1994).

—, *Cornelius Van Til – An Analysis of His Thought* (Phillipsburg, N. J.: Presbyterian & Reformed, 1995).

—, *The Doctrine of the Knowledge of God* (Phillipsburg, N. J.: Presbyterian & Reformed, 1987).

FREI, H., 'The Doctrine of Revelation in the Thought of Karl Barth, 1909 to 1922' (PhD diss., Yale University, 1965).

FURNISS, N. F., *The Fundamentalist Controversy, 1918–1931* (Hamden, Conn.: Archon, 1954).

GAFFIN, R., 'Old Amsterdam and Inerrancy' [part 1], *Westminster Theological Journal* 44 (1982), pp. 250–289.

—, 'Old Amsterdam and Inerrancy' [part 2], *Westminster Theological Journal* 45 (1983), pp. 219–272.

GASPER, L., *The Fundamentalist Movement* (The Hague: Mouton, 1963).

GEISLER, N. L. (ed.), *Inerrancy* (Grand Rapids: Zondervan, 1979).

GILLQUIST, P. E., *Becoming Orthodox* (Ben Lomond, Calif.: Conciliar, 1992).

GILLQUIST, P. E., *Coming Home: Why Protestant Clergy Are Becoming Orthodox* (Ben Lomond, Calif.: Conciliar, 1992).

GRAVE, S. A., *The Scottish Philosophy of Common Sense* (Oxford: Clarendon, 1960).

GRENZ, S. J., *Revisioning Evangelical Theology: A Fresh Agenda for the 21st Century* (Downers Grove: IVP, 1993).

—, *Theology for the Community of God* (Nashville: Broadman & Holman, 1994).

GRENZ, S. J., and FRANKE, J., *Beyond Foundationalism: Shaping Theology in a Postmodern Context* (Louisville: Westminster John Knox, 2001).

GUNTON, C. E., *A Brief Theology of Revelation* (Edinburgh: T. & T. Clark, 1995).

—, *Father, Son and Holy Spirit: Toward a Fully Trinitarian Theology* (London: T. & T. Clark, 2003).

HALL, D. W. (ed.), *The Practice of Confessional Subscription* (London: University Press of America, 1995).

HAMILTON, I., *Calvin's Doctrine of Scripture: A Contribution to Debate*, Rutherford Monographs (Edinburgh: Rutherford House, 1984).

HARPER, M., *The True Light* (London: Hodder & Stoughton, 1997).

HELM, P., 'Thomas Reid, Common Sense and Calvinism', in H. Hart, J. Van Der Hoeven and N. Wolterstorff (eds.), *Rationality in the Calvinian Tradition* (Lanham, Md.: University Press of America, 1983), pp. 71–89.

HENRY, C. F. H., *God, Revelation and Authority*, 6 vols. (Carlisle: Paternoster, 1999).

—, *The Uneasy Conscience of Modern Fundamentalism* (Grand Rapids: Eerdmans, 1947).

HERON, A. I. C., *A Century of Protestant Theology* (Guildford: Lutterworth, 1980).

—, *The Holy Spirit: The Holy Spirit in the Bible, the History of Christian Thought, and Recent Theology* (Philadelphia: Westminster, 1983).

HESLAM, P., 'Faith and Reason: Kuyper, Warfield and the Shaping of the Evangelical Mind', *Anvil* 15.4 (1998), pp. 299–313.

HODGE, A. A., and WARFIELD, B. B., 'Inspiration', *Presbyterian Review* 2 (1881), pp. 225–260.

—, *Inspiration*, ed. R. R. Nicole (Grand Rapids: Baker, 1979).

HODGE, C., 'Inspiration', *Biblical Repertory and Princeton Review* 29 (1857), pp. 660–698.

—, *Systematic Theology*, vol. 1 (London: James Clarke, 1960).

HOEFEL, R. J., 'The Doctrine of Inspiration in the Writings of James Orr and B. B. Warfield: A Study in Contrasting Approaches to Scripture' (PhD diss., Fuller Theological Seminary, 1983).

HOWARD, A., *Basil Hume: The Monk Cardinal* (London: Headline, 2005).

JENKINS, P., *The Next Christendom: The Coming of Global Christianity* (New York: Oxford University Press, 2002).

JENSEN, P., *The Revelation of God* (Leicester: IVP, 2002).

JUSSELY, D., 'The Puritan Use of the Lectio Continua in Sermon Invention (1640–1700)' (PhD diss., University of Southern Mississippi, 1997).

KANT, I., *Critique of Judgment* (Mineola, N. Y.: Dover, 2005).

—, *Critique of Practical Reason* (New York: Liberal Arts, 1956).

—, *Groundwork of the Metaphysics of Morals* (Cambridge: Cambridge University Press, 1997).

—, *Religion within the Limits of Reason Alone* (New York: Harper & Row, 1960).

—, *The Critique of Pure Reason* (Cambridge: Cambridge University Press, 1999).

KUHN, H. B., 'Fundamentalism', in E. Harrison (ed.), *Baker's Dictionary of Theology* (Grand Rapids: Baker, 1960), pp. 233–234.

KUYPER, A., *Calvinism: Six Stone Lectures* (Edinburgh: T. & T. Clark, 1989).

LETIS, T. P., *The Ecclesiastical Text: Text Criticism, Biblical Authority and the Popular Mind* (Philadelphia: Institute for Renaissance and Reformation Biblical Studies, 2000).

— (ed.), *The Majority Text: Essays and Reviews in the Continuing Debate* (Philadelphia: Institute for Renaissance and Reformation Biblical Studies, 1987).

LIEBMAN, R. C., and WUTHNOW, R. (eds.), *The New Christian Right: Mobilization and Legitimation* (New York: Aldine, 1983).

LINDSAY, T. M., *A History of the Reformation*, vol. 1, 2nd ed. (Edinburgh: T. & T. Clark, 1907).

LOETSCHER, L. A., *The Broadening Church* (Philadelphia: University of Pennsylvania Press, 1954).

MACHEN, J. G., *Christianity and Liberalism* (Grand Rapids: Eerdmans, 1923).

MARCIL-LACOSTE, L., *Claude Buffier and Thomas Reid, Two Common Sense Philosophers* (Montreal: McGill-Queen's University Press, 1982).

MARKARIAN, J. J., 'The Calvinistic Concept of the Biblical Revelation in the Theology of B. B. Warfield' (PhD diss., Drew University, 1963).

MARSDEN, G. M., *Fundamentalism and American Culture: The Shaping of Twentieth Century Evangelicalism: 1870–1925* (New York: Oxford University Press, 1980).

—, *Reforming Fundamentalism: Fuller Seminary and the New Evangelicalism* (Grand Rapids: Eerdmans, 1987).

MARSHALL, I. H., *Biblical Inspiration* (London: Hodder & Stoughton, 1982).

—, *The Pastoral Epistles*, International Critical Commentary (Edinburgh: T. & T. Clark, 1999).

MARTIN, W., *With God on Our Side: The Rise of the Religious Right in America* (New York: Broadway, 1996).

McCORMACK, B. L., 'The Being of Holy Scripture Is in Becoming: Karl Barth in Conversation with American Evangelical Criticism', in V. Bacote, L. C. Miguelez and D. L. Okholm (eds.), *Evangelicals and Scripture: Tradition, Authority and Hermeneutics* (Downers Grove: IVP, 2004), pp. 55–75.

McCOSH, J., *The Scottish Philosophy* (New York: Charles Scribner's Sons, 1890).

McDONALD, L. M., *The Biblical Canon: Its Origin, Transmission and Authority* (Peabody, Mass.: Hendrickson, 2007).

McDONALD, L. M., and SANDERS, J. A. (eds.), *The Canon Debate* (Peabody, Mass.: Hendrickson, 2002).

McGOWAN, A. T. B. (ed.), *Always Reforming: Explorations in Systematic Theology* (Leicester: IVP, 2006).

McGRATH, A. E., *Christian Theology: An Introduction*, 2nd ed. (Oxford: Blackwell, 1997).

MEETER, J. E., and NICOLE, R. R., *A Bibliography of Benjamin Breckinridge Warfield, 1851–1921* (Nutley, N. J.: Presbyterian & Reformed, 1974).

METZGER, B. M., *The Canon of the New Testament: Its Origins, Development and Significance* (Oxford: Clarendon, 1987).

—, *The Text of the New Testament: Its Transmission, Corruption and Restoration* (New York: Oxford University Press, 1992).

MULLER, R. A., *Post-Reformation Reformed Dogmatics*, vol. 2: *Holy Scripture: The Cognitive Foundation of Theology* (Grand Rapids: Baker, 1993).

NEUHAUS, R. J., and CROMARTIE, M. (eds.), *Piety and Politics: Evangelicals and Fundamentalists Confront the World* (Washington, D. C.: Ethics and Public Policy Center, 1987).

NEWMAN, J. H., *The Idea of a University* (London: Longmans, Green, 1931).

NIXON, L., *John Calvin, Expository Preacher* (Grand Rapids: Eerdmans, 1950).

NOLL, M., 'A Brief History of Inerrancy, Mostly in America', in *The Proceedings of the Conference on Biblical Inerrancy 1987* (Nashville: Broadman, 1987), pp. 9–10.

—, *Between Faith and Criticism: Evangelicals, Scholarship and the Bible in America* (San Francisco: Harper & Row, 1986).

— (ed.), *The Princeton Defense of Plenary Verbal Inspiration* (New York: Garland, 1988).

NOTARO, T., *Van Til and the Use of Evidence* (Phillipsburg, N. J.: Presbyterian & Reformed, 1980).

OLD, H. O., *Worship*, Guides to the Reformed Tradition (Atlanta: John Knox, 1984).

ORR, J., *Revelation and Inspiration* (London: Duckworth, 1909).

—, *Revelation and Inspiration* (New York: Charles Scribner's Sons, 1910).

—, 'Science and Christian Faith', in R. A. Torrey (ed.), *The Fundamentals*, vol. 1 (Grand Rapids: Baker, 1970), pp. 334–347.

—, *The Christian View of God and the World* (Vancouver: Regent College Publishing, 2002).

—, 'The Early Narratives of Genesis', in R. A. Torrey (ed.), *The Fundamentals*, vol. 1 (Grand Rapids: Baker, 1970), pp. 228–240.

—, 'The Holy Spirit and Modern Negations', in R. A. Torrey (ed.), *The Fundamentals*, vol. 1 (Grand Rapids: Baker, 1970), pp. 94–110.

—, *The Problem of the Old Testament* (New York: Charles Scribner's Sons, 1906).

—, *The Ritschlian Theology and the Evangelical Faith* (London: Hodder & Stoughton, 1898).

—, 'The Virgin Birth of Christ', in R. A. Torrey (ed.), *The Fundamentals*, vol. 2 (Grand Rapids: Baker, 1970), pp. 247–260.

— (ed.), *The International Standard Bible Encyclopaedia* (Chicago: Howard-Severance, 1915).

OSBORNE, G., *The Hermeneutical Spiral: A Comprehensive Introduction to Biblical Interpretation* (Nottingham: Apollos, 2006).

Oxford English Dictionary (Oxford: Clarendon, 1959).

PACKER, J. I., *God Has Spoken* (London: Hodder & Stoughton, 1965).

—, 'What Did the Cross Achieve? The Logic of Penal Substitution', *Tyndale Bulletin* 25 (1974), pp. 1–43.

PANNENBERG, W., 'Amor Vincit Omnia – or Does it?', *Church Times* (June, 1996).

PARKER, T. H. L., *Calvin's Preaching* (Edinburgh: T. & T. Clark, 1992).

PHILIP, J., 'Expository Preaching: An Historical Survey', in N. M. de S. Cameron and S. Ferguson (eds.), *Pulpit and People* (Edinburgh: Rutherford House, 1986), pp. 5–16.

PICKERING, W. N., *The Identity of the New Testament Text* (Nashville: Nelson, 1977); updated version available free online at <http://www.revisedstandard.net/text/WNP/>.

PLANTINGA, A., *God and Other Minds: A Study of the Rational Justification of Belief in God* (Ithaca, N. Y.: Cornell University Press, 1990).

—, *Warranted Christian Belief* (Oxford: Oxford University Press, 2000).

REID, J. K. S., *The Authority of Scripture: A Study of the Reformation and Post-Reformation Understanding of the Bible* (London: Methuen, 1957).

RIDDERBOS, H., *Studies in Scripture and Its Authority* (Grand Rapids: Eerdmans, 1978).

RIPLINGER, G., *New Age Bible Versions* (Munroe Falls, Ohio: A. V., 1993).

RITSCHL, A., *Justification and Reconciliation* (Edinburgh: T. & T. Clark, 1900).

ROGERS, J. B., *Scripture in the Westminster Confession: A Problem of Historical Interpretation for American Presbyterianism* (Grand Rapids: Eerdmans, 1967).

ROGERS, J. B., and McKIM, D. K., *The Authority and Interpretation of the Bible: An Historical Approach* (New York: Harper & Row, 1979).

ROSS, J. W. (ed.), *The Westminster Confession of Faith* (Glasgow: Free Presbyterian, 1986).

RUCHMAN, P., *Why I Believe the King James Version Is the Word of God* (Pensacola: Bible Baptist Bookstore, 1988).

RUNIA, K., 'Preaching', in, S. B. Ferguson and D. F. Wright (eds.), *New Dictionary of Theology* (Leicester: IVP, 1988), pp. 527–528.

RUSSELL, C. A., *Voices of American Fundamentalism: Seven Biographical Studies* (Philadelphia: Westminster, 1976).

RYLE, J. C., 'The True Church', in R. A. Torrey (ed.), *The Fundamentals*, vol. 3 (Grand Rapids: Baker, 1970), pp. 315–319.

SANDEEN, E. R., 'The Princeton Theology: One Source of Biblical Literalism in American Protestantism', *Church History* 31 (1962), pp. 307–321.

—, *The Roots of Fundamentalism: British and American Millenarianism 1800–1930* (Chicago: University of Chicago Press, 1970).

SCHAEFFER, FRANK, *Dancing Alone: The Quest for the Orthodox Faith in the Age of False Religions* (Brookline, Mass.: Holy Cross, 1994).

SCHAEFFER, FRANCIS A., *The Complete Works of Francis Schaeffer*, vol. 4: *A Christian View of The Church* (Westchester, Ill.: Crossway, 1982).

SCHAFF, P., *The Creeds of Christendom*, vol. 1: *The History of the Creeds* (New York: Harper & Brothers, 1877).

—, *The Creeds of Christendom*, vol. 2: *The Creeds of Christendom* (Grand Rapids: Baker, 1983).

SCHLEIERMACHER, F., *On Religion: Speeches to its Cultured Despisers* (Cambridge: Cambridge University Press, 1996).

—, *The Christian Faith* (Edinburgh: T. & T. Clark, 1960).

SCOFIELD, C. I. (ed.), *The New Scofield Reference Bible* (New York: Oxford University Press, 1967).

—, *The Scofield Reference Bible* (New York: Oxford University Press, 1909).

SHELLEY, B., 'Fundamentalism', in J. D. Douglas (ed.), *The New International Dictionary of the Christian Church* (Grand Rapids: Zondervan, 1974), pp. 396–397.

SMITH, H. P., *Inspiration and Inerrancy: A History and a Defense* (Cincinnati: Robert Clarke, 1893).

SPROUL, R. C., GERSTNER, J., and LINDSLEY, A., *Classical Apologetics* (Grand Rapids: Zondervan, 1984).

THISELTON, A., *New Horizons in Hermeneutics* (Carlisle: Paternoster, 1992).

TORRANCE, D. W., and TORRANCE, T. F. (eds.), *The Second Epistle of Paul the Apostle to the Corinthians and the Epistles to Timothy, Titus and Philemon*, Calvin's Commentaries (London: Oliver & Boyd, 1964).

TORRANCE, T. F., *God and Rationality* (Oxford: Oxford University Press, 1971).

—, 'Review: The Inspiration and Authority of the Bible. By B. B. Warfield', *Scottish Journal of Theology* 7 (1954), pp. 104–108.

—, *Space, Time and Incarnation* (Oxford: Oxford University Press, 1969).

—, *The Christian Doctrine of God, One Being Three Persons* (Edinburgh: T. & T. Clark, 1996).

—, *The Ground and Grammar of Theology* (Belfast: Christian Journals, 1980).

—, *The Hermeneutics of John Calvin* (Edinburgh: Scottish Academic Press, 1988).

—, *Theological Science* (Oxford: Oxford University Press, 1969).

—, *Theology in Reconstruction* (Grand Rapids: Eerdmans, 1965).

TORREY, R. A., *The Fundamentals* (Grand Rapids: Baker, 1970).

TOWNER, P. H., *The Letters to Timothy and Titus*, New International Commentary on the New Testament (Grand Rapids: Eerdmans, 2006).

UROFSKY, M. I., and MAY, M. (eds.), *The New Christian Right: Political and Social Issues* (New York: Garland, 1996).

VAN DUSEN, H., 'The Third Force in Christendom', *Life* 44 (9 June 1958), pp. 113–121.

VANHOOZER, K. J., *First Theology* (Leicester: Apollos, 2002).

—, *Is There a Meaning in This Text?* (Leicester: Apollos, 1998).

—, 'On the Very Idea of a Theological System: An Essay in Aid of Triangulating Scripture, Church and World', in A. T. B. McGowan (ed.), *Always Reforming: Explorations in Systematic Theology* (Leicester: IVP, 2006), pp. 125–182.

—, *The Drama of Doctrine: A Canonical Linguistic Approach to Christian Theology* (Louisville: Westminster John Knox, 2005).

VAN TIL, C., *A Christian Theory of Knowledge* (Phillipsburg, N. J.: Presbyterian & Reformed, 1969).

—, *The Defense of the Faith* (Philadelphia: Presbyterian & Reformed, 1976).

—, 'Volume 2 – A Survey of Christian Epistemology' (unpublished class syllabus) (den Dulk, 1969).

VROOM, H. M., 'Scripture Read and Interpreted: The Development of the Doctrine of Scripture and Hermeneutics in Gereformeerde Theology in the Netherlands', *Calvin Theological Journal* 28N (1993), pp. 352–371.

WALLS, A. F., *The Cross-Cultural Process in Christian History: Studies in the Transmission and Appropriation of Faith* (Maryknoll: Orbis, 2002).

—, *The Missionary Movement in Christian History: Studies in the Transmission of Faith* (Maryknoll: Orbis, 1996).

WARD, T., *Word and Supplement: Speech Acts, Biblical Texts, and the Sufficiency of Scripture* (Oxford: Oxford University Press, 2002).

WARE, T., *The Orthodox Church* (London: Penguin, 1993).

WARFIELD, B. B., *Limited Inspiration* (Philadelphia: Presbyterian & Reformed, 1962).

—, 'Professor Henry Preserved Smith, on Inspiration', *Presbyterian and Reformed Review* (January 1894), pp. 600–653.

—, *Revelation and Inspiration* (New York: Oxford University Press, 1927).

—, 'The Deity of Christ', in R. A. Torrey (ed.), *The Fundamentals*, vol. 2 (Grand Rapids: Baker, 1970), pp. 239–246.

—, *The Inspiration and Authority of the Bible* (Philadelphia: Presbyterian & Reformed, 1948).

WATSON, F., *Text, Church and World: Biblical Interpretation in Theological Perspective* (Edinburgh: T. & T. Clark, 1994).

WEBSTER, J., *Holy Scripture: A Dogmatic Sketch* (Cambridge: Cambridge University Press, 2003).

WEINANDY, T. G., *The Father's Spirit of Sonship* (Edinburgh: T. & T. Clark, 1995).

WELLS, P., 'The Doctrine of Scripture: Only a Human Problem', in R. Gleason and G. L. W. Johnson (eds.), *Post Conservative Evangelicals: A Critique* (Wheaton: Crossway, forthcoming).

WHITE, J. R., *The King James Only Controversy: Can You Trust the Modern Translations?* (Minneapolis: Bethany House, 1995).

WILLIAMS, D. H., *Evangelicals and Tradition: The Formative Influences of the Early Church* (Milton Keynes: Paternoster, 2005).

WILLIAMS, D. H., *Retrieving the Tradition and Renewing Evangelicalism: A Primer for Suspicious Protestants* (Grand Rapids: Eerdmans, 1999).

WOLTERSTORFF, N. P., *Divine Discourse* (Cambridge: Cambridge University Press, 1995).

WOLTERSTORFF, N. P., and PLANTINGA, A. (eds.), *Faith and Rationality: Reason and Belief in God* (Notre Dame, Ind.: University of Notre Dame Press, 1984).

WOODBRIDGE, J. D., *Biblical Authority: A Critique of the Rogers/McKim Proposal* (Grand Rapids: Zondervan, 1982).

WOODBRIDGE, J. D., and BALMER, R. H., 'The Princetonians and Biblical Authority: An Assessment of the Ernest Sandeen Proposal', in D. A. Carson and J. D. Woodbridge (eds.), *Scripture and Truth* (Leicester: IVP, 1983), pp. 251–279.

ZWIER, R., *Born-Again Politics: The New Christian Right in America* (Downers Grove: IVP, 1982).

INDEX OF NAMES

Abraham, W. J. 39–41, 127, 183
Agobard of Lyon 157
Aland, B. 104
Aland, K. 104
Alexander, A. 136
Althaus, P. 73
Ammerman, N. T. 90
Amyrald 151
Augustine 100, 180, 199, 200

Bacon, F. 145
Badcock, G. D. 22
Bahnsen, G. L. 32, 109–111
Balmer, R. H. 99
Barr, J. 58, 96
Barth, K. 10, 31, 35, 46, 61, 62–64, 65, 98, 143, 155–156, 162, 180, 187
Barton, J. 58–60
Bartsch, H.-W. 23
Battles, F. L. 19

Bavinck, H. 31, 87, 106, 120, 126, 137, 138, 139–164, 165, 172, 184, 211–212
Bell, M. C. 167
Berkeley, G. 51
Berkhof, L. 28, 115
Berkouwer, G. C. 18, 34, 97, 98, 99, 105, 111–112, 139, 161–162
Blocher, H. 126
Bloesch, D. G. 22, 65, 98, 100–101, 105, 138
Bloom, A. 172–173
Boston, T. 89, 180
Braaten, C. E. 105
Bray, G. 14
Briggs, C. 86
Bromiley, G. 63
Bruce, F. F. 13
Bruce, R. 180
Bruce, S. 93
Brueggemann, W. 105

Brunner, E. 34–35

Bucer, M. 200

Buffier, C. 101

Bullinger, H. 27, 191

Bultmann, R. 22, 23, 70, 105

Burgon, J. W. 95

Calvin, J. 18, 19, 26, 37, 46, 63, 65–68, 77, 81,
    100, 106, 124, 125, 134, 143, 150, 151,
    152, 153, 162, 163, 180, 184, 188, 191,
    192–195, 198–199, 200–203

Campbell, J. M. 180

Carnell, E. J. 96

Carson, D. A. 95, 172, 182–183

Childs, B. 61

Chrisope, T. A. 74

Chrysostom, J. 199

Clark, T. 39

Cochrane, A. C. 191

Cole, G. 22

Cole, S. C. 90

Colet, J. 197, 198

Colson, C. W. 93

Congar, Y. M.-J. 179, 184

Coon, G. 115

Cox, H. 93

Cromartie, M. 93

Cunningham, W. 180

Dabney, R. L. 102

Darby, J. N. 91

Davis, D. C. 101

Dawkins, R. 172

Descartes, R. 52, 69

Dilthey, W. 56

Dixon, A. C. 88

Dodd, C. H. 105

Dollar, G. W. 90

Duncan, J. T. 101–102

Duns Scotus 100

Edgar, R. 145, 146

Ehrman, B. D. 104

Einstein, A. 69, 70, 71, 72

Ellingsen, M. 90

Enns, P. 120, 121

Erasmus, D. 198

Erdman, C. R. 88–89

Falwell, J. 93

Farrer, A. 59, 60

Feinberg, P. 107–108

Ferguson, S. B. 22

Fleming, D. H. 204

Fowl, S. E. 14

Frame, J. M. 32, 33, 38

Franke, J. 183–184

Frei, H. 61, 62

Furniss, N. F. 90, 91

Gaffin, R. 138

Galileo, G. 69

Gasper, L. 90, 91

Geisler, N. 106, 107

Gerson, J. de 100

Gerstner, J. 34, 107

Gillquist, P. E. 167

Gore, C. 65

Graham, B. 96

Grave, S. A. 101

Grenz, S. J. 24, 182, 183–184

Gunton, C. E. 22, 105

Hall, D. W. 174

Hamilton, I. 199

Hargis, B. J. 92

Harnack, A. von 10, 55

Harper, M. 167

Hebert, A. G. 65

Helm, P. 101

Henry, C. F. H. 93, 96, 114–115

Henry, M. 134

Hepp, V. 139

Hermann, W. 10, 55, 61, 62, 74

Heron, A. I. C. 22, 63

Heslam, P. 137

Hodge, A. A. 85, 87, 98, 99, 115, 117, 126, 136, 146, 211

Hodge, C. 85, 102, 116, 144, 145, 146, 163

Hoefels, R. J. 128

Holmes, M. W. 104

Howard, A. 181–182

Hume, D. 37, 51, 52

Huygens, C. 69

Jenkins, P. 24

Jensen, P. 131

Jenson, R. W. 105

Jussley, D. 201

Kant, I. 51, 52–53, 54, 55, 62, 69, 70–71, 72, 77–78, 82, 163

Kierkegaard, S. 72

Kik, J. M. 86

Knox, J. 180, 204

Krabbendham, H. 111

Kuhn, H. B. 90

Kuyper, A. 14, 87, 126, 137, 138, 139, 144, 158, 159, 160, 162, 164

Laws, C. L. 90

Leibniz, G. W. 52, 69

Leighton, R. 180

Lessing, G. E. 58

Letis, T. P. 95, 103

Liebman, R. C. 92

Lindsay, T. M. 197

Lindsell, H. 114

Lindsley, A. 34

Lloyd-Jones, M. 201

Locke, J. 51, 52

Loetscher, L. A. 86

Luther, M. 65, 66–67, 100, 125, 134, 191

Machen, J. G. 61, 74–77, 170

Marcil-Lacoste, L. 101

Markarian, J. J. 86

Marsden, G. M. 88, 89, 93, 96

Marshall, I. H. 42, 106, 112–113

Martin, W. 92

Marty, M. E. 93

May, M. 93

McCormack, B. L. 64

McCosh, J. 101

McDonald, L. M. 13

McGowan, A. T. B. 169

McGrath, A. E. 196, 197

McIntyre, C. 92

McKim, D. K. 97, 98–103, 123, 124, 125, 138, 139, 146, 148, 161–162, 212

Meeter, J. E. 86

Metzger, B. M. 13, 104

Meyer, L. 88

Molina, L. de 151

Moltmann, J. 22

Muller, R. A. 26, 27, 68, 163

Murray, J. 180

Needham, N. 41, 55

Neuhaus, R. J. 93

Newman, J. H. 171

Newton, I. 69–70, 71

Nicole, R. 85, 86

Nixon, L. 205–206

Noll, M. 85, 86, 95

Notaro, T. 33

Ockenga, H. J. 96

Old, H. O. 200

Orr, J. 14, 87, 89, 94, 106, 108, 126–137, 139,
        143, 148, 161, 162, 164, 170, 212
Osborne, G. 14

Packer, J. I. 103, 115, 117
Pannenberg, W. 170
Parker, T. H. L. 191, 193, 199, 201, 202,
        205
Philip, J. 201
Pickering, W. N. 95
Plantinga, A. 37

Reid, J. K. S. 62, 64–68
Reid, T. 37, 101, 102
Ridderbos, H. 112, 113, 119
Riplinger, G. 95
Ritschl, H. 10, 55–56, 61
Robertson, P. 92
Rogers, J. B. 97, 98–103, 123, 124, 125, 138,
        139, 146, 148, 161–162, 212
Rollock, R. 180
Ross, J. W. 19, 170
Ruchman, P. 95
Runia, K. 191
Russell, C. A. 90
Rutherford, S. 180
Ryle, J. C. 89

Sandeen, E. R. 90, 91, 97
Sanders, J. A. 13
Schaeffer, F. 167
Schaeffer, F. A. 10
Schaff, P. 25, 26, 184–185, 186
Schlatter, A. 61
Schleiermacher, F. D. E. 10, 54–55, 56,
        61
Scofield, C. I. 91
Scopes, J. T. 91
Shelley, B. 90
Smith, H. P. 86

Spinoza, B. 52
Sproul, R. C. 34
Stewart, L. 88
Stewart, M. 88
Still, W. 201
Strauss, D. F. 70

Thiselton, A. 14
Tholuck, F. A. 120
Thomas Aquinas 32, 100
Thornwell, J. H. 102
Torrance, T. F. 22, 61, 62, 65, 68–73, 77, 120,
        129, 142, 180, 192
Torrey, R. A. 88
Towner, P. H. 42
Troeltsch, E. 56
Turretin, F. 98, 151
Tyndale, W. 197

Urofsky, M. I. 93

Van Dusen, H. 21–22
Van Til, C. 32, 33, 34, 35–36, 37, 71, 74,
        77–82, 131, 143
Vanhoozer, K. J. 14, 57, 116, 117, 145,
        184
Vroom, H. M. 159

Wallis, J. 93
Walls, A. F. 23
Ward, T. 117
Ware, T. 177
Warfield, B. B. 11, 14, 39, 41, 42, 85–87, 88,
        89, 97, 98, 99, 102, 106, 110, 111, 114,
        116, 117, 120, 124, 125, 126, 128, 137,
        146, 164, 211–212
Watson, F. 14, 105
Webster, J. 20–21, 30, 121, 172
Weinandy, T. G. 22
Welker, M. 22

Wells, P. 161

White, J. R. 95

Wilkins, J. 181–182

Williams, D. H. 180, 182

Williams, S. N. 126

Wilson, A. 41

Witherspoon, J. 37

Wolterstorff, N. P. 37

Woodbridge, J. D. 99–100, 101, 124–125, 162–163

Wright, D. F. 41

Wuthnow, R. 92

Wycliffe, J. 100

Zwier, R. 93

Zwingli, H. 180, 199–200